THE JEWISH BACKGROUND
OF CHRISTIANITY

THE
JEWISH BACKGROUND
OF CHRISTIANITY

A MANUAL OF THE POLITICAL, RELIGIOUS, SOCIAL AND LITERARY LIFE OF THE JEWS FROM 586 B.C. TO A.D. 1

BY THE

REV. N. LEVISON

AUTHOR OF
'THE PARABLES : THEIR BACKGROUND AND LOCAL SETTING'
'PASSIONTIDE' ETC.

EDINBURGH : T. & T. CLARK, 38 GEORGE STREET

1932

PRINTED IN GREAT BRITAIN BY
MORRISON AND GIBB LIMITED
FOR
T & T. CLARK, EDINBURGH
LONDON: SIMPKIN MARSHALL, LIMITED
NEW YORK: CHARLES SCRIBNER'S SONS

TO

THE SACRED MEMORY

OF

MIRIAM LEVISON
MY MOTHER

AND

JANE NISBET NICHOL
MY MOTHER-IN-LAW

PREFACE

THE period that our book covers is a very difficult one, presenting, indeed, problems so formidable that it has been avoided by many Biblical scholars. The material from which the facts have to be disentangled is so copious and uncertain and so many-sided, that failure to deal adequately with the problems is excusable.

I undertook the study of the period because I was personally interested in it. This interest was created in the home where my mother and her friends wove their stories for our childish love round the heroes of the Old Testament and the Maccabean house, and was stimulated in me by my honoured teacher, Professor A. C. Zenos, of the Presbyterian Theological Seminary, Chicago. Dr. Zenos was able to supply the Greek background of the period as few teachers can, for he had inherited Greek traditions in his blood, and he brought to bear upon the subject a clear mind, quick to grasp the historical and philosophical values of the movements of the time. This, combined as I have said with my early home life in the midst of the best Jewish traditions, contrived to make the period when Greek and Jew met in the world's historical fields the subject of a very attractive spare-time exercise.

The realisation by many Christian bodies that our period has a very special importance for the better understanding of Christianity has provided me with an opportunity of setting my studies of the times down in writing. Much of the material in this book has been delivered in lecture form. The section dealing with Jewish Worship was delivered to the Scottish Ecclesiological Society ; the section dealing with ' The Passover and the Lord's Supper ' was given as a paper to the Society for New Testament Study of Aberdeen and to the ' Renaissance Society ' of the former Church of Scotland ; and much of the other material in the book has been delivered in lecture form before ministers and Sunday-school teachers in Scotland. Some of the material has also appeared in a somewhat different form in the *Holborn Review* : I am grateful to the editors of that periodical for their kindness in giving me the privilege of their columns for these studies.

One cannot help feeling conscious that the book falls far short of the ideal. But the ideal history is still in the mind of the ambitious schoolboy ; for those who endeavour to put it into print only its shortcomings are evident. I have confined myself to a large extent to the material I have given to inquirers from time to time.

Had there already been a book covering the period from the point of view that is here presented, I should have hesitated to add yet another book. But I do not know of any work which covers the various matters arising from the thoughts and actions of the period in the same manner in which I have dealt with them.

My personal and chief interest lay in the desire to understand Christianity more fully. I sought to get at the origin of some of its beliefs and conceptions. I sought to get into the atmosphere in which the Church was born. I wanted most of all to find out the truth about the contentions so often met with, especially in Jewish writers, that Jesus added but few original thoughts to the teaching of the Jewish pre-Christian thinkers, and that the writers of the New Testament borrowed their ideas from here, there and everywhere. I have come to a decided conclusion on the foregoing factors, and although I shall discuss it in the body of the book, I should like to have it stated here briefly and clearly.

Judaism was the theological sponge of the ages. It absorbed knowledge from every nation with which it came in contact, rejecting that which seemed superfluous and holding fast to the best that it had acquired. It added to its acquisition a personal and individualistic contribution which was of no small value. Christianity inherited that legacy, and in its turn added something that far surpassed the Jewish one; Jesus possessed an originality that Judaism did not. The prophetic, the numinous of pure reason, love objective and subjective, were so merged in His teaching and personality that Judaism could not

contain Him; it cast Him without the gate. Jesus
Himself, though a son of the race, was far greater than
anything racial; and though He must have been familiar
with the teaching of Hillel and the other great teachers
of the nation, He taught out of the fulness of the Divine
Man, and had no need to borrow. His own mind and
heart overflowed with things new, and if He had respect
for the old, it was because the old was also of God.

The case of the other New Testament personalities is
different, and in the writings of the Gospels, Epistles and
the other books of the New Testament we find much of
the past taken over and with truly Jewish genius given
a new content. That there should be a mixture of Greek
and Roman thought in the Apostolic mind is no wonder,
and that the sub-apostolic Church should have emphasised
the Græco-Roman side and neglected the Jewish side is
equally comprehensible, but it is sadly evident that the
Semitic genius is lacking in the syncretism of the Patristic
Church. Behind Jehovah in the Jewish scheme and in
the Apostolic scheme there is room for no other, nor is
there room for any alongside of Him. Behind the Patristic God there lurks Mithraism, Orphic and Eleusinian
mysteries and forms of worship. If, then, we want to
know the background of the Apostolic Church, the Judaism
of our period furnishes that; and if we want to know the
reason for that religion and its central factor, it is the
personality and individuality of Jesus, incomparable and
unique in itself and in its contribution to that period and
to all times.

My aim in writing this book will have been achieved if
I succeed in stimulating the interest of Christians, to whom
the religion of Jesus means everything. While the Jewish
background appeals to me more than the Greek or Roman,
I have not neglected to acquaint myself with the contribution that these great civilisations have made to some
aspects of sub-Apostolic Christianity. But, since my
object is to give the background of Christianity and not
its subsequent development, I have refrained from com-
menting upon Christianity in the modern manner indifferent
alike to the Jewish, Greek or Roman contributions, seeking
to accommodate Christianity to its own viewpoint, instead

of applying it to the many serious problems awaiting solution. These problems will remain unsolved until it is learnt that the ethics of Jesus, His theology, and He Himself are the final revelation of God to man, for obviously God could give no other revelation of Himself than Himself.

Necessity has forced me to be concise and sparing with my references to the works of other scholars. I have been tempted often to throw all caution to the winds and to argue instead of stating the facts and thus letting the reader draw his conclusions. The difficulty of stating what appear to be facts lies in the consideration that mathematical precision has not as yet been reached in historical matters, especially in ancient history. There are yet many things to be learned from the unearthed treasures of the world, but for the present it seems that life consists in every department, not excepting science, of unlearning to-day what yesterday seemed settled for ever. As my reading in this particular line has extended over twenty years, I have not been able to give credit to every author from whom I have learned, nor to quote every authority on whom I have relied.

I trust that this book will give a slight idea of the vast amount that remains to be done in the full exposition of the religious value of this period. Dr. Oesterley is working on this period, and we can look forward to some valuable contribution from his pen. But the period requires more study ; it requires fresh minds to collect its treasures ; and, above all, it requires that students for the Christian ministry should be most fully instructed in its great contributions to humanity's greatest study, ' Theology.' The general Christian worker, the Sunday-school teacher and the leaders of Young People's classes would come to appreciate their Bible more fully if they filled the gap that is left between the Old and the New Testaments with the thought and life of the period.

My reward for this work is already paid in the pleasure I have had and continue to have in the demands that come to me from so many societies, Sunday School Unions and Study Circles to lecture to them on the subjects dealt with in this book.

I have already mentioned the sources of inspiration that

drew me to this period. I can only reiterate my deep and grateful acknowledgment to the circle of pious and learned Jewish women who filled my young and impressionable mind with the stories of the heroes of Israel. To Professor A. C. Zenos of Chicago I owe very much which I cannot state in words. I acknowledge with very great and heartfelt gratitude my indebtedness to the Very Rev. Principal W. M. Macgregor of Trinity College, Glasgow, for reading the MSS. and making many valuable suggestions. I have also to thank the Rev. Professor A. C. Baird, Dean of the Faculty of Theology and Professor of Biblical Criticism at Aberdeen University, for his interest in this work and the help he gave me.

My very sincere thanks are due to the Rev. Professor W. Manson, D.D., of New College, Edinburgh, for his careful reading of the proofs and his many valuable suggestions.

N. LEVISON.

June 1932.

CONTENTS

PAGE

PREFACE vii

CHAPTER I

THE POLITICAL ASPECT

INTRODUCTORY 1

FROM THE EXILE TO THE END OF THE PERSIAN
 PERIOD, 597–333 B.C. 3
 The Jews under the Persian Rulers—The Hagio-
 cracy (The Priestly Rule)—Nehemiah—Ezra.

SUMMARY OF THE NEO-BABYLONIAN AND PERSIAN
 PERIODS, 586–333 B.C. 9

THE JEWS IN EGYPT, 650 B.C.–A.D. 1 . . . 10

THE JEWS UNDER ALEXANDER, THE PTOLEMIES AND THE
 SELEUCIDS, 332–142 B.C. 12
 The Rise of the Power of Greece—Ptolemy Lagi,
 320–285 B.C.—Ptolemy II. (Philadelphus), 285–
 247 B.C.—Ptolemy III. (Euergetes), 247–221 B.C.
 —Ptolemy IV. (Philopator), 221–203 B.C.—
 Seleucus I. (Nikator), 311–280 B.C.—Antiochus I.
 (Soter), 280–261 B.C.—Antiochus II. (Theos),
 261–247 B.C.—Seleucus II. (Callinicus), 247–
 226 B.C.—Seleucus III. (Keraunus), 226–223 B.C.
 —Antiochus III. (The Great), 223–187 B.C.—
 Seleucus IV. (Philopator), 187–175 B.C.—Anti-
 ochus IV. (Epiphanes), 175–163 B.C.—Hellenisation of Judea—Judaism or Hellenism—First Blow
 for the Covenant—The Hashmonaim, 165–63 B.C.
 —Judas Maccabæus—Death of Antiochus—The
 Rise of Jonathan and Simon.

PAGE

PALESTINE INDEPENDENT UNDER SIMON AND HIS SUC-
CESSORS, 142–63 B.C. 30
Simon — Hyrcanus — Aristobulus — Jannæus —
Alexandra.

PALESTINE UNDER ROME, 63–4 B.C. . . . 33
Antipater—Herod—Division of Kingdom.

CHAPTER II
LITERATURE OF THE PERIOD

INTRODUCTORY 43

THE APOCRYPHA AND PSEUDEPIGRAPHA . . 45
Epistle of Aristeas—Book of Enoch—Tobit—
Jubilees—Testaments of Twelve Patriarchs—Books
known as Maccabees—Wisdom and Psalms of
Solomon—Zadokite Fragments and other Books.

THE MISHNAH 52
Divisions and Contents—Elements.

THE TALMUDS 56

CHAPTER III
THE RELIGIOUS BACKGROUND

INTRODUCTORY 57

PRE-EXILIC THEISM 57
Earlier Forms of Theism—El Shaddai and El
Elion—Yahwism and Mosaism—The Religion of
the Prophets—The Theologians of Israel—The
Priestly School or Schools—The Theology of the
Pentateuch.

DOGMAS OF POST-EXILIC JUDAISM . . . 67
The Nature, Character and Relation of God to
the World—The Nature of Man ; his Duty to
God and to Society—Sin and Redemption—
Messianism—Judaism and Zoroastrianism—Angelology and Demonology—The Future of Man and
the Future Life.

the Exile onwards is ' Jew,' and that it applies to those who profess the Jewish religion as such. To state the case clearly, we ought to call Jews those who believe the Jewish religion as recorded in the Old Testament and the teaching of the Rabbis, while the term Hebrews is to be applied to those who are descendants of the nation, no matter what their religious beliefs be. Thus we might say that this people is Semitic by race, Hebrew by tribe or nation, and Jewish by religion. As to their language, its classical tongue is Hebrew ; its exilic tongues are those of the countries in which they find themselves ; and a common language which they use among themselves in most parts of the world is Yiddish, or Jewish.

From the Exile to the End of the Persian Period (597-333 B.C.).

The exilic period is generally considered as commencing in 597 B.C., the date when the first party of the Judeans were carried into exile with their king, but it should be remembered that there was an earlier exile of the northern tribes which extended over a period of years, but culminated with the fall of Samaria in 722 B.C., when Sargon II. carried 27,290 of the inhabitants of the northern kingdom into exile. A late tradition, found in 2 Kings xviii. 11, gives the names of the cities to which these exiles were dispersed. Judaism in the proper sense has its beginnings in 586 B.C., when the Neo-Babylonian general, Nebuzaradan, was given orders by Nebuchadrezzar to burn the Temple, destroy the capital (Jerusalem) and carry the majority of the inhabitants of Judah into exile.

The Jews under the Persian Rulers.

The Neo-Babylonian Empire did not continue long after its conquest of Judah, and the period which elapsed between that achievement and its own fall is very uncertain historically, so far as the Jews are concerned. I am of the opinion that Professor A. C. Welch is nearer the truth regarding the history of this period than are most of the other Old Testament scholars ; but Dr. Welch has not yet worked out fully his own theory, and till we get his views in fuller and in more concrete form we must suspend judgment. As long as the Neo-Babylonian Empire continued its existence there was little hope of the exiles returning to their homeland, though the promises of the prophets were all in that direction. The long years which elapsed between 586 and 540 B.C. must have dispirited these exiles, and when about 540 B.C. the exilic prophet announced the dawn of their deliverance, they must have felt very sceptical. But the prophet saw the disintegration of the Neo-Babylonian Empire very clearly, and in words that seem extravagant hailed the Median conqueror as the anointed of Jehovah.

Cyrus, the son of Teispes, king of Anshan, began his conquests about 550 B.C. : by the month of October 538 B.C. his general, Ugbaru, entered Babylon : and in the following month Cyrus himself entered the capital of the once mighty Empire and thus became ruler of the Middle East, including Palestine.

It is not clear what specific religion Cyrus followed. It is quite probable that he was a Zoroastrian, but whatever his private beliefs were, he was a syncretist, for he accommodated his beliefs to those of his subjects, and we must not be surprised to find him including Jehovah among the gods he worshipped.

The story of the restoration of the exiles is given us in two passages, namely, Ezra i. 1–4, 2 Chron. xxxvi. 28. Exception has been taken to the language of these passages by many Old Testament students, who maintain that they are too monotheistic and Jehovistic. It should be remembered, however, that the writer, taking the Jewish viewpoint of history (which looks upon events not as mere dates for historians to tabulate, but as the working of the providence of God through human agencies), could not escape from the view that Jehovah had accomplished the conquest for Cyrus. The writer of Isa. xlv. takes the same sane and wholesome view. The ' Edict of Cyrus,' which may be examined in the *Encyclopædia Biblica*, col. 982, and the comments of Professor Whitehouse in his commentary on 2 Isaiah, or the comments in the *Cambridge Ancient History*, vol. iii. pp. 480 ff., and vol. iv. pp. 13 ff., will suffice to show that the language used in the Old

Testament is anything but extravagant, for Cyrus talks of Marduk, the chief deity of the Neo-Babylonians, in very respectful terms. The tradition is, however, given most fully in the Greek Esdras (1 Esd. ii. 11–14). ' Now when Cyrus king of the Persians had brought them forth ' (*i.e.* the vessels of the Temple which Nebuchadrezzar had carried off) ' he delivered them to Mithridates his treasurer, and by him they were delivered to Sanabassar the governor of Judea. And this was the number of them : A thousand golden cups and a thousand of silver, censers of silver twenty-nine, vials of gold thirty, and of silver two thousand, four hundred and ten, and a thousand other vessels. So all the vessels of gold and silver which were carried away were five thousand threescore and nine.' It is asserted that Cyrus did not give these vessels back, but if he did not, who did ? This statement must be accepted at its face value till a better is forthcoming.

That the exiles did not take advantage of the ' Edict of Cyrus ' is quite probable. The reason for their not doing so is not far to seek. The country was unsettled by the wars that Cyrus was carrying on, and Egypt had yet to be won for the Persian Empire. As long as that task remained unaccomplished Judea was not safe.

Cyrus died fighting in the regions of the Caspian Sea, and was succeeded by his son Cambyses in 529 B.C. There was another son, Bardia, but he was put to death by his brother Cambyses before Cambyses set out for Egypt. Though this was done secretly, it must yet have been known to the Jewish leaders, and therefore the exiles did not trust Cambyses. Of Cambyses' attitude to the exiles in his own kingdom we have no information, but we learn from the Elephantine papyri that he was favourably inclined to the Jewish Colony at Yeb, in the island of Elephantine. Cambyses carried on his wars in Egypt till early in 522 B.C., and, during the spring of that year, whilst returning home, he died. The exact place of his death is not known, but it was probably in Syria.

As has already been indicated, the death of Bardia, Cyrus' second son, was not generally known, and so a pretender by the name of Gaumata proclaimed himself as Bardia and started a revolt while Cambyses was still alive. The people rallied round him, but his reign was shortlived, for there was an abler man than himself seeking the kingdom.

Darius, the son of Hystaspes, who was a relative of Cyrus, and was governor of the satrapy of Parthia and Hyrcania, overthrew the pretender and made himself master of the kingdom of Cyrus, and also of the part of Egypt which Cambyses had just won. This happened in 521 B.C.

The rapid and masterly conquest by Darius gave all within the Empire a sense of security, and the Jewish exiles shared in this. Thus we find the prophet Haggai coming forward in September 520 B.C. and rebuking the slackers, and making a strong appeal for the commencement of the rebuilding of the Temple at Jerusalem. Haggai followed his September appeal by two others that year and one in January 519 B.C. His appeal was strengthened by the appeals of the prophet Zechariah in that year, and the efforts of these prophets bore fruit. The ' Edict of Cyrus ' was appealed to, and Darius gave the necessary permission to rebuild the Temple.

It would be interesting to trace the political affairs of the Persian Empire after the entry of Cyrus into Babylon, for it would make it evident that the state of the Empire was such that those who studied it carefully could not but sense its instability. The Jewish exiles could not help feeling that to return to Palestine while things were so unsettled was to court trouble, and they wisely refrained from taking advantage of the permission of Cyrus to return, till they deemed it quite safe to do so. With Egypt as part of the Empire, however, they could count on peace within their own borders, and as the prophets at least were sure of the stability of the Empire under Darius and imparted their views with authority to their brethren, the result of Haggai's and Zechariah's assurance was that the Temple was rebuilt by 516 B.C. How complete this rebuilding was we are not told.

The Persian Empire was divided into satrapies. The Satrap was the civil and military ruler of his province, and the province was again divided into smaller sections for administrative purposes. Judea was in the Abar-

Nahara (beyond the river) satrapy. According to the Jewish records, Zerubbabel, a scion of the house of David, was local governor (Phacha or Pasha). Many Old Testament students are disinclined to accept the Zerubbabel story because of the great uncertainty which envelops his after life. But later tradition and story centre so much round his personality that I cannot help feeling that he was, as the Books of Haggai and Zechariah maintain, a real historical person who played the part related of him. The priestly cults of every land exercised and still exercise great power among the people and influence the records of their countries. Zerubbabel seems to have been unfortunate enough to have got involved in one of their quarrels, and it is no wonder that he disappears so completely from the records of his people. He sided with the priestly cult, which had returned from the exile, against those who remained in the land during the captivity, and was roundly rebuked by the prophet Zechariah. And, since Zechariah is our only source of information for that period, it is no wonder that the man whom he rebuked should find no further place in his scheme of things.

The Hagiocracy (The Priestly Rule).

The Jews contrived at that early stage in their history to maintain, as they have been able to maintain to this day, their separate existence as a community within the communities among whom they live. This is due to the influence of their religious outlook upon their lives. The Jews did not believe in ' doing in Rome as Rome did,' for they could not do so and remain true to their religious ideals. Thus it mattered not who the rulers were politically ; they maintained themselves as a religious community, whose aim and duty was to give to God what was God's and to Cæsar what was his. The community which established itself in Judea after 519 B.C. was ruled by the priestly cult till A.D. 70, when the Temple was destroyed. The priestly cult did not always rule or guide well. The Book of Malachi gives us a very sad picture of the Hagiocracy, and right down to the time of Mattathiah and his sons, with one or two exceptions, the priestly rule is unrelieved by any worthy or capable ruler.

Nehemiah.

Some of the exceptions to the above rule are, however, worthy of special mention. About 444 B.C., Nehemiah, an official in the court of Artaxerxes I. (Longimanus), hearing of the sad plight in which the Judean community found itself owing to the misrule of the priests, obtained leave of absence from his master and went up to Jerusalem. He did not waste time preaching, but set about reorganising and reforming the community. His task was a formidable one, for he had to contend with opposition from within and without ; but by dint of hard work he managed to reform some of the abuses, especially those of inter-marriage of Jews with Gentiles and the non-observance of the Sabbath and feasts. Nehemiah was anxious to have the city walls round Jerusalem rebuilt, and obtained permission to do so.

The community which settled in Samaria after the exile of the Northern tribes was of mixed origin ; some were descendants of the Israelites, others (and these were in the majority) were Assyrians who had been colonised there, and who had accepted the local religion because of the belief that the local gods must be worshipped if prosperity were desired. The Jews who rebuilt the Temple did not think that these people, who were called ' Samaritans,' were good enough Jews to be associated with them in their great work. They therefore refused the Samaritans any share in the rebuilding of the Sanctuary, and because of this the Samaritans obstructed Nehemiah in the rebuilding of the walls. The Samaritans contrived to get the ear of the Satrap, and they also had the help of Sanbalat the Hurranite, the Arabs, Ammonites and Ashdodites. Thus Nehemiah had a very formidable opposition, but he was not discouraged, and by making half his workmen a military guard and the other half builders he accomplished his task. Nehemiah had to return to his master's court, but after some time he obtained long leave and returned to Judea, where he died. The services he rendered were very great, and their full account in the Books of Ezra and Nehemiah must be studied with care if a proper estimate is to be reached. One of the great services of a lasting nature was the list of the returning exiles which he compiled. This list and the list in the Book of Ezra, as also that of the Greek Ezra (Esdras), give us a fair account of the people who returned. While there are certain minor differences in the lists mentioned, they do not differ so widely as to require special comment. We may put the number of returning exiles at 49,492.

Ezra.

Biblical criticism is centred round the person of Ezra, and opinions about him differ very much. Some would have it that there was no such person at all; others that there was some one of that name, but that he did not contrive to do what has been claimed for him, either by the Book which is called after him or by earlier critics. Yet others would place him before Nehemiah, and make him the compiler of the Book which bears his name and the Books of the Chronicles. My own reading of the literature of the period leads me to believe, with many others, that Ezra was a real person of importance who lived in the reign of Artaxerxes II. (Mnemon), and that he came up to Judea in the seventh year of the reign of the aforesaid, that is in 397 B.C. His work was mainly scribal, and he collected such writings as were then found and compiled the books as we now have them.

Regarding the Hagiocracy of the intervening period little can or need be said, so we shall have to pass over this period and content ourselves with a list of the names of the high priests to be given at the end of this book.

Summary of the Neo-Babylonian and Persian Periods (586-333 B.C.).

It must be quite evident to all serious students of the time when Judaism emerged into its full existence that the political life was greatly affected by the religious life, and it must further be recognised that in the main the religious life was of the priestly type.

Jeremiah soon passed out of the influential sphere. Then Ezekiel came to the fore, and with him the priestly cult. This cult influenced Judaism so much that they found it necessary to offer a new theory of creation itself and a new history of the world. The fact that the people were in exile helped to give the priests the predominant position they sought, and when they returned to their native land it was not as a political entity, but as a religious sect. The Temple inevitably became the centre of Judaism, and with the Temple the priests became supreme. Even such a person as Zerubbabel, son of David as he was, was shelved when he appeared unfriendly to the priestly cult.

The prophets of the period are left in some obscurity, with the exception of those who were favourable to the priestly cult, such as Ezekiel, Haggai, Zechariah and probably Malachi. It is true that the last of these, though he was not at all partial to the shortcomings of the priests, was yet priestly. Other prophets, like the author of the second part of Isaiah, and the author of Isa. lii. 11–13, liii. 1–12, do not even get their names handed down to us. Like the Egyptian priests in the case of Ikhnaton, the Jewish priests tried, with better success than the Egyptians, to efface the very names of these great prophets from the monuments, and they even dared to pass off their own writings as those of Moses. But, in spite of them, Judaism did not allow itself to be diverted from its course, and the Synagogue sprang up alongside the Temple and in time was found within the Temple precincts itself. Old Testament criticism has been able to restore the personalities of the prophets whom the priestly cult tried to obscure, but it has not yet been able to get at either the names or times of some of them. Still, these prophets live because Judaism had not been altogether dominated by the priestly cultus.

The religious influence of the Neo-Babylonian and Persian periods will be indicated when we deal with that section of our theme, but it cannot be too strongly emphasised that both Babylonia and Persia contributed much to the religion which was to give the world a pure monotheism and a firm moral grip of the realities of pure religion.

The Jews in Egypt (650 B.C.-A.D. 1).

We noted that when Cambyses was waging his wars in Egypt he came across a Jewish community there, and that he treated them well. We must take time to investigate the history of this community, as it is important for our understanding, not only of the political, but also of the religious situation.

Old Testament evidence for a Jewish settlement in Egypt is not wanting. In Jer. xliii. 7–9, xliv. 1 and xlvi. 14 we have clear support of the existence of a Jewish colony in Egypt, and though this settlement is confined to Tachpanes ('house of the negro,' modern Tel-ed-Defenneh), yet there may, even in Jeremiah's time, have been more than one settlement. In 1901 Professor Sayce bought from some Egyptian diggers a papyrus which they said they found on the island of Elephantine, which is situated in the first cataract of the Nile. This papyrus, which is dated 471 B.C., tells of a settlement of Jews in Yeb, and gives us a new view of the spread of the Jews in Egypt. In 1904 Lady Cecil bought three and a half papyri at Assuan ; in the same year Mr. Robert Mond bought five and a half papyri ; other papyri of the same nature were bought by Professor Sachau. Thus the evidence became overwhelming for the existence of the Jewish Colony in Egypt at an early date after the Exile. These papyri are written in Aramaic and are mostly dated, both by the Hebrew month and the Egyptian month, allowing us to arrive at the year in which they were written with a certain amount of assurance. The questions arise, When did these Jews come to Egypt, and for what purpose did they come ? Many opinions are prevalent, but the following is my own conclusion.

Egypt was conquered by the Assyrians on the 18th of Tammuz (July) 671 B.C. by Esarhaddon. Ashurbanipal, who succeeded Esarhaddon, was favourably inclined towards the son of the late king of Egypt, and reinstated him in his father's dominions. The reinstatement of this Egyptian prince (Psammetikus I., also known by the Assyrian name Nebu-shezibanni) meant that the Assyrian king had to provide him with troops to protect himself from the invasion of the Upper Egyptian people and also the tribes of the Sudan, and it seems to me that it was at that time that Jewish soldiers who had been carried into captivity by the Assyrians from the Northern Kingdom were sent by Ashurbanipal to his protégé in

Egypt. We find a military colony established at Yeb in Elephantine, and in November 406 B.C. they complain to the Satrap Bagoas that a certain Nephayan, the son of a man called Waidrang, had destroyed their sanctuary, which had existed there in the days of Cambyses, and they ask for the Satrap's help. The political issues of this petition are complicated. Bagoas was Satrap of the Abar Nahara satrapy, but it is the fifth satrapy, while Egypt was in the sixth satrapy. It is possible that they appealed to him because he was satrap of the section which included Judea, and that would mean that he had special knowledge of the right of the Jews in the Persian Empire to worship their own God.

Two points of importance emerge from the study of these papyri. One is that these soldiers were not monotheists in the strict sense of that term, for along with Jehovah they worshipped other gods in the sanctuary at Yeb. The second point is that as soon as they could they tried to establish contact with their brethren in Judea, and that they address themselves to the high priest there.

The papyri throw a great deal of light on the life and outlook of the people, but into this we cannot enter here. We shall come back to the Jewish influence and activities in Egypt, but we must now turn to a more important factor in Jewish history.

The Jews under Alexander, the Ptolemies and the Seleucids (332-142 B.C.).

The Rise of the Power of Greece.

The coming of Alexander to Palestine, and the subsequent rule of the Ptolemies and Seleucids had a profound influence politically, religiously and metaphysically upon the Jews. The influence was especially great culturally, and so far as Christianity was to be concerned, that influence is incalculable. Greece was the link between East and West. Its influence upon Egypt was great and, if it is true that the Philistines came from the Island of Crete, its influence upon Palestine goes back to about 1500 B.C.

The decisive battle for the supremacy of Greece in the

East was fought on the Issus between Darius ' Codomannus ' and Alexander, the son of the Greek king, Philip of Macedon. The battle took place in 333 B.C., and from that date Greece was the mistress of the Near East.

The Jews were thus faced with a formidable situation. They had felt the Persians kindly disposed towards them, so far as we know, and they could not accept this new conqueror with open arms. They had learned their lesson of exile and desolation, and wanted nothing better than to be left alone. Had they been tucked away in some corner of the globe to which access was difficult, no doubt they would have been left alone ; but they were in the centre of faction of the world in those days. Having Syria on one side, and Egypt on the other, both prizes worth fighting for, they could not help being an important factor in the political moves of the day.

Alexander turned his steps towards Egypt as all the conquerors of the past had done, and thus Palestine was in his line of march. He was too astute a general to leave a hostile people in his rear, and so would have turned aside to reduce Jerusalem, but he was forestalled by the reigning high priest Jaddua, who met him and assured him of the friendly sentiments that the Jews entertained for him. Josephus has woven a miraculous element around the story of Alexander's visit which we need not heed. Jaddua's diplomacy saved Jerusalem from invasion, and Alexander continued his march to Egypt.

We cannot follow the great world-conqueror in his triumphs, nor need we speculate what other changes would have taken place in the history of the world had he lived. Alexander died in Babylon on 29th June, 323 B.C. His death had very unfortunate results for the vast Empire he conquered. The troops, who alone had the power, were divided regarding the succession. The infantry wanted to wait for the child of Roxana, Alexander's wife, that was not yet born, but the cavalry favoured a half-witted brother of Alexander. A compromise was reached and Perdiccas, a scion of the ruling family in Orestis (Macedonia), was elected regent. The generals who fought under Alexander were too powerful and too ambitious to allow the regency to continue for very long, and soon trouble ensued. One of the most astute of Alexander's generals, Ptolemy Lagi (who is also known as Ptolemy Soter=Saviour), made himself master of Egypt, and with Egypt went Palestine. Thus was the link between the Jews and Egypt established.

The Jews under the Ptolemies (320-199 B.C.).

Ptolemy Lagi (Soter), 320-285 B.C.

While the Empire of Alexander was supposed to be governed by the Regent Perdiccas on behalf of the child that was to be born from the marriage of Alexander and Roxana, the leading generals tacitly divided the Empire between them. Ptolemy Lagi took possession of Egypt and Palestine, which step was contested by the Regent, but without success. The Jews, being in a dilemma, tried to keep clear of all political entanglements, so that when Ptolemy arrived in Jerusalem on a Sabbath day, about 320 B.C., they offered no opposition to his making the Sabbath a pretence of their neutrality. In spite of this, Ptolemy deemed it necessary to make sure of the continued goodwill of the people, and had a goodly number of Judeans transported into Egypt. He evidently considered that this hold upon their relatives would keep the Judean Jews on their best behaviour. Sir Flinders Petrie concludes from papyri discovered in the Fayyum district that it was to that district that the Jews were transported.

Ptolemy Lagi ruled with all the energy and craft that had made him one of the leading generals in Alexander's army, but on reaching the age of eighty-two he felt that his day was over, and he abdicated in favour of his younger son by Berenice. He lived for two years after his abdication.

Ptolemy II. (Philadelphus), 285-247 B.C.

Ptolemy the Second was fortunate in his heritage, for the Empire that was handed over to him was well organised and fairly secure. He was thus able to devote himself to the advancement of the liberal arts. He gathered round himself many notable scholars of his day, among whom was the Egyptian priest Manetho, who translated into Greek many of the extant Egyptian records. Other well-known scholars and poets of his day, like Theocritus, Apollonius, Rhodius and Callimachus, were among his court favourites.

The most notable deed of his reign, so far as we are here concerned, was his inauguration of the movement to translate the Old Testament into Greek. The extent of the translation is a disputed matter, but all competent scholars agree that at least part of the Pentateuch, and some of the other books of the Old Testament, were translated. We have records from two sources, namely, ' The letter of Aristias ' and the writings of one Aristobulus. Both these writers would like us to believe that the entire Greek version known as the LXX or Septuagint was completed during the reign of Philadelphus, but this is impossible since some of the books in the LXX were not in existence at that time. We do not detract from the effort of this enlightened monarch by not granting the thesis of these writers ; we recognise gratefully his accomplishment, and are conscious of the aid rendered by this step to the Judaism of the Dispersion, and afterwards to the spread of Christianity. The Jews in Egypt enjoyed perfect liberty under him, and, as is made apparent from the Petrie papyri, they spread to many other districts than those mentioned, and especially gravitated to Alexandria.

Ptolemy III. (Euergetes), 247-221 B.C.

The tranquil period that lasted through the reign of Ptolemy II. did not continue, for Ptolemy was hardly down from his chair of enthronement when he was faced with a war in Syria. We cannot follow all his fortunes there, but we know that all ended well for him. His attitude to his Jewish subjects in Egypt itself was friendly. His Judean affairs did not go quite as smoothly. The high priest at Jerusalem from 250-219 B.C. was a man named Hananias (Onias) II.—a very miserly person. His meanness caused him to withhold the twenty talents of silver (£5000) due in tribute to Ptolemy III. The king sent an envoy by the name of Athenion to demand the tribute. Hananias still refused, but a nephew of his by the name of Joseph went down to Egypt, and not only paid the tribute, but bought up the tributes of Phœnicia and Cœlosyria. The end of the story in regard to Joseph's treatment of the Syrians is full of his cruel abuse of his position. He became the tax-gatherer of Euergetes, and was no doubt justly hated by all Syrians.

Ptolemy IV. (Philopator), 221-203 B.C.

It is said that Philopator (lover of the father) assassinated his father. Polybius and Strabo, our Greek authorities, tell us that this king was a worthless character. It is no wonder that Antiochus the Great took this chance to invade Philopator's dominions. The first attempt, which culminated in the battle of Raphia, did not go well for Antiochus (see House of Seleucus, Antiochus III.). Philopator behaved as was to be expected of him. His head was turned still further by his victory at Raphia, which led to his committing great excesses both in Syria and Palestine. He invaded Jerusalem, and entered the Holy of holies, which enraged the Judean Jews and made them his bitter enemies. We leave the Jews in Egypt and the Ptolemies at this point and turn our thoughts back a hundred years to events in Judea under the house of Seleucus.

House of Seleucus and its connections with Judea.

Seleucus I. (Nikator), 311-280 B.C.

Among Alexander's generals was one Seleucus, the son of Antiochus, a Macedonian nobleman, and, though he was only a cavalry commander of the Imperial Horse Guards, he was also one of Alexander's staff officers. Seleucus did not at first get part of the kingdom of Alexander ; he got the governorship of Babylonia which he administered to the satisfaction of the inhabitants of the province. He was, however, feared as a future rival, and had to flee for his life to Egypt, where he became a captain in the army of Ptolemy Lagi. When the Regent Perdiccas came against Egypt, and was beaten in battle, Seleucus led his troops into the Regent's tent and ran him through with the sword. His equitable rule as governor of Baby-

Ionia had gained him the friendship and support of the inhabitants of Babylon, and when he came against the city he was received by the populace with open arms and began his conquest.

By 311 B.C. Seleucus was well established in his kingdom, and from that date the House of the Seleucids may be said to begin. With the other conquests of Seleucus we are not concerned. Suffice it to say that by 302 B.C. he was master of that part of the Empire which stretched from the Jaxartes and Indus on the one side to Syria on the other. We might mention here a notable fact about Seleucus' building activities: he had two cities built, namely, Seleucia, the port from which the first Missionaries of the Cross set out to preach the Risen Christ, and Antioch, the story of the building of which is told fully by Malalas, *Chronog.* viii. Seleucus allowed the Jews to settle in his newly founded cities and gave them full rights of citizenship.

The fortunes of Judea during the years of conflict between Alexander's generals were not very happy. While Ptolemy Lagi was virtually the ruler, his rule was contested by Antigonus, another of Alexander's generals; and it was not till after the battle of Ipsus in 301 that the Ptolemies became masters of Palestine. Seleucus governed Syria and made his capital there, so that Palestine was always coveted by the Seleucids. They had to wait long before they got it, but in the end they got not only Palestine, but part of Egypt also. It was, however, a Ptolemy (Keraunos) who between November 281 and March 280 ended Seleucus' life. Seleucus was making his way into Europe; he had just crossed the Hellespont and turned aside to examine a traditional spot connected with the host of Agamemnon when this Ptolemy came up from behind him and cut him down.

Antiochus I. (Soter = Saviour), 280-261 B.C.

This monarch does not come into our special sphere of interest, for he was mostly concerned with wars in the West. Family strife, that bane of so many of the ruling houses of the world, leading to their downfall and even their extermination, began in the time of this Seleucid, and this so-called 'Saviour' had his own son Seleucus murdered because of suspicion that was fanned against him. This much may be said about Antiochus I., that he was engaged in many wars, and that he was no poltroon, but was often found in the thick of the battle.

Antiochus II. (Theos), 261-247 B.C.

This ' god ' was rarely sober, and, so far as governing was concerned, he did very little. Had there been any strong man opposed to him he would have lasted but for a very short time. As it was, the ladies of his harem did the governing ; and this could not but have had very bad results for the Empire. Still, the Greeks exalted this drunkard into a god, and he and his mother, who was the grand-daughter of Antigonus, were worshipped in Melitus as gods !

Seleucus II. (Callinicus=the Victorious), 247-226 B.C.
Seleucus III. (Keraunus=Thunderbolt), 226-223 B.C.

These two kings only come into our review at odd times.

Regarding the victory of the Victorious, the less said the better. He did not try to wrest Palestine from Ptolemy Euergetes, but the latter, in spite of being known as the ' Benefactor,' was not beneficent enough to allow the ' Victorious ' to help himself to parts of his kingdom. The ' Thunderbolt ' hurled his bolts too long ago for us to hear their roar, and to tell the truth they hit such unimportant objects that we would need an historical microscope to find any traces of them.

Palestine under the Seleucids, 199-135 B.C.

Antiochus III. (' The Great '), 223-187 B.C.

A courtier of this king, who put up a monument to his patron at Delos, styles him as ' Antiochus the Great,' and adds the further information—a ' Macedonian.' This may only mean being great as Macedonian greatness goes.

That some very noteworthy things happened during his reign cannot be denied. One matter of great interest was the defeat of Antiochus at Magnesia ad Sipylum (modern Manissa) by Lucius Scipio (Asiaticus) in 189 B.C. This battle is historically very important as it was the beginning of the assertion of the power of Rome in the East.

But things to the credit of this king must also be recorded, especially as they concern the people of Palestine. In 217 he attacked Egypt after conquering Palestine and Transjordania, but instead of pushing his attack against Ptolemy Philopator he allowed him time to recover, and though Antiochus himself, commanding the right of his army, defeated the left wing of the Egyptian army, the rest of his troops gave before the Egyptians and all the fruits of victory were lost. Antiochus had to turn his attention for a time to the West, where he did very well, taking all things into consideration. In 202 Antiochus came to an understanding with Philip of Macedon at Pella, when it was agreed to give Antiochus a free hand in Egypt. Having now gained great experience in the field, he found it an easy matter to overcome the armies of Egypt, where a minor, Ptolemy V. (Epiphanes), reigned. In 198 Antiochus defeated Ptolemy V. and wrested from him Southern Syria, of which Palestine was part. Other parts of the Egyptian possession fell to Antiochus. The Jews, who had come to detest the Egyptians because of the violation of their sanctuary by Ptolemy Philopator, received Antiochus with open arms. Antiochus removed two thousand families of Jews from Mesopotamia and Babylon and settled them with full rights as citizens in the regions of Lydia and Phrygia. This transplantation was of great importance in the spread of Christianity, as it formed the nucleus of the settlement to which Saul and Barnabas went with John Mark and was also the source of the further dispersion westward, especially to Ephesus and Troas, and probably the other cities which St. Paul visited on his second and third missionary journeys.

By 188 B.C. Rome had gained a firm footing in the world of that day, and Antiochus was nothing more than a tool in the hands of that rising power. He struggled manfully against it, but in that year he had to conclude a very humiliating treaty with Rome, and in the following year he died, probably in the Elymæan hills.

Seleucus IV. (Philopator), 187-175 B.C.

Rome had taken good care that the Seleucids would not raise their heads for many days to come. She had levied a very heavy war indemnity, which had to be paid in annual instalments, and had made sure that this would be paid, by taking as hostages many important personages, among them Antiochus, the king's son, so that when Seleucus IV. came to the throne he was but a figure-head. He sent one of his generals, Heliodorus, to Jerusalem to bring away the Temple treasure, which was reported to him to be four hundred talents of silver and two hundred of gold (in English money, £602,500). A full account of this incident is given in 2 Maccabees ii. It would seem that this Heliodorus was responsible for the murder of Seleucus in 175.

Antiochus IV. (Epiphanes=God Made Manifest, also Illustrious), 175-163 B.C.

The natural successor of Seleucus Philopator was his boy Demetrius, who was a hostage in Rome for the good behaviour of his father. And it would seem that Heliodorus proclaimed him king, for this suited his plans best since he would be the virtual ruler. But the son of Antiochus III., who had also been a hostage in Rome, was set free and was in Athens at the time that his brother Seleucus IV. (Philopator) was murdered. He made his way to Syria with the aid of some friends and took charge of the kingdom. He saw to it that the infant son of his brother was cleared out of the way, and he had the murderer of him also put to death.

It is very difficult to do justice to this man, for it is not easy to judge the good points of a man who was, on the whole bad, yet we shall try to do him justice, for what we are concerned with is history and not partisan estimation.

Antiochus was a religious enthusiast, and he tried to impose his religion upon the conquered peoples, not only Jews, but all his subjects. The peoples of the East had learned from a very early period that the gods of the conquerors had to be accepted into their pantheon. Another god made very little difference to them ; they had nothing to lose by such acceptance. Antiochus was a

Hellenist, and though his Hellenism was tainted with much of the Eastern view-point, he yet meant to impose Hellenism upon his subject peoples. He himself, as appears from the fact that halos are found on his coins—the sure sign of deification—wanted to be counted among the gods; indeed he claimed to be an incarnate god. His subjects generally did not mind this new form of worship, for it only meant the worship of Antiochus instead of some other Seleucid. But Hellenisation was quite a different matter from that of acceptance of another god. For the Jews both these things were of course impossible, and trouble was bound to result.

Hellenisation of Judea.

Even on the showing of the Jewish account, the Hellenisation of Judea took place at the express desire of the Hellenistic party in Jerusalem, especially the house of Tobias. No sooner had Antiochus taken charge of the kingdom than he deposed the high priest Hananias III. and put Jason, his brother, into office. Jason was anxious to please his patron and did what he could to Hellenise his brethren. The Book of the Maccabees gives us a true and lurid picture of matters : ' In those days went there out of Israel wicked men, who persuaded many, saying, Let us go and make a covenant with the heathen that are round about us : for since we departed from them we have had much sorrow. So this device pleased well. Then certain of the people were so forward herein that they went to the king, who gave them licence to do after the ordinances of the heathen. Whereupon they built a place of exercise at Jerusalem according to the customs of the heathen, and made themselves uncircumcised, and forsook the holy covenant, and joined themselves to the heathen, and were sold to do mischief ' (1 Macc. i. 11–15). To this we only need add a passage from 2 Maccabees to give us a complete view of the state of things :

' Beside this, he (Jason) promised to assign an hundred and fifty more, if he might have licence to set up a place for exercise, and for the training of the youth in the fashion of the heathen, and to write them of Jerusalem by the name of Antiochians, which when the king had granted, and he had gotten into his hands the rule, he forthwith brought his own nation into the Grecian fashions' (2 Macc. iv. 9–10). These quotations, taken from Jewish documents, leave us no choice but to assign the blame to the hellenistic party among the Jews themselves. I do not want to exonerate Antiochus from his share in the matter, but we have to be just.

The movement towards Grecian culture and fashion did not go unchallenged. The orthodox Jews formed themselves into a party to counteract this Hellenistic party, and brought to their task hearts aflame for the Law and traditions of the fathers. The party was known by the name of Hasidim (*i.e.* the pious ones) because of their fidelity to the Covenant. The period we are entering upon may well be called the period of the Covenant.

Hananias III. was put to death by the governor of Syria at the instigation of Jason. Jason himself was deposed, and the high priesthood was conferred on one Menelaus, in spite of the fact that he belonged to the tribe of Benjamin and was therefore ineligible for the high priesthood. It is said that when Antiochus heard of the shameful way the high priest Hananias was put to death, he wept. Yet he was king and had an opportunity, which he did not use, to punish the guilty parties, and history cannot set much value upon his tears. The hellenising party had the king's ear; the king was vain and uninformed; and the road of the Hasidim was bound to be a hard one. A deputation was sent by the Hasidim to Tyre, where the king was at the time, to plead their cause against Menelaus. The king ordered the deputation to be put to death. Henceforth Antiochus looked upon every effort of the Hasidim as personal opposition, and with the unreasoning frenzy of a fanatic poured out his might against the faithful to the Covenant. The news of the butchery of their deputation to the king at Tyre threw Jerusalem into confusion, and they declared open revolt against him. Antiochus, on hearing of this, set out for Jerusalem with his Syrian troops. These troops had but little love for the Jews, and though the king's orders were strong enough in mercilessness, the troops went even beyond these orders. The needs and avarice of the king took him to the Temple itself, which he plundered and burned in part. He entered into the inner sanctuary, into which only the high priest was allowed to enter once a year. These acts could not but strain to the utmost the relations between Antiochus and the Jews ; indeed he became intolerable to the Hasidim and to any of the others who had a shred of love or respect left for their religion. Antiochus had to turn his attention to other fields of conflict, and from 170 to 168 B.C. it was left to the hellenisers to do the work of forcing others to apostatise.

Judaism or Hellenism.

In 168 B.C. Antiochus determined to put an end to Judaism. He sent his general Apollonus, commander of the Mysian corps, to Judea with orders that he must eradicate all Jewish worship and practice, at the point of the sword. The general's task was not very formidable, for he had the help of the apostate high priest from within and his troops from without. The Hasidim were put to the sword. A strong castle (the Akra) was erected on Mount Zion in which the royal troops were stationed. The statue of Zeus was placed in the Temple, and the worship of Zeus was identified with worship of the king, swine being offered as sacrifice in the Temple. What was done in Jerusalem was also done in Samaria, and there no opposition was offered.

The struggle was a very unequal one ; the might of the Seleucid empire was pitted against a few thousand men who were without leadership, and who refused to protect themselves on the Sabbath day when attacked. The Syrian commanders soon learned of this and waited for the Sabbath to launch their attacks against these defence-less folk !

The First Blow for the Covenant.

Jerusalem was soon turned into an apostate city. The task was now that of bringing the rest of Judea into line, but this was not so easy to accomplish, as the king was soon to find. When those who were appointed to complete the task of hellenising reached the town of Modin (present site unknown), a man by the name of Mattathiah slew a

Jew, who was in the act of offering to the king's statue, and his officer who was in charge. For this he had to fly to the hills, which have been the places of refuge for all those who have fought for liberty and true religion. Their mists have given shelter from enemy eyes, their caves from Nature's hardships, and their own isolation has reminded those who have had to take shelter within their bosom of the everlastingness of the Creator of the hills.

The Hashmonaim (165-63 B.C.).

Mattathiah was of priestly origin and belonged to the Jeorib section of the priestly divisions. He was a grandson of one Hashmon, and it was after this progenitor that the family was named ' Hashmonaim ' or Hasmonaim. He was the father of five sons who took to the mountains with him. I can find no parallel in history to the fortune of this patriarch. There was no black sheep among his five sons ; all were worthy of the father as he was worthy of them. Mattathiah made it clear to the Hasidim that if the Sabbath was worth fighting for, it was worth while fighting on the Sabbath, that God's covenant had to be defended on the Sabbath as well as on week-days. Old age and the hardships of mountain life told on Mattathiah, and he laid down his task in the confidence that his sons would carry it on worthily.

Judas H'machbi (Maccabæus).

Though Judas was the third of the sons in point of age, yet he was appointed to organise and lead the struggle. The surname ' Maccabee ' was applied to him, but its meaning is not clear. Two explanations are given, the most common that it means ' hammer,' the other ' extinguisher.' The latter, though not so commonly accepted, seems to me the more likely one, but it matters very little which signification the word has ; either would suit equally well. It is the surname of Judas that we find very often applied in ancient literature to the family, so that readers need not be surprised when writers on this period use either the name ' Hashmonaim ' or ' Maccabees.' Both are worthy names and deserving of honour.

Antiochus, being engaged in other quarters, gave

command to his kinsman, Lysias, to put an end to Jewish opposition. Lysias sent a force which he thought would once and for all complete the task. The two generals whom he placed in command of the troops divided them, Gorgias leading his troops into the mountains with the view of making a surprise attack upon Judas, the other commander, Nicanor, remaining in the plain near Emmaus to finish the fleeing Hasidim as they emerged from the hills. Judas, however, was not caught sleeping, and, acting on the principle that surprise attack gives the smaller forces a better chance of success, he attacked Nicanor's forces when they believed themselves quite safe, and this attack, which was made after prayer and fasting, was a complete success : Nicanor's forces were routed. Thus the first engagement was won, and its effect upon those who were still hiding, or refraining from helping because of the seeming inequality of the contending forces, was to rally them to Judas.

Death of Antiochus.

Lysias knew that Antiochus would not forgive him for this humiliating failure ; indeed it is said that when Antiochus heard of the defeat of his generals he wept. Lysias took the field against Judas in person. He entered the country from the south because he could trust the inhabitants there to remain loyal to him. He started his work of devastation, but before he could achieve a pitched battle with Judas's troops he heard of the death of Antiochus. This altered matters, for Lysias was now regent on behalf of Antiochus's son, and there were others who he knew would claim the kingdom of the Seleucids. Rome, of course, had to be reckoned with.

One cannot agree with Professor M. Rostovtzeff's remarks that the heroic efforts of the Jews did not achieve much in themselves (see *Camb. Hist.*, vol. vii. pp. 188 ff.). Lysias offered Judas honourable terms, first and foremost of which was liberty to worship according to the dictates of his own conscience, and also a certain amount of political liberty. Judas accepted these conditions, and in December 164 B.C. (by Jewish reckoning the 25th of Kislev) he entered Jerusalem, cleansed and rededicated the Temple to the service of Jehovah amidst the frantic joy of his people, who to this day observe an eight-day feast known as Chanuka, that is to say ' Dedication.' This feast is also known as the feast of lights, for special lights are kindled in every pious Jewish home during the days of the feast, beginning with one light the first night of the feast, and increasing by one every night till they reach the number seven.

During the days of exile from their homes many Jews had found their way into neighbouring principalities. They had fled to Edom and territories in Transjordania. There were in these places small settlements of Jews, but, as in days of old, the Edomites turned against the Jews in their times of trouble, and other tribes did the same. Judas therefore felt it his duty to teach these people a lesson for future times. He set out with a punitive force, and he aimed not only at punishment but also at converting these people to Judaism. He was successful in his expeditions, but he felt it necessary to bring back as many of his brethren as he could to the vicinity of Jerusalem, for he was aware that the battle was far from won so far as the Seleucids were concerned. Judas was anxious to be rid of the troops stationed in the Akra in Jerusalem, and he therefore proceeded to invest it.

Religious factions are a very difficult and unknown quantity. As soon as things looked secure from the outside the Hasidim felt it wrong for Judas to hold the office of high priest, and quarrels ensued which alienated some of the Hasidim from his side. Still, Judas was not anxious for any title of honour for himself; he was concerned for the security of the country, and, instead of feeling hurt at the slight offered him, he set about getting help for his country. He turned to Rome, now the power that every country had to reckon with. His deputation was received kindly by the Senate, and promises were made, but at this particular time Rome was not in a position to do very much.

Lysias was aware of the embassy to Rome, and was also angered by the siege of the Citadel. He therefore came up against Judas in company with his ward, the young son of Antiochus, in 163. The army that was marching against Judea was the strongest that had come up against it so far. With the defection of some of the Hasidim, and the influence of the Hellenisers, which was still strong, for Menelaus was still in Jerusalem, the struggle was a hopeless one. But the lion-hearted Maccabee was undaunted by numbers. He met them first at Beth Shur, then at Beth Zechariah, but the odds were against him. His brother Eliezer fell in the latter battle. Judas continued the fight, and the Lord fought for him. A usurper by the name of Philip appeared in the capital of Syria and claimed the kingdom. On hearing of this, Lysias again made peace with Judas, and he and the king came into Jerusalem as friends, sacrifices being offered on their behalf.

Lysias and the young king returned to Syria to find things worse than they expected. Rome favoured the claim of Demetrius Soter and sent a mission to Syria to straighten out outstanding differences. One of the deputation (Octavius) was murdered in Laodicea, and though the government had no hand in the murder, Rome set its face against Lysias and his ward, but did not begin actively to support the other claimant who had been an hostage with them. On the advice of the historian Polybius, Demetrius did not ask for the Senate's aid, but took matters into his own hands and escaped from Rome. He was well received by the people of Syria, and before long the army joined him and, knowing the wish of the new ruler, put Lysias and the young king to death.

Thus, in 162 B.C., Judas had a new power to reckon with. He had now to fight on two fronts. There was the internal opposition which was based on the inacceptability of the Hashmonaim as high priest, and there was the Seleucid king, who, having been brought up in Rome, had learnt that divided power means weakness. Demetrius would have been quite content to give the Jews all the religious liberty they wanted, but he could not allow the Hashmonaim to exercise any political power : and we cannot but see that the policy that the Hashmonaim were now pursuing was religious liberty and political freedom, with their house as the leaders in both the religious and political

life. Demetrius, however, found his opportunity for
curtailing the Hashmonaic power when an appeal was made
to him by a delegation from Judea about the high priesthood. He had one, Jakim (Hellenised into Alcimus), who
was of high priestly descent, appointed high priest, and he
commanded his general, Bacchides, to see that Jakim
was installed in office. Judas was driven out of Jerusalem
in 162. He was not so easily disposed of, but made things
very difficult for Jakim and his party. Jakim appealed
to Demetrius, who sent a general by name of Nicanor to
settle affairs in Judea. Nicanor, however, came round to
favour Judas's cause; he admired him as a man and a
fighter, and advised the king to support him. But the
king would have none of the Hashmonaic dominance, and
ordered Judas to be brought to Antioch, his capital, as a
prisoner. Nicanor, in spite of his liking for Judas, could
not but obey orders, and tried to capture Judas. Judas
met Nicanor's forces at Adasa in March (13th Adar)
160 B.C., defeated them, and returned to Jerusalem. He
again sent envoys to Rome, but Rome had its own axe
to grind, and could not or would not help Judas. The
Hasidim also had ceased to support him. Bacchides came
up again with a large force and offered Judas honourable
terms of surrender, which Judas refused. He met
Bacchides's forces at Elasa near Birrah, and though he knew
it was a hopeless battle, he fought and lost his life. Thus,
in April 160, died the mighty Maccabee.

The Rise of Jonathan and Simon.

There were still three sons of Mattathiah left to carry
on the struggle—Jonathan, Simon and John. These fled
to the wilderness of Tekoah, which is in the Dead Sea
district, and there they carried on guerilla warfare against
the king's forces. John lost his life in one of these
skirmishes.

Jonathan and Simon carried on their struggle for nearly
ten years, gaining many over to their cause, and becoming
once more a force to be reckoned with. The death of
Demetrius Soter in 152 B.C. improved matters for them.
A usurper by the name of Alexander Balas established
himself on the throne of Antioch ; Demetrius II. contested

Balas's claim; and a dual kingship was created in the kingdom. Each of the claimants sought the support of the smaller units in their kingdom, and Judea was among the countries deemed worth having as friend by each of the kings. Demetrius offered Jonathan political freedom within the kingdom, but Balas offered the high priesthood as well, and Jonathan accepted Balas's offer and promised his support.

In October 152 B.C., during the Feast of Tabernacles, Jonathan entered the Temple as high priest and political head of Judea. All that Judas had fought for was now won, though Jonathan, unlike Judas, was politically ambitious for himself, and less so for the nation. Jonathan kept his contract with Balas, who in turn showered favours upon him, giving him among other things the town of Ekron as a personal gift. But Balas was too much disliked by the people of his kingdom, and, in spite of the aid that Jonathan gave him, he could not maintain himself. Balas was killed by an Arab chief (Zabdiel) in 146 B.C.

During Balas's reign, Jonathan and Simon pursued a policy of extension of their territory, and succeeded in extending it considerably. When Demetrius (Nicator) came to the throne he seemed favourably inclined to Jonathan, but could not overlook the fact that the Maccabees were spreading their wings with the intention of freeing themselves from the Seleucid kingdom. Jonathan was at that time blockading the Akra in which a garrison of Seleucid troops was stationed. The king called Jonathan to account for this, but the promise of a yearly tribute of £75,000 made the king enlarge Jonathan's province considerably. Both to the north and south did this enlargement extend, but the fly in the Jewish ointment was the heathen garrison in the Akra, which the king refused to move. Thus when a son of Balas was brought forward by one Trypho, who claimed the kingdom for him, the Jews supported this claim against the king. Jonathan again sent a deputation to Rome, seeking its aid for complete freedom from the Seleucids. Trypho did not mean to let Jonathan have anything in return for his help; indeed he meant to curtail much of his power. He sent an invitation to Jonathan to come and meet him at

Ptolemais. Jonathan came with a bodyguard of about a thousand men. Trypho had these murdered and took Jonathan prisoner. Trypho demanded £25,000 as ransom for Jonathan, and also stipulated that Jonathan's two sons should be sent as hostages. Simon had no alternative but to comply with these demands. He was anxious for the life of his brother, but the sending of the money and hostages did not save Jonathan's life, for the treacherous Greek had Jonathan murdered.

Simon and Independence.

Simon threw off the yoke of Antiochus after the murder of his brother, made peace with Demetrius and declared his province independent of the Seleucid. And from this year (142 B.C.) to the year 60 B.C., when Rome took over the kingdom, Judea remained an independent state. The heathen garrison was cleared out of the Akra, and Joppa and Gazara were occupied by Simon's soldiers.

The occupation of these towns could not be overlooked by Antiochus VII. (Sidetes, 137–129 B.C.). He sent Cendebæus to demand a fine of £250,000. This Simon would not pay, and so Sidetes sent the commander of Syria against him. Simon's age made it necessary that his military duties should devolve on to other shoulders, and never had a father more capable shoulders to lay his burdens on than had Simon in those of his son, John Hyrcanus. John, who was at Modin (his grandfather's home), made an attack upon Cendebæus's forces and drove them into Ashdod, where they took refuge in the towers, which John set on fire. A son-in-law of Simon's, Ptolemaius, son of Habub, invited his father-in-law, Simon, to Duk, and murdered him there in January 134 B.C. Ptolemaius had designs upon the high priesthood and civil authority, but Hyrcanus was too able a man to be so easily outwitted.

Hyrcanus was now faced with a stronger force headed by Sidetes, who came up against him, pushed him back into Jerusalem, and laid siege to the city during the Feast of Tabernacles, 134 or 133 B.C. While besieging Jerusalem, Sidetes offered Hyrcanus a truce, and even sent offerings

to the Temple. Difficulties within, and the kindness of
Sidetes, led to surrender. The terms of peace were the
payment of £135,000, hostages for future good conduct
(one of whom was to be Judas, the brother of Hyrcanus),
and the dismantling of the wall round Jerusalem. To
obtain this money, Hyrcanus had the tombs of the kings
opened up, and from the tomb of David he removed
sufficient treasure to enable him to pay the fine to Sidetes
and to hire some foreign troops to accompany him to
the war of Sidetes against the Parthians. This campaign was fatal for Sidetes, and Hyrcanus took advantage of the unrest which followed his defeat and death
to throw off the Seleucian yoke. Hyrcanus, after a year's
fighting, conquered the whole of Judea and Samaria, and he
destroyed the Samaritan Temple on Mount Gerizim. He
also turned his attention to the Nabateans in Transjordania
and occupied their territory as far as Maddabah. In the
south he conquered the Idumæans.

In all these conquests Hyrcanus compelled the Gentiles
to become Jews. This is especially noteworthy, as the
Herods came from the south country and belonged to
these forced converts to Judaism. The destruction of the
Temple on Mount Gerizim had an echo in Egypt where a
number of Samaritans were settled. The dispute became
so troublesome that Ptolemy Philometor caused representatives of the factions to appear before him to thrash
the matter out. The Jews were represented by one
Andronicus, the Samaritans by Sablæus and Theodosius.
The Jew was declared right, and the Samaritan champions
were put to death. This naturally did not improve the
relationship between Samaritans and Jews.

Hyrcanus had also to contend against internal troubles
mainly of a religious nature. He met these with courage
and firmness, but what he was able to do for his people he
was unable to do in his own house. His five sons he knew
were not of the old Hashmonaic stamp, and thus when he
was making his preparations for the future of the state,
he nominated his wife as his successor, and Aristobulus,
his eldest son, as high priest. Hyrcanus died in 104 B.C.
His wife was imprisoned by his high priestly son, Aristobulus I., and starved to death. This Aristobulus assumed

the title of 'King,' successfully invaded and conquered Galilee
and Ituria, and forced the inhabitants to become Jews.

The court of the king was very corrupt, and intrigues
played havoc with his family affairs. Aristobulus was
set against his brother Antigonus, of whom he was fond,
and had him murdered. Aristobulus reigned only one
year. He accomplished much in his conquests, but he did
much in that year to show how characterless he was,
and he saddled the Hashmonaim with the title of ' Kings,'
which was only a hindrance to them. With Aristobulus
the best Jewish tradition for which the house of Hashmon
stood came to an end. The Pharisees and Sadducees were
not a little to blame for this.

The LXX (see p. 15) now came into its own, for the
Galileans, who were forced into Judaism, used it extensively.

Aristobulus died childless, and his widow, Alexandra
Salome, liberated his three brothers and married Jonathan,
the eldest surviving brother, who succeeded Aristobulus
in 104. Jonathan is known as Jannæus, and to this name
must be added the Greek name of Alexander. He proceeded to put one of his brothers to death because he was
afraid of him ; the other, who took no interest in politics,
he left alone.

Jannæus was determined to own the entire country
from Dan to Beersheba, and did so, though not without
opposition from Ptolemy X. (also known as Lathyrus).
This Ptolemy, who was king of Egypt and Cyprus, 117–88
B.C., was desirous of winning back Palestine and helping
his Gentile brethren, and might have done so had he not
had a difference with his own mother, Cleopatra, who drove
him out of Egypt into Cyprus. Jannæus was not, however, destined to enjoy peace, for there were many internal
revolts ; Josephus sets down the number of killed by him
as ' many ten thousands.' The Pharisees disliked Jannæus
and fomented trouble for him. He met this by having
many of them (800 ?) crucified. He died in 88 B.C., after
having won for his country all the cities of modern Palestine,
with the exception of Ashkelon.

Jannæus died in Ragaba in Transjordania ' of hard
drinking and ague ' (see Josephus, *Antiquities*, Book xiii.
ch. xv. p. 5). He was succeeded by his pious wife,

Alexandra Salome. She reversed his policy of hostility to the Pharisees to one of friendship, as he had advised that course before he died. Antipater, one of the nobles of Idumea, who was a person of importance at court, also advised this friendly attitude to the Pharisees, and it proved the best for the country. Alexandra appointed her eldest son, Hyrcanus, as high priest. The Pharisees did not use their influence with moderation for they had most of the former advisers of Jannæus murdered.

Aristobulus, the younger son of the queen, took up the cause of the Sadducees. The queen was in a difficult position, and trouble would have followed had not political events in Syria, where Tigranes an Armenian was conquering the country, taken Aristobulus out of the centre of the trouble. The storm, however, could not be long delayed. The queen died in 69 B.C. and civil wars raged in the country until 63 B.C. Hyrcanus II. was not a politician, and he would have been quite satisfied to have remained high priest and to have allowed his brother to wear the crown. Antipater and the Pharisees on the one hand, with Hyrcanus as their tool, and Aristobulus and the Sadducees on the other, made conflict inevitable. Antipater played the game for his own ends and won the day.

Palestine under Rome.

Rome was now mistress of Europe, and having made her influence felt in the East in the day of Judas Maccabæus, as already indicated, she was now conquering the East. The Jewish parties appealed to her representative, Pompey. This appeal was threefold. Firstly, the appeal of Hyrcanus II., or rather Antipater and the Pharisees ; secondly, the appeal of Aristobulus and the Sadducees ; and, thirdly, that of the rank and file of the people, especially those in Galilee who had been forced into Judaism. Pompey came to Jerusalem in 63 B.C., entered the Temple and even the Holy of holies. He confirmed Hyrcanus in the high priesthood, put the civil powers into the hands of his governor of Syria, and took Aristobulus prisoner with him. When he was later accorded a triumph in Rome he

3

had Aristobulus marching beside his chariot as one of the
tokens of his victories. Some of the territories conquered
by the former members of the house of Hashmon were
taken from the kingdom. Josephus mentions the following cities—Gadara, Hippos, Scythopolis, Pella, Dios and
Samaria, Marissa, Ashdod, Jamnia, Arethusa, Gaza, Joppa,
Dira and Strathius' Tower. Pompey also carried off a
number of Jewish prisoners who formed themselves into a
colony and soon became a community within Rome as
they were in other cities. Thus ended the glory of the
Hashmonaim.

While Hyrcanus II. remained the ecclesiastical ruler,
Antipater was the virtual guide of the affairs of the country.
When Scaurus, the governor of Syria, was engaged in the
Sinai peninsula with the Arabs, Antipater supplied the
wants of his troops out of Judea's resources. Down to
56 B.C. matters in Palestine went on quietly. The
governors that followed Scaurus, namely, M. Philipus,
61–60 B.C., and Lentulus Marcellinus, 59–58 B.C., ruled in
the equitable Roman fashion. In 57 B.C. Gabinius came
to Syria. He was anxious to gain fame and fortune.
Apart from his campaign in Egypt, he was the cause of
strife in Palestine. Alexander, a son of Hyrcanus, raised
a revolt which Gabinius put down, with a loss to the Jews
of about 3000 killed and 3000 prisoners. The most
notable feature of this incident is that Antipater made
friends with Mark Antony who was then serving under
Gabinius. Gabinius divided the Palestine which was
under the ecclesiastical domination of Hyrcanus unto five
sections, with the following towns as their centres—Jerusalem, Jericho, Amathus, Gadara and Sepphoris (with
Gadara as capital for Transjordania, and Sepphoris for
Galilee). Aristobulus meanwhile escaped from Rome
with his son Antigonus. They came to Palestine, wasted
the lives of five or six thousand of their countrymen and
were sent back in bonds to Rome. Another revolt by
Alexander, son of Hyrcanus, culminated in the battle of
Mount Tabor, where ten thousand Jews were lost, and
resulted also in Antipater strengthening his hold on the
affairs of Palestine.

M. Licinius Crassus followed Gabinius as governor of

Syria. He sacked the Temple, carrying off gold to the value of about £530,000, but he was murdered in June 53 B.C. by Parthians who were pretending to make peace with him.

We may note here the marriage of Antipater to a woman of Idumæan blood by the name of Cypros, who was the mother of Herod (The Great). We may also note from Josephus's account that the Syrian governor, Cassius Longinus, 53–51 B.C., carried off 30,000 Jews as captives.

Julius Cæsar came over in 47 B.C. to conduct his Egyptian campaign, and Antipater joined him with three thousand Jewish troops. This service Cæsar rewarded by restoring to Hyrcanus II. civil powers under Antipater, who was made procurator of Palestine. He also freed the Jews from paying tribute to Rome, and authorised the rebuilding of the wall round Jerusalem which Pompey had destroyed, sending a record of this to Rome to be lodged in the Capitol. In 44 B.C. he reaffirmed this reward.

Antipater did not wait long to take command of the whole situation. He appointed his elder son Phasael governor of Jerusalem, and Herod the younger son to the governorship of Galilee. Both the sons of Antipater must have been fairly young, but Herod at least was very capable, and made many friends in Galilee. No doubt most of his friends were forced converts or descendants of Judaised Greeks and Syrians. He ruled with much firmness and executed the leader of a band of rebels, Hezekiah by name, and also some of his followers. For this the Sanhedrin summoned Herod to appear before them, a very foolish and spiteful measure, for Herod had every right to do what he did. Herod appeared, not as a suppliant, but in full armour, and did not wait to hear the sentence of the court. Indeed, had he been allowed, he would even then have taught the Sanhedrin a lesson of respect for his civil authority. He, however, went off to Damascus to wait his opportunity.

The murder of Cæsar in 44 B.C. had a disturbing effect upon the East. C. Cassius Longinus came back as governor of Syria in that year, but as he belonged to the Brutus faction, Mark Antony attacked the Brutus forces and defeated them at Philippi. Antony was now joint master of the East with Octavius. The Jews were not long in appealing to Antony for help against the sons of Antipater.

The captive Jews whom Cassius had sold into slavery in 52 B.C. were released by Antony on the appeal of Antipater and Hyrcanus.

Herod obtained the consent of Hyrcanus to become engaged to his grand-daughter, Mariamne (the daughter of Alexander).

The Jews, however, would have nothing to do with the son of Antipater, and sent deputation after deputation to Antony. At last, when a deputation of nearly a thousand Jews met him at Daphne, he was so incensed at them that he would have put them all to death had not Herod saved them.

Antony restored the kingship to Hyrcanus and appointed Phasael and Herod as tetrarchs under Hyrcanus.

Another Jewish deputation of a thousand went to Tyre to plead with Antony again against the sons of Antipater. This time Antony treated them very harshly, and further vented his anger by putting a hundred of the former deputation to death.

Antipater had done his sons good service by befriending Antony in his earlier days in Palestine, for Antony never forgot this kindness. In 43 B.C. Antipater was poisoned by one Malichos.

Antony returned to Rome, and Antigonus, the son of Aristobulus, the Sadducean champion, appeared in Palestine. With the aid of Barzapharnes, the king of the Parthians, he took possession of Jerusalem and had Hyrcanus's ears cut off so that he could no longer serve as high priest. Phasael, whom they intended to murder, committed suicide. Herod escaped and went first to Egypt to seek Cleopatra's help. He would have got her aid willingly, but he realised that the Senate at Rome was the only power that could offer a crown that would be secure, and so he went on to Rome. The help his father, Antipater, had given to Cæsar, and the favourable impression he had made on Antony, stood Herod in good stead. Octavius and Antony supported his claim, and within a very short period he had the promise of the coveted kingship.

With the promise of the crown by the Roman Senate,

Herod had by no means achieved his goal. The conditions in Palestine were against him, for the Hashmonaim were yet a power to be reckoned with. The leaders of the great Rabbinical schools (Shemaia and Abtalion) were also against him, as, too, were the Pharisees. He was no son of David and only a half Jew. Nicolas of Damascus, his future treasurer, tried to prove a pure Jewish descent, but no one could be made to believe his story. Herod had, however, certain factions in the country on whose aid he could count. These were the Galileans, whose governor he had been, and by whom he had been greatly appreciated. The Galileans were half Jews like himself, and so were not concerned so much with Jewish traditions as with good government. They were less fanatical and much kindlier than the Judeans; and as Herod was a capable ruler, they were ready to give him their support.

The Samaritans had no love for the Hashmonaim, who had destroyed their temple on Mount Gerizim, nor for the Judeans, who held them in contempt, and therefore they also could be counted upon to support Herod.

Jerusalem was in the possession of Antigonus; and Herod, before he could put on the crown, had to take Jerusalem. Herod counted upon Roman help, and in this he was not served well. He appealed to Ventidius, governor of Syria, 39–38 B.C. Ventidius was engaged in a war against the Parthians, yet he detached some of his troops and sent them under the command of P. Silo to aid Herod. Antigonus bribed Silo, who retired on reaching Jerusalem, and demanded provisions for his army from Herod. Silo's soldiers sacked Jericho, and this deed was charged to Herod's account. Herod's aim was to raise the siege of Jerusalem and turn towards Galilee. To this end he made his way towards Sepphoris and occupied it. The country between Sepphoris and the Lake of Galilee is very wild and hilly, and is honeycombed with caves. In these caves bands of robbers lived and terrorised the countryside. Herod proceeded to rid the country of these robbers, and so won the gratitude of the country-folk around.

In the following year, 38 B.C., Ventidius sent another of his commanders to help Herod, and though this commander (Machærus) was, like Silo, bribed by Antigonus, he yet attacked the city, but did Herod more harm than good.

Herod went off to Samosata, where Antony now was, and put his case before him.   Antony did little to aid him, but gave orders to C. Sosius (governor of Syria, 38–37 B.C.) to do so.   Herod now took the field himself and subjugated the whole country, save Jerusalem, which he blockaded. The tide now turned in his favour.   The rabbis, seeing the inevitable, advised the surrender of Jerusalem to him. During the winter period of inactivity, Herod married Mariamne, the daughter of Alexander, son of Hyrcanus II., and the Samaritans, in whose country the marriage took place, made the wedding a royal affair.

In June 37, Sosius' troops entered Jerusalem, and he had to be bought off to avoid plundering the Temple and city.   Antigonus was taken prisoner, and, instead of being treated as a prince, he was treated as a slave, was scourged and then beheaded.   This action was most dishonourable both to Sosius and to Herod.

Herod was now in Jerusalem secure in his kingship, but again his Roman friends brought him trouble.   Mark Antony had come to the East to prosecute the war against the Parthians and to see Cleopatra.   He needed money, and Herod had to furnish part of it.   Resorting to murder and confiscation to obtain it, he proscribed a number of the richest inhabitants of Jerusalem, confiscated their property and executed them.   In addition to the money thus raised, all the treasures of the Hashmonaim, even to the gold plate, went to Antony.   The only return Herod had for this was to see Antony give to Cleopatra the whole of the southern coastal region of Palestine.

Herod was too clever to object to Antony's demands and actions, but as soon as opportunity offered itself he went over to Octavius's side.   He visited Octavius at Rhodes in 30 B.C., placed his army at his command and contributed £192,000 to his needs.   He also supplied him with food.

Herod's Domestic Troubles.

The question of the high priesthood had to be settled without delay.   Hyrcanus II., having had his ears cut off, was ineligible for the post, and any other of the remaining Hashmonaim would have been unwelcome. So, on the advice of a friend from Antioch (Samaralla), Herod appointed one Hanamal as high priest. Hanamal was unacceptable to priests and rabbis alike, and Herod's mother-in-law strongly urged the appointment of her own son Aristobulus. Herod could not withstand this national and family pressure, and in 35 B.C. Aristobulus was appointed high priest. He did not remain long in the priesthood, for, by command of Herod, he was drowned whilst bathing in the swimming-baths at Jericho. Herod was made to answer for this by Antony, but even though Cleopatra was against him, Antony did not punish him for this crime. Further family troubles caused Herod to execute his brother-in-law, Joseph.

Down to the battle of Actium (31 B.C.), Herod had Cleopatra to contend with—a difficult task which he managed with great skill.

Antony delegated Herod to keep the Nabatean Arabs in check while he was engaged in his other battles. Herod fought for his own ends in this campaign as well as for those of Antony.

In this year an earthquake of great violence shook Palestine. Herod did what he could to relieve his suffering subjects.

Antony's demand for money and his giving of a large part of Herod's kingdom to Cleopatra justified Herod in withdrawing his support and throwing in his lot with Octavius, and in pursuit of this Herod prevented Antony's gladiators from passing through his territory to join their master in Egypt. The defection of Herod from Antony's cause is said to have surprised Antony very much, but as we view things as a whole we cannot but see that it was inevitable.

Before leaving Palestine to meet Octavius, Herod had Hyrcanus II. put to death, and appointed his brother Pheroras regent of the kingdom. Octavius returned to Herod all the former territory held by him and showed him favour.

On his return home Herod found that, though high politics could win him a kingdom, they could not win him

peace in his family affairs. The intrigue of Herod's sister
on the one hand, and the foolish behaviour of his wife on
the other, followed by the base conduct of her mother,
who shamelessly deserted her, sealed Mariamne's fate, and
she was put to death. Alexandra herself was the next
victim, and these two Hashmonaim were followed by the
sons of Babas, also of Hashmonaic descent.

During the next few years (28–25 B.C.) Herod had to
meet many internal troubles, for the Pharisees did not
forget that he was half Idumean, half Jew. Herod, while
trying to meet the just demands of his subjects, showed
great consideration for them when a famine overtook the
country. He gave his own plate and furniture to buy
food for the starving, for of cash he had but little left,
having used it up in an elaborate policy of building palaces
and towns. He built a large palace, theatre and amphi-
theatre in Jerusalem, and rebuilt Samaria, which he named
Sebaste. Later he built Cæsarea on the coast, midway
between Acre and Joppa, and also had a large break-
water built there, which made it an important port, as we
read in the Acts in connection with St. Paul's journey.
Amongst other towns he built were Antipatris in honour of
his father, and Aggripeum in honour of his friend Agrippa,
after whom he also named one of his sons. He also started
the rebuilding of the Temple, which was not completed
at his death.

The favour of Augustus continued towards him, and the
districts of Hauran, Batania, Trachonitis, the east of the
Jordan, and part of Cœlesyria, which included Panias
(modern Banias, Old Testament Dan), were added to his
domain. Herod showed care for his people by remitting
their taxes twice during his reign. Had his family affairs
gone better, Herod might have done a great deal for
Palestine. But his family life, together with the hatred
of the Pharisees which manifested itself in plots against
him, made him bitter and revengeful. While he was on a
visit to Rome, his family engaged in plot and counter-
plot ; and from the date of his return from Rome
(circa 10 B.C.) his life was full of sorrow and strife. He
first had his sons, Alexander and Aristobulus, strangled at
Sebaste. A revolt followed, the leaders of which were

Judas, son of Seriphius, and Matthias, son of Margalothus. Herod suppressed it with the utmost energy, and this was followed later by the execution of his son Antipater.

We must now stop to consider a very important event, namely, a census with which the names of P. Sulpicius Quirinius (Luke ii. 1–2) and Sentius Saturninus (Tertullian, *Adv. Marcion*, iv. 19) were associated. Its importance to us in this connection is that our Lord was born at the time of the taking of this census. The facts are briefly as follows : The governor of Syria from 8–6 B.C. was C. Sentius Saturninus. Conjoint with him in some capacity was P. S. Quirinius, who was ' Legatus Cæsaris proconsulari potestate.' In Cilicia there was a people known as the Homonades who were proving troublesome to the Empire, and Quirinius went out to suppress them. While on this campaign he was properly styled by Luke governor of Syria. Tacitus (*Ann.* iii. 48) bears this out in part. Sir Wm. Ramsay (*The Bearing of Recent Discovery on the Trustworthiness of the New Testament*) makes it conclusive. He further points out that the taking of the census was an established practice in the Roman Empire. The mention by Tertullian that our Lord was born during the governorship of Sentius Saturninus, which we know was from 8–6 B.C., settles the date within those two years. The actual date of His birth was probably March or April 7 B.C. What is not commonly understood is the decree that people should go to their native towns. I have no special information on this point, but in view of Herod's Idumean descent, and taking into consideration the treatment meted out to the descendants of the Hashmonaim, Herod could not feel himself safe on the throne until he had exterminated not only the descendants of the Hashmonaim, but also all those of Davidic descent, and the only, or at least the easiest, way of doing this was to get the people to go to their tribal towns. The Davidic descendants would go to Bethlehem, and he would then be able to put them out of the way.

Herod died in 4 B.C., after an actual reign of thirty-three years. That Josephus should be biased against him is not to be wondered at, for he was a Pharisee, and his party suffered much at the hands of Herod. That at least one

New Testament writer presents him in a very bad light is due to his actions in general, which are not at all out of keeping with those of the murderer of his own children. Yet we must grant that, as kings of those days went, Herod was ' great ' as a politician, an administrator, and a constructor of cities and palaces.

Herod lived wisely according to worldly wisdom, but died foolishly. He had a great many eminent people put to death before he himself died. In his will he divided his kingdom into three parts—Archelaus to be king of Judea and Samaria, Antipas to be tetrarch of Galilee and Peræa, and Philip to be tetrarch of Trachonitis and Panias. Archelaus was deposed by the Romans in A.D. 9, but the others retained their positions. Antipas remained until A.D. 39 when he was followed by Herod Agrippa, who obtained the title of king from Rome ; and Philip remained tetrarch till A.D. 34.

CHAPTER II

LITERATURE OF THE PERIOD

I WANT to keep clear of Biblical controversies, but this is impossible when we come to deal with the literature of our period. The battleground of Criticism and Orthodoxy has been the question of the authorship of certain books of the Bible, or, more strictly, the date of compilation or redaction of some books. A misunderstanding arose in this matter which neither school has taken the trouble to clear up. In many cases in which the critical school has assigned a date for a book or portion of a book, its contention concerned the date of that book's compilation in its present form, and not the actual date of its coming into existence. For instance, no well-informed critic maintains that the document known as J dates entirely from the eighth or seventh century B.C. It is fully recognised that J had material before him belonging to a period much earlier than his own time. The document known as JE also shares in this antiquity of the originals from which it was compiled. And so one might go on illustrating, but it will be wasting the reader's time to go over the old and almost worn-out shibboleths. The controversy is one between traditionalists who reject all tradition save the one that lends itself to the formulation of a pet theory, and a school which, using similar methods for the same purpose, arrives at very different conclusions.

The solution of the problem is not to be found in adding yet another note of a controversial character, but in appealing to those who hold a theory that has been handed down to us from the ' Dark Ages ' to reconsider their position on the basis of the findings of men and women who have a sincere love for the Word of God, and whose only desire is to promote truth and an accurate knowledge of that Word. It should be clearly understood that Jewish

sources do not support those who hold that, because a
book appears under a certain name, the person under
whose name it appears wrote it. While many passages
might be cited from Jewish writings in this connection,
only one will be quoted, for it is the most comprehensive.
The passage is found in the tractate *Baba Bathra* 15a.
' And who wrote them ? Moses wrote his book and the
Balaam section and Job. Joshua wrote his book and
eight verses of the Torah. Samuel wrote his book, Judges
and Ruth. David wrote his book with the help of ten
patriarchs—Adam, Malkitzedek, Abraham, Moses, Aiman,
Yeduthan, Asaph and the three sons of Korah. Jeremiah
wrote his book, the books of the Kings and Lamentations.
Hezekiah and his associates wrote Isaiah, Proverbs and the
Song of Songs. The men of the Great Assembly wrote
Ezekiel, the twelve (minor) Prophets, Daniel, Esther.
Ezra wrote his book and the genealogy of the Chronicles.'

This tractate belongs in its present form to about A.D.
200, but much of its substance may go back to about
200 B.C., so that even at that time the Jewish rabbis did
not assign the authorship of the first five books to Moses.
They claimed that Moses did write a certain book and the
account of Balaam, but the extent of this book we have no
means of knowing. And what shall one say about the
books of Isaiah and the twelve prophets, which are assigned
to different schools of composers or redactors ? It is
surely a very unworthy attitude on the part of those who
claim the stamp of ' Orthodoxy ' to make belief in an
ignorant dogma a test of faith. The rabbis who handed
down the tradition quoted above were not less jealous of
preserving the Word of God than are those who to-day
claim the only right to speak for that Word. These rabbis
lived by faith in God ; sought very earnestly to regulate
their lives by His Word ; and many of them died for their
faith and for the commandments. Let us be done with
these controversies ; join in making the Word of God
effective, apart from who wrote the portions of this, that
or the other book ; and leave it to those who by diligent
study, backed by earnest Christian witness in their lives,
strive to teach the truth, unafraid of the consequences.

So far as we are here concerned, we need not consider

the question of the authorship of Old Testament books. This has been done for us by many competent students. We will confine our studies to books belonging to this period which are not included in our canon, but which are very vital to the understanding of the development of Judaism and the doctrines of Christianity.

The Apocrypha and Pseudepigrapha.

The above-named writings have been divided into two classes by somewhat arbitrary methods. The reason for the division is that the Apocrypha had been accepted by the Early Church and put into the Bible, whereas the Pseudepigrapha had not received such recognition. But the influence of the latter upon Judaism of the pre-Christian period was as strong as the former, and in many respects more so. The Pseudepigrapha are so called because they are written under assumed names, or in the names of others, or in the names of historical or traditionally historical persons. But the Apocrypha shares in this characteristic. We have, for instance, the books of Ezra (Esdras), Wisdom of Solomon and so on. In fact, there is no distinction between these two classes ; neither of them have canonical standing, but both have very valuable information as to the history and religious thoughts of our period. I shall deal with them here in chronological order in so far as that is possible.

Epistle of Aristeas. *Circa* 200 B.C.

Concerning the date of this book, there is much controversy. Some scholars would bring its present form down to the beginning of the Christian era. The arguments are too complicated to be gone into at length. My own opinion is that there are interpolations in the book, but that it belongs in its original form to about 200 B.C.

Historically its value is to be found in the information it affords about the state of the Palestinian Jews in and about Jerusalem. The period which the epistle portrays can be no other than the latter part of the third century B.C., a date prior to the battle of Raphia (see p. 19). The information regarding the Temple services is also valuable. These matters are dealt with in chapter iv., sections 83–

120. In section 16 the writer seeks to prove that the gods of the Ptolemies, namely, Zeus and Dis, are only another form of the God whom the Jews worship. The epistle breathes a spirit of ethical monotheism. Its magnification of the Law is quite in keeping with the teaching of the rabbis of that period. The epistle is very well worth reading, and though direct influence on the New Testament may not be apparent, it can nevertheless be traced in many passages.

Enoch.

This book, which consists of 105 chapters, belongs to various periods. It may be that it covers a period of about two hundred years, beginning with about 200 B.C. (to which chapters six to thirty-six belong) and going down to the last half-century B.C. The influence this book had upon the New Testament is incalculable. It is the first document which covers the periods of transition from the Old to the New Testaments, the first to develop the doctrine of the Messiah as we find it among the contemporaries of our Lord and His disciples. Its importance for those who wish to read the New Testament as an open and intelligible book cannot be too strongly emphasised. The Messianic doctrine, the doctrine of Redemption, its Angelology, its Demonology, its doctrine of the Future Life, must be studied if a real estimate of the teaching of our Lord and the other writings in the New Testament are to be fully appreciated. Its doctrine of intercession by the angels for man, and by man for man, is also very illuminating. Its Midrashic comments on such passages as the story of the fallen angels of Genesis vi., its exposition of the idea of ' The Son of Man ' and the ' Elect One,' are invaluable for New Testament enlightenment. While unequal in value, and historically untrustworthy in parts, it is yet one of the most important books of our period.

The Wisdom of Jesus, the Son of Sirach (or Ecclesiasticus).

Here we have a book which belongs to the first quarter of the second century B.C. A good translation, with notes in English, is that found in Archdeacon R. H. Charles's edition in two volumes. The treatment of the book by

Canon Box and Dr. Oesterley is sound, though one cannot agree with everything they say.

The author of this book was Jesus ben Sirach, who lived in the third century B.C., and the edition we have is that of his grandson, who lived in Egypt 132 B.C. The style of the book is that commonly found in the Biblical writings known as Wisdom Literature, and it is quite a worthy representative of that class. He gives us a very illuminating view of Palestinian life in his time. This has been set forth for us by Dr. Schechter in *Studies in Judaism*, Second Series, pp. 55-102, ' A Glimpse of the Social Life of the Jews in the Age of Jesus, the Son of Sirach.' Ben Sirach's theology is very difficult to analyse, and often most unacceptable. His doctrine of the future life is thoroughly Sadducean. There are, nevertheless, portions in the book that rise to very noble heights. His doctrine of God is very clearly monotheistic. He also reaches a very exalted conception of the relationship of God with man. God is man's father and friend. That this book should have influenced the rabbis is not to be wondered at ; that it influenced writers of the New Testament is generally admitted ; that a study of it is necessary for the understanding of the development of Judaism of our period and early Christianity goes without saying.

Tobit.

Tobit is part of the Apocrypha and belongs to the class which, for want of a better term, we may describe as a religious-historical novel. Though the plot of the novel is laid in Babylonia and Media, and the date of the scenario of the book is that of the fifth century B.C., yet its date of production is the early part of the second century B.C. It would seem that the plot of the book is built upon a story called ' The Story of Achikar ' that was current among Semitic peoples, and is known in Arabic, Aramaic, Syriac and Ethiopic, as well as Armenian. The historical value of the book for the time it is supposed to portray is not great, it is indeed very untrustworthy, but its angelology and demonology, as well as the superstitious beliefs of the people, are very well set forth. The main value of the book is to be found in the theological view-point expressed

in the last two chapters. These are helpful as guides to
the religious beliefs of those times.

Books belonging to the Second Half of the Second Century B.C.

It is unfortunate for us that we are unable to date most
of the books more definitely than by half centuries. Even
the extended period allotted does not quite cover the
possible dates within which the books, or at least portions
of them, which follow were written.

The Book of Jubilees.

It is also known as the ' Smaller Genesis,' and is called
' Jubilees' because of the author's attempt to divide the
period with which he deals, namely from the creation of the
world till the Exodus, into periods of forty-nine years.
The book purports to be a vision which Moses received on
Sinai, but there can be little doubt that it belongs to about
180 B.C.   Its value to those interested in the development
of Judaism as against hellenistic influences in Judaism is
very great.   The doctrinal teaching of the book is of the
greatest importance, and it may be said that this book
is the most important in the whole range of literature
of the period. Its glorification of the Law is a feature
that stands out on every page. Its glorification of the
priestly cult is also noteworthy. But one cannot con-
vey adequately its many-sided interests and important
contributions. The book must be read to be appreciated.

The Testaments of the Twelve Patriarchs.

This book, which in the main belongs to the middle of
the second century B.C., deals with the character of the
twelve sons of Jacob. Certain interpolations bearing
upon the Incarnation have influenced many students in
dating it as post-Christian ; but this date, while applicable
to many interpolations, is certainly not true of the book
as a whole. The general teaching about Messianic times,
which the author assumes will only affect the Jewish
people, is contrary to the Christian ideal. Again, the
author's interest in the sacrificial system, for which he
claims divine origin, indicates that he lived before the
destruction of the Temple. There is in this book the

forerunner of later Jewish teaching about a Messiah coming from the tribe of Levi, or rather a conjoint Messiah from the tribes of Judah and Levi.

The book is of the Midrashic type and deals with many ethical and religious subjects. It probably contains much that was found in tradition about the various tribes, and also some historical incidents which the author couches in Midrashic form. It is a valuable book for students of the New Testament.

The Books of the Maccabees.

Of the four books that have come down to us under the title 'Maccabees' the second is the most important. It is an abbreviation of a much larger work, the author of which is known as Jason of Cyrene. Dr. J. Moffatt's treatment of the book in Charles's edition is like all the work that we have from him, very good ; though I cannot agree with all his conclusions. I think that historically 2 Maccabees is of the greatest value, and is far superior to 1 Maccabees. As Dr. Moffatt rightly points out, it is not a sequel to 1 Maccabees, but an independent document, and covers part of or nearly all the period of the first book. In comparing the two books I would say that 1 Maccabees is the journalistic treatment of the period. The sensational and spectacular are to the fore, and in the main it is a report without a conclusion. 2 Maccabees pays stricter attention to facts, draws conclusions, and at times gives the ethical implications of events, thus showing us the struggle of the soul which enabled Judaism to uphold the Covenant of Jehovah, and to come through the terrible time of its trial. For the student who wishes to understand the soul of Judaism, and what it is capable of in suffering and sacrifice for its ideal, the study of 2 Maccabees is indispensable.

Enough has already been said about 1 Maccabees. Dr. Oesterley's treatment of this book in both Charles's volume and in his own book on the Apocrypha is very full and suggestive.

The third Book of Maccabees has nothing to say about the Maccabees ; it deals with the events belonging to the time of the battle of Raphia, 218 B.C. It is not clear why it is classified under that name—a name I feel sure it did

4

not originally have. It is possible that the name 'Maccabees' is applied to it because it was written during the period of Maccabean rule. It is Egyptian in origin, and breathes the spirit of the early Hasidic Judaism. It is worthy of a place in the Canon of Scripture.

The fourth Book of Maccabees belongs to a much later date than the other books, probably to the beginning of the first century A.D. It deals with the martyrdom of one Eleazar and seven brothers and their mother. It is a homily in which Jewish and Greek thought are intertwined, philosophy and religion being made to serve the author's purpose. In spite of the graphic manner in which it sets forth the martyrdoms, it is unreal, and leaves one with the feeling that he has been reading a modern 'blood-and-thunder' novel.

The theology of these books naturally differs both as regards value and expression. The resurrection idea is found in the three earlier books. The noblest conception of the life hereafter is that found in the fourth book. In this book it is not the resurrection of the body but the continuity of life beyond the grave that is taught. Of other doctrines, that of the vicarious sufferings of martyrs is set forth—a doctrine which is held by many Jews to-day—and prayer for the dead—another of those still held by many Jews, if not by all.

The Wisdom and Psalms of Solomon.

Many other books in the Apocrypha and Pseudepigrapha might be dealt with, but space forbids our doing this here. The student of Christian background and doctrine must go direct to these books to get at the heart of things. The above two are, however, of special importance, and must receive special notice.

The Wisdom of Solomon belongs to the beginning of the first century before our era. It follows closely the style of the books of Proverbs and the Wisdom of Ben Sirach, but it is more hellenistic than either of these books. It consists of nineteen chapters, which are of unequal value. The first ten chapters are homiletic and purport to be addressed by Solomon to the rulers and judges of the earth. While Solomon is the mouthpiece, 'Wisdom' itself talks. Wisdom in the view of the author is a personality which had an independent existence from God, it is the ' Memrah ' and the ' Logos ' of later thought. The addresses are very noble in thought and diction, and in spite of its hellenisms it is very Jewish in outlook and conception. The transcendence of God is stressed in the book. God is very far removed from the universe: Wisdom is the connecting link between God and man. The impression that the book leaves upon the mind is that God is very far away but can be reached through Wisdom ; that God has given Wisdom the mission of mediation between Himself and man ; and that when man becomes fully possessed of the qualities of Wisdom he will enter into full fellowship with God.

The last nine chapters are a very good example of man seeking to be heard by lengthy repetitions and complicated addresses to the Almighty. There is a good deal that is of liturgical value in these prayers. Some of them when taken by themselves breathe a spirit of true communion, but taken as a whole the prayers are not attractive and fail to inspire a worshipful spirit.

The Psalms and Odes of Solomon.

About the Odes little need be said, for there is no doubt that many, though not all, are post-Christian. The Psalms, eighteen in number, are in different case. While it is impossible to claim unity of authorship for the collection, and therefore no date can be assigned to the whole, it is yet possible to say that some of the Psalms belong to about 40–50 B.C. Some may belong to a date earlier in the century. The 17th Psalm, as given in Dr. J. Rendel Harris's book, *Odes and Psalms of Solomon*, pp. 152–154, gives us a very deep insight into the Messianic hopes of the times, and helps us to understand the outlook of the disciples of Jesus. It also helps us to realise why the rejection of Jesus was inevitable upon the basis of current Messianism.

Many of these Psalms might have found their way into the Canonical Psalter, and one is at a loss to understand why they did not. If the Psalms, which are claimed to be Maccabean in origin, were in time for inclusion in the Canonical Psalter, it is surprising that some of these Psalms were left out, especially since they were said to have been Solomon's work.

The Zadokite Fragments.

These fragments, which were edited by Dr. Schechter, and presented by him to the Cambridge Library, are very interesting from the view-point of Messianism, for they evince belief in a Messiah, or the Messiah as a descendant from the tribe of Levi. It is true that the phraseology is somewhat ambiguous, for it speaks as though he were to come from the tribe of Levi and Israel generally. But the addition of the word ' Israel ' is merely generic, although it may have been used in the sense of Israel as against Judah. The MSS. are badly mutilated, and the attempts of Dr. Schechter and Archdeacon Charles to emend them are not altogether satisfactory, though vastly improving the existing readings.

Other Books.

As we have already said, there are a great many more books in the Apocrypha and Pseudepigrapha which might have been commented upon, and should certainly be read by those interested in the formative thought of Christianity. But though they do not add much to our knowledge as a whole, after the books mentioned have been studied carefully they add individual points of great importance and will repay the reader for the trouble of careful study.

The Mishnah.

The books so far mentioned are illuminating and instructive, but the books known as the ' MISHNAH ' are the true guide to the Jewish soul, outlook and belief.

To the average non-Jew the Mishnah will be not only most uninteresting, but in many places unintelligible. With some of its principles they will profoundly disagree, of some of its maxims they would feel ashamed, but with its main teaching they would feel satisfied.

The Divisions and Contents.

The Jew has for the last twenty-three centuries held the view that the will of God was made known to man in two ways—through the Prophets, Legislators, Seers and Priests, and through the nation's teachers who sought to interpret the Law. Hence the MISHNAH—the word means the second or duplicate—is every whit as authoritative as the Scriptures themselves, and naturally deals with the material contained in the Scriptures. It is not a commentary, but an amplification of the Scriptures of the Old Testament.

It was recognised at a very early stage in Judaism that, to keep it true to the letter of the Law, a fence had to be made round the letter that would make it impossible for any one to transgress it, and it was with this object in view that the Mishnah was compiled. Alas for human safeguards ! In time this fence-making had developed to such an extent that the original object was lost sight of, and instead of the safeguards being the servants of the Law they became its master, and it was against this that our Lord strove. The result of the making of these Laws was to lose sight of the spirit of the Law and to become entangled in the letter. It also tended to make the rabbis the dictators of the national conscience ; and though many of them were of humble spirit, looking upon themselves as vessels used by God, others deemed themselves indispensable to God and man alike, and their arrogance was overbearing in the extreme.

The Mishnah consists of sixty-three tractates or booklets, and is divided into six sections.

(1) Zeraim = seeds. This consists of eleven tractates of which the following are examples : (a) Beracoth = blessings. Blessings to be made when different fruits, vegetables or meats are eaten ; also at times of prayer. It contains nine divisions. (b) Pheah = the corner. This tractate deals with the rights of the poor to gather the left-over part of the crops after the harvest. Up to a very recent time Lakat (i.e. pickings) was practiced by the poor of Palestine. As most of the harvesting was done with the sickle there were quite a number of ears of corn left over, and these the poor were entitled to gather for themselves. The extreme edges of the field were not cut, but were also left over, and this practice was in vogue among not only the Jews but also Arabs. For early practice of Lakat see the Book of Ruth. This tractate consists of eight divisions. (c) Demai = things doubtful.

This tractate deals with matters pertaining to tithes and sheave-offerings, and consists of seven chapters.

I have given an example of the subject-matter of the tractates in the first section, but I do not think it necessary to detail all the tractates.

(2) The second section, Moed = festivals. It consists of twelve tractates and deals with all the festivals and parts in the Jewish calendar, the sacrifices needed for various festivals and various agricultural matters.

(3) Nashim = women. This section consists of seven tractates and deals with things pertaining to women, such as betrothals, divorces, laws of marriage and respect to be paid to women's vows. It also contains laws for the Nazarite.

(4) Nezekim = injuries. It consists of ten tractates, including a very important tractate on the constitution of the Sanhedrin and their rules of procedure. It is impossible for any one to understand how illegal the so-called 'trial of Jesus' was until this tractate with its humane and just enactments is read.

(5) Kedashim = holy things. This section deals with the various types of sacrifices, and consists of eleven tractates.

(6) Theoroth = laws of purification. This section deals with sanitation and purification, and consists of twelve tractates.

While the Mishnah is considered to consist of sixty-three tractates, there are three others which are sometimes included in one of them, dealing with general etiquette.

The Elements in the Mishnah.

There are eight elements in the Mishnah which go to make up its contents :

(1) Mishnaic material. This material amplifies and elucidates the text of the five books of the Law and decides how the enactments in the five books should be applied. The authority of these Mishnaioths is equal to that of the Law itself.

(2) Halachoth. The Halachoth are details of the usages as sanctioned by custom, and approved by the general conscience of the community.

(3) Dibreh Chachamin. This element is, as the Hebrew

words indicate, the sayings of the wise men of the nation whose opinions were sought and considered of weight by reason of the standing of these sages in the general esteem of the nation.

(4) Dibreh Yechidim. The sayings of individuals. In the case of the third element the question under consideration was argued out by the various schools ; in the case of the fourth section it was accepted as settled by the individual whose opinions were deemed of great enough value to be made law.

(5) Massioth. Time and circumstances demanded changes in the regulations about conduct and practice, and this element dealt with such changes and sanctioned departures from former usages.

(6) Gezeroth. It was occasionally found necessary to make decisions on the spot for which there could be found no former precedents. Once the decision was made it became legal in common practice.

(7) Tekinoth. Modification of usages.

(8) Elalim, general principles on which any decisions that might be necessary might be based. It should be noted that these elements contain the principle of progressive revelation.

Having given a very rough idea of the contents of the Mishnah, it only remains to add that in these tractates which deal with every aspect of life of the Jewish nation are found the true Jew as he is seen in everyday life. The consolation that the Jew derives from the Mishnah is that his life is regulated for him and every phase of it, even to the very minutest thing, is legislated for, so that if he is conscientious he cannot go wrong in his daily life and practice as regards the demands of God upon him or his fellowmen. It need hardly be added that such a life as the pious Jew is expected to live is devoid of freedom and action and is very burdensome. As a pious Jew, one lives in constant dread lest any of the many thousands of laws or requirements have been trespassed. Having been brought up according to the requirements of the Mishnah (for I was taught the Mishnah before I was taught the Prophets), I realise to some extent the grave objections which our Lord had to much of its teachings. It is bound to create formalism, to make the letter live and to kill the spirit. Christians can only know what Judaism means through studying the Mishnah, and comparing it with the liberty of the Gospel and the realisation by St. Paul of the impossibility of observing the Law and of yet living a free life in the willing service of God.

Though the date of the final collection of all the tractates into one volume is only A.D. 219, there can be no doubt that many of the usages and laws of the Mishnah are as old as Judaism itself, and some of its sayings and rules older than Judaism. Great care must be exercised when setting forth Mishnaic usages in relation to the New Testament. Many Christian scholars have erred very lamentably in the application of usages to the time of our Lord and to the Apostolic Church, when, as a matter of fact, the practices they claimed as pre-Christian and contemporary with Apostolic times are of much later date.

The Talmuds.

Though, strictly speaking, these commentaries on the Mishnah do not belong to our period, a word must be said about them, since no Jew reads his Mishnah without the Talmuds.

The Palestinian Talmud.

This commentary, which is also known as ' the Jerusalem Talmud,' belongs to about the fourth century A.D. The principle it follows is to comment in Aramaic upon Mishnaic passages. It does not cover all the books in the Mishnah. Much of its material belongs to the Rabbinical school of Tiberias.

Babylonian Talmud.

This commentary, which belongs to about the sixth century A.D., follows on the same lines as the Palestinian Talmud, though it is very much larger than it. It was the work of Babylonian Jews, and its language is Aramaic.

No one who does not know these commentaries can or ought to claim a knowledge of Judaism.

CHAPTER III

THE RELIGIOUS BACKGROUND

THIS phase of our studies brings us to the most important as well as the most difficult issues. For the study of the sources of the Christian background, the many difficult and varied issues inherent in the Old Testament become intensified and much more complicated. There are those who honestly believe that Christianity is independent of Judaism, that it is an original revelation of God made by Jesus of Nazareth. There are others who maintain with equal honesty, force and scholarship that Christianity is but an appanage of Judaism with very little originality or value. There are still others who look upon Christianity as the logical conclusion of Judaism in a progressive revelation of God. The last of these viewpoints seems more in keeping with the verdict of history, and we shall examine it in detail—a task which will demand the student's patience with what at first may appear as irrelevant material.

Pre-Exilic Theism.

The Earlier Forms of Hebrew Theism.

It is generally agreed that the Hebrews were part of the Semitic race, though the prophet Ezekiel casts some doubt on this conclusion when he twice tells his people, ' Your father was an Ammurite, your mother a Hittite ' (Ezek. xvi. 3, 45). The Hittites were not, strictly speaking, Semites, and close investigation of the subject supports Ezekiel's view-point. The religion of the Hebrews, so far as it can be comprehended, seems to have followed the general Semitic lines. There are traces of Animism, Spiritism and even Polydemonism in it. At the time when we come in contact with the Hebrews (*circa* 2100 B.C.) religious concepts are in an advanced state among the larger branches of the Semitic peoples ; and since tradition insists that Ur in Mesopotamia, and Aram Mahnaim in Amurru, were the homes of the Hebrews, we must look for their religious background in these districts.   Briefly stated, the situation was as follows : The earliest civilised religion of Mesopotamia was made up of a triad of gods and their consorts, Anu=the god of the upper regions (heaven), who was the father of the gods, and presumably Antu, his consort, the mother of the gods ; Enlil=the god of the earth ; Ea=the god of the seas and nether regions. Anu was accorded pre-eminence over the pantheon, but just what that meant is very uncertain.   If we grant that Anu's position was something like that of Marduk, the supreme deity of the Babylonians, we may conclude that Anu was in a sense a god who possessed the qualities and attributes of all the gods in some indefinable measure. The Semitic conception of deity is expressed in the words ' Ilu,' ' El ' and ' Ilahi.'   The Western Semites, Hebrews, Phœnicians, etc., used the term El.   The etymology of the terms Ilu and El is not generally agreed upon by Semitic scholars and need not detain us, for at the time when our studies begin, the original meaning of El is no longer part of the religious concept.   Ilu, El, etc., signify deity and nothing more.   These forms, Ilu and El, have their plurals, Illani and Elim ; they also have feminine formations.   An El may be a place deity, for instance, Jacobel, Josephel, El-Bethel, Penuel, etc.   It was also part of the names of persons such as Eliab=the deity is the father, Abiel=my father is the deity, Elimelech=the deity is king, etc.   It should be quite clear from the way those names are used that it is in a metaphysical rather than a physical sense that the deity is associated with the names of persons or people.

El Shaddai and El Elion.

These two names for the deity are associated with the earliest forms of the Hebrew religion.   We are told in Ex. vi. 3 that the Patriarchs knew the deity by the name ' El Shaddai.'   In Gen. xiv. 18–20 we are told Abram came into contact with the deity ' El Elion ' through Melchizedek, priest of the cult and king of Shalem= Urusalim=Jerusalem.   We are further informed exactly what concept there existed about this deity—'Possessor of heaven and earth.' A very advanced theistic concept, to be sure, but the uncertainty of its origin, of its historical contents, and of its date, make it very difficult to place too great reliance upon its contents. From verse 22 we learn that Abram identified El Elion with his own god.

The etymology of El Shaddai, or rather Shaddai, is very uncertain ; the most reasonable explanation appears to be that the word is derived from the Assyrian 'Shadu,' which means mountain. Among the Sumerian and Accadian peoples we come across deities which are specially associated with mountains, but just what this association meant for these people is not easy to say. It may have meant that the deity so associated had special care over the mountain ; it may, on the other hand, have meant that this deity had its seat in the mountains. Among the Sumerians the worship of this deity goes very far back, and suggests that they were a people that had come into the plains of Meso-potamia from a country that was mountainous. Be that as it may, we do know that the Sumerians divided the universe between the three deities.

Anu, the chief of this triad of gods, gave Enlil the title Kur-Gal=the great mountain, or rather the god of the great mountain. Among the Babylonians, Marduk in time became the god *par excellence*. This god absorbed into himself all the functions and attributes of the other gods, and among his titles is Shadu Rabu=the great mountain. Old Testament scholars have sought the explanation for the word Shaddai in Hebrew stock words ; but none of these words is in the least satisfactory, for they assume that the Hebrew language was in existence before the Hebrew people—an assumption that does not strike one as logical. When the fact that the Hebrew religion is inti-mately connected with mountains is considered, *e.g.* Sinai, Horeb, Gerizim and Jerusalem, the conclusion that El Shaddai was an El who had something to do with mountains is not unreasonable.

Yehowism and Mosaism.

Some time between 1500 and 1400 B.C. a people known in the monuments as Habiru appear on the horizon of history in special connection with Palestine ; it is believed with reason that these Habiri were the Hebrews. The arguments for and against this theory are too involved to be gone into, but examination of the facts leads to the conclusion that the identification is very probable. That this people were looked upon by their neighbours as polytheists is shown from the way they speak of their gods in the plural, ' Illani Habiri.' The records so far recovered have little information to offer us about this people, save that they were trying to wrest Palestine from the occupants, who owed allegiance to the kings of Egypt. The Old Testament is therefore our only source of information, and we must turn to it.

The information that the Old Testament offers is very simple if one stream or narrative is followed, but as we must take into account several strata in the narrative, the problem becomes involved. We shall keep to the obvious, combining our sources as we go along in so far as they agree in the main.

Moses, a son of Amram and Jochebed, was brought up in the court of Egypt, and being sympathetic towards his brethren who were enslaved by the Egyptians, he had to flee from Egypt. He fled into the Sinai desert and there came into contact with a Midianite tribe known as the Kenites. The priest of this tribe, whose name is given as Jethro, Hobab and Reuel, took Moses into his family and gave him one of his daughters in marriage. Like all nomadic peoples, the mainstay of this people or tribe was their herds ; and Moses, having been taken into the family circle, was given a herd to pasture. While engaged in tending the herd, Moses was vouchsafed a special revelation of God (through the angel of Yahweh, see Ex. iii. 2), which like that of Saul of Tarsus made a great impression upon him. This revelation enabled him to face the future without fear and caused him to return to Egypt to plead or demand the liberation of his brethren. The revelation led him to one conclusion : that Yahweh (or Yehovah) was the only God, there was no other beside Him, nor could there be any other alongside of Him. The vision in the wilderness of Sinai imbued Moses with a personality which the ages have not been able to efface or belittle. It has been suggested by many Old Testament scholars that Moses got his religion from the Kenite tribe of which his father-in-law was priest; others have suggested that Moses got his ideas from the Egyptian reformer and king Ikhnatan, but both these suggestions or theories lack force and conviction. The theism of Moses has come down to us, and we are witnesses of it, but the suggestion that any other religion influenced him is a matter of speculation, and very far from proven. The only possible explanation in the light of history is that Moses was so fired by the vision that he received that he was able to collect the scattered tribes around him, and so to impress them with his own vision that time has not been able to efface it. This vision Moses interpreted into Monotheism, *i.e.* there is but one God and He only is worthy of man's worship and devotion. Whether it was to strengthen his position, or that he recognised that the Patriarchs worshipped this same God under a different form, we cannot tell, but there can be no doubt that the appeal to the tribes was, that this God Yahweh was the God of their progenitors, Abraham, Isaac and Jacob, and He would be their God too if they obeyed His commandments and served Him whole-heartedly. Moses set down ten commandments as the ideal towards whose fulfilment they were to strive, and these we have in the decalogue. The ten commandments (or ' words ' as they are called in Hebrew) were carried about by the Hebrews in an ark, and remained their code of laws, rule of faith and standard of life till the rise of the Prophets. It has been suggested that Moses was not a monotheist, but a monolatrist—that is to say, he taught that Israel must serve one God only, but he did not look upon Yahweh as the God of all the earth ; it is further suggested that he was a Henotheist, that is to say, he taught that Yahweh was the tribal God of the Hebrews ; but these theories, which are but different names for the same idea, have no sound historical basis. Moses was a Monotheist in the same sense as was Muhammad, which conclusion explains best his place in the history of religion, and especially in Judaism.

The Religion of the Prophets.

The prophets were not theologians in the sense that we understand that word. They were ethical Monotheists, by which expression is meant that they preached a line of conduct consistent with belief in Yahweh as the only true God. They met the needs of their day by speaking from a consciousness that felt the impulse of the divine power. Of course there were Prophets and prophets, but the Prophets whose writings have reached us were the Prophets of Yahweh and not of the dervish type which worked itself up into a frenzy or ecstasy which made them babble incoherently. They were men with a message which they often called ' a burden,' and they were always hesitant in undertaking the mission entrusted to them. Their religious teaching consisted of a call to holiness of life and honest dealing between man and man. The love of God for Israel held a great place in it, but their belief that Yahweh was a universal (though not universally worshipped) God is evident from the fact that they taught that He was able to punish the other nations. Israel was God's people because they accepted the covenant of the Patriarchs, and Moses and the Gentiles were to be brought into that covenant.

The Theologians of Israel.

Theology and History were combined by the authors of the first five books of our Bible. Theology and History are inextricable in the Pentateuch. The basis of their theology was Mosaism. The basis of their history was the traditions, legends and sagas of the tribes. To combine these into a unity was no mean undertaking, and to be true to both was an almost impossible task. The history had to be gathered from north and south, and not only that, but Yahweh had to be proved as the Creator and originator of the universe and all that was in it. That the Hebrews possessed such a theory of the universe may well be doubted, and that it had to be borrowed from the older and more theologically inclined nations is probable. The stories of these peoples were gathered, put through the sponge of Monotheism, and made into a continuous story from Creation downwards. It is therefore not surprising that post-exilic Judaism magnified the Law to a foremost place in its thought and teaching. Even to this day portions of the Pentateuch are read thrice weekly in the Synagogue, while the other writings of the Canon are read only in small portions on the Sabbaths, feasts and fasts. The collection of the various strata of tradition makes the Pentateuch appear a bundle of contradictions, but Old Testament scholars have been able to trace back these strata to their sources, and by literary and historical criticism to demonstrate that we have in these books, not a mass of contradictory material, but an honest record of different periods, coming from different schools of thought, and from different parts of Palestine.

The Priestly School or Schools.

It has been already pointed out that the Deity was known and worshipped under different names, El being the general Semitic term with its equivalents in the other Semitic languages. El Shaddai and El Elion were the names by which the Patriarchs knew and worshipped God. Moses introduced Yahweh, and Yahweh held the field among the Prophets. While the Prophets preached Yahwism, the people went their own way, the courts often setting the fashion of worship. If the court worshipped Baal, the majority of the people did likewise, in spite of the remonstrance of the Prophets. The Priesthood was in closer contact with the people, and it was able to mould their thought more effectively. Among the various traditions that existed in Israel, the Priestly school offered the most complete theory and theology, and that formed the real historical theology of the people after the exile. It is remarkable that the Priestly theology should have obtained the place it did among the people, seeing that it was a late-comer compared with Yahwistic and Elohistic traditions, but the others held their place alongside the Priestly lore and so the Pentateuch has reached us, not as a document written down by Moses, but as a combination of tradition and theology in which Moses is the central figure, and Yahweh the God of the people.

I am not sure if it has yet been fully realised among

scholars that the Pentateuch, in spite of its late date of composition, is the norm of Jewish theology. Scholarship has not been careful enough in its examination of the theological aspect of the Pentateuch. It has not explained its theological problems, which in a sense seem very much more contradictory than its literary or historical ones.

I shall cite just a few passages which seem to me to go to the root of the matter. ' And He (Yahweh) said, Thou canst not see My presence (or face) and live. . . . For no human being can see Me and remain alive ' (Ex. xxxiii. 20). Historical criticism has rightly followed the clue offered in Ex. vi. 3, and developed its science of criticism, but it has not taken into full consideration the theological issues involved, and has explained away, or not troubled itself very much to explain, the theological problems of the Pentateuch or Hexateuch. If the statement made in our verse be right, then whom did the Patriarchs, Moses and the Prophets see ? Anthropomorphism does not solve the problem, but confuses it very much, and to no purpose. The oft-repeated plural used in connection with deity cannot be solved by the answer, ' It is a plural of Majesty.' Nor does the explanation that ELOHIM is plural of majesty solve the theological problem. Theology must ask one or two very vital questions :

(1) How does historical criticism explain the passage quoted from Exodus ?

(2) Why did a writer or school of writers in the fifth century select the name Elohim, seeing that at that time Yahweh was the specific name of the God of Israel ; and why choose Elohim, seeing that it is a plural ? Historical criticism may answer that it is not concerned with these matters ; it gives the best explanation that it can for the text as it finds it. That would be a just answer were it not for the fact that the Pentateuch is the basis of a religious system, and as such, every aspect of its study must have reference to that factor.

To answer these questions in detail would require a volume much larger than this can hope to be, so the answer will have to be stated in a few sentences.

The Theology of the Pentateuch.

The Exilic theologians recognised that a transcendent God, such as some of the Prophets declared, could not hold the affection of the nation, especially since the nation was in exile, and was apt to accept the dicta of such poets as the one who wrote Psalm 137 : ' How shall we sing the song of Yahweh in this foreign land ? ' The Prophets were idealists who felt God and needed no further proof of Him or His interest in the nation. Jesus could teach that God was Spirit, and the Prophets might have taught it too—and did in so many words. But the people could not be brought to realise this noble conception, and, while the Prophets preached their idealistic Monotheism, were moving farther and farther from them and their teaching. Judaism in its exile had to be brought into touch with God, or cease to be.

The Angel of God and the Spirit of God were set forth as the representatives of God, and they formed the point of contact between God and the people. God Himself could not be seen, but He could be seen through a mediating power, the Angel (Malach). Thus, when Moses is vouchsafed his great vision, it is not Yahweh that he sees, but the Angel of Yahweh (Ex. iii. 2). When Abram is visited, angels are the visitors, but it is Yahweh who speaks (Gen. xviii. 9, 10). (Notice especially the change from the plural to the singular.) When Jacob wrestles he does so with a ' man,' but he is quite certain that it was ' Elohim ' (God) that he saw face to face. Many other instances might be given, but these will suffice. Naturally those who would have us think that we have in these cases ' Anthropomorphism ' and Polytheism have their answer for these passages, but an honest attempt to understand the Pentateuch can leave no doubt in the mind that its writers and readers must have realised that they were debasing Monotheism if they mixed it with anthropomorphism and any other isms. The solution that the Pentateuchal writers offered was that Monotheism meant, not the transcendence of God which made Him a bundle of attributes that was very far removed from experience and reality, but a Divine Economy in which

5

other selves that could be experienced were part. 'Elohim said, Let us make man in our images and forms (so the Hebrew reads, Gen. i. 26)! Elohim is not a plural of majesty as some scholars would have us believe. It is this Divine Economy which is meant by Rashi (a very famous Jewish commentator of the twelfth century), who explains the plurals used here as being addressed to the angels. It is quite true that Jewish colonists at Elephantine did worship other gods alongside of Yahweh, but here we are dealing with official Judaism, and it is unbelievable that it should have gone back to what on the face of it looks like Polytheism and Anthropomorphism. A century or two after the Pentateuchal theology was closed we find Wisdom exalted to a place incompatible with strict Menotheism. Still later we have the doctrine of the Memrah (saying or Word of God) playing a part which strict Monotheism could not allow, and lastly we have the doctrine of the Logos (Word) developed by Philo of Alexandria, which is very near that of the Logos of St. John's Gospel.

The reversion by this late writer 'P' to the term Elohim is inexplicable save on the basis formulated here, namely, a Divine Economy. The inextricability of Yahweh and the Angel of Yahweh cannot be explained on any other ground, at least I have not come across an explanation that really explains. Most of the explanations offered explain away the problem and do not explain it. I know that this explanation will be criticised on the basis that it is a retrogression from the Prophetic Monotheism, but is it that? Does it not lead to Christianity, and is it not really an advance on that of the past which portrays a deity that is far removed from man and that is made up of attributes—Love, Mercy, Righteousness, Holiness, etc.

I do not wonder that Christians cannot find God in the Old Testament, a God that is personal, a God Who is Father. I do not for one moment claim that we have here a revelation such as Jesus gives of God, but I do say that the reading of the facts points to a preparation of the way for that greater revelation which was to come through Jesus of Nazareth.

The theology of the Pentateuch may not be of much

interest to the Christian who has an open book in the New Testament, but for the history of religion the points brought out are of the utmost importance. For progressive revelation the theology of the Pentateuch furnishes the only link between the Old and the New Testaments, and between the Old Testament, the Apocrypha and Pseudepigrapha. That there is woven into that theology much of the folklore, tradition, legend and saga of the people is merely an indication of the skill of its authors, who realised more than many of us realise to-day, that you can only teach theology by dressing it up in the garments of story, popular traditions and legends. The theologian of to-day may well take a leaf out from the book of the Priestly school if he is desirous that his theology should reach down to the man in the street.

The Dogmas of Post-Exilic Judaism.

In spite of the fact that Judaism had no Creed (in the sense that Christianity has one) till the thirteenth century, it had some very definite dogmas, and these we shall now turn to. We may place them under five headings, namely :

(1) The Nature, Character and Relation of God to the World.
(2) The Nature of Man : his Duty towards God and his Fellow-man.
(3) Sin and Redemption.
(4) Angelology and Demonology.
(5) The Future of Israel in History, and the Life beyond the Grave.

For a clear understanding of these dogmas it will be as well to give actual quotations from relevant literature, so that the reader can judge for himself just what the authorities have to say on the matter.

The Nature, Character and Relation of God to the World.

We shall take our first quotation from Ecclus. xliii. 28 f. :

' How shall we be able to magnify Him ? for he is great above all his works.

The Lord is terrible and very great, and marvellous in his power.

When ye glorify the Lord, exalt him as much as ye can; for even yet will he far exceed : and when ye exalt him, put forth all your strength, and be not weary; for ye can never go far enough.

Who hath seen him, that he might tell us ? and who can magnify him as he is ?

There are yet hid greater things than these be, for we have seen but a few of his works.

For the Lord hath made all things ; and to the godly hath he given wisdom.'

God's relation to the world at large was governed by love, justice, mercy and a desire for righteousness in man. His relation to the Jews was on a different basis : He was still considered as the God of the Jews in a special sense. The following quotation from a prayer that is very definitely pre-Christian will set forth that relationship clearly (this prayer is included in the Jewish prayer-book of to-day) :

> ' Thou hast loved us with great love, Jehovah our God.
> With great and overflowing compassion hast Thou had compassion on us,
> Our Father and our King, for the sake of the patriarchs who trusted in Thee.
> And Thou didst teach them the statutes of life, so also, be gracious unto us and teach us.
> Our Father, Father of mercy Who art merciful, have mercy upon us and grant our hearts to discern and acquire wisdom,
> To attend to, learn and teach, to observe and do and to make effective all the teaching of Thy Torah in love.
> Enlighten our eyes with Thy Torah, and cause our hearts to cleave to Thy commandments.
> Unite our hearts to love and reverence Thy name, that we may never be put to shame.
> For in Thy holy, great and awe-inspiring name have we trusted.

> We will rejoice and be glad in Thy salvation,
> For thou art a God Who workest wonders,
> And us hast Thou chosen in preference to every
>   nation and tongue, and drawn us near to Thy
>   great and holy name (Selah) in truth,
> That we might praise Thee, and be united to Thee
>   in love.
> Blessed are Thou, O God, Who choosest Thy people
>   Israel in love.'

There is a verse which I have left out, as it seems to me to be a later insertion. The words ' Father ' and ' love,' should be carefully noted in view of the fact that they are so constantly used both by our Lord and many of the New Testament writers.

It will be seen from the quotations that in the literature of the last three centuries before Christ's advent, the nature and character of God were viewed from a very highly developed standpoint. His Fatherhood and love for Israel were taught as the theological dogma of Israel's heritage which it must ever keep in the forefront of its thought. The doctrine of Man and his duty to God and to Society is not less exalted, and though in this as in the case of the doctrine of God it was the Jew who was mostly concerned, yet the idea that the Messiah would gather the nations into the commonwealth of Israel enlarged the outlook of the writers so as to include the Gentiles in the ultimate applications of these doctrines.

The Nature of Man: his Duty to God and to Society.

Man was the summit of God's creative energy, and during the last two centuries before the Christian era the belief that man was the last and highest of God's creations, and that he was intended to be immortal, was firmly established in the minds of the rabbis. Freedom of the Will was also part of their dogmatic teaching. Man was endowed with a free will and used his freedom in an independent manner, as the following two quotations will show. The first one, taken from Ecclus. xv. 11–20, belongs to about 180 B.C. :

> ' Say not thou, It is through the Lord that I fell away :
> for thou oughtest not to do the things that He hateth.

> Say not thou, He hath caused me to err: for He hath no need of the sinful man.
> The Lord hateth all abomination; and they that fear God love it not.
> He Himself made man from the beginning, and left him in the hand of his counsel,
> If thou wilt, to keep the commandments, and to perform acceptable faithfulness.
> He hath set fire and water before thee: stretch out thy hand unto whether thou wilt.
> Before man is life and death; and whether he liketh shall be given him.
> For the wisdom of the Lord is great, and He is mighty in power, and beholdeth all things:
> And His eyes are upon them that fear Him, and He knoweth every work of man.
> He hath commanded no man to do wickedly, neither hath He given any man licence to sin.'

This second quotation belongs to about 50 B.C., and together with the above gives a very accurate view of the idea about free will.

> ' For we work by free will and the choice of our own souls to do either good or evil by the work of our hands. And in Thy righteousness Thou dost visit the children with the Lord, and he who does wickedness incurs judgment upon his soul in perdition.' (*Psalms of Solomon*, p. 147, vers. 7–10. J. Rendel Harris.)

Individualism was a highly developed doctrine. The saying in the Epistle of Jas. v. 20 is not a stray thought, but it is reflected in the general teaching of our period, and emphasised in the Mishnah. In the teaching of Jesus it finds its highest expression in the parables of the lost sheep, the lost coin, and the prodigal son. The nationalistic tendencies were very strong and the individual was lost sight of by the leaders, but the greatest teachers of Biblical and extra-Biblical literature emphasised the value of the individual soul. The rabbis were wont to point out that God created one man that it might be clear that the individual was the unit round whom the world centred.

These two doctrines were in great part responsible for the Genesis stories of creation and the fall of man. The battle between fundamentalists and evolutionists would not be raging if the doctrinal teaching on the subject was clearly understood. Man is the special creation of God for the purpose of glorifying Him and manifesting His attributes of love, mercy, goodness, holiness, truth and justice. In making manifest these divine qualities, man's daily dealings with his fellows must be regulated by these attributes. The sum of Jewish teaching regarding man's duty to man is found in Leviticus, chapter xix., of which verse 18 is the high-water mark : ' Thou shalt not be revengeful nor sulky with your co-nationals, and thou shalt love thy neighbour as thyself : I am Jehovah.' And also in the teaching of Hillel : ' That which is hateful to thee, do not unto thy neighbour.'

Man's duty to God was the occupation of his life. He had to think, act, live and move in one direction, namely, toward God. The idea of drawing a line between secular and religious was outwith the Jewish conception. God was concerned in every act, thought and deed : there was nothing outside the sphere of God's interest in the Jew's life. God was so much concerned in the action of every Jew that He made provision for him even when he had acted contrary to His will, to enable him to make amends. Thus the idea of Atonement in its deeper sense arose, and, while but insufficiently developed in Judaism, found full expression in Christianity.

Sin and Redemption.

Professor G. F. Moore, in his very valuable book, *Judaism*, vol. i., p. 460, quotes the definition of Sin from the Shorter Catechism with approval : ' Sin is any want of conformity unto, or transgression of, the law of God.' I find that not only in this terse definition but in the detailed conception of it do the Presbyterian Churches, especially the Scottish Presbyterian, regard the matter from the Jewish point of view. Yet a great difference exists. Judaism held and still holds views of sin which Christ and Christians have ceased to hold.

The earliest conception of sin was failure in one's social

duties. Hence the word Chata (=to sin), means to miss the mark. In primitive Semitic society, as Professor A. Bertholet points out, sin was considered as a breach of social obligation : ' Deeds that are not done, and therefore ought not to be done ' (Gen. xx. 9, xxxiv. 7 ; 2 Sam. xiii. 12). While the recognition as sinful of acts towards God and man which ought not to be done came at an early stage in Judaism, yet one of the main ideas underlying most of the Old Testament terms for sin carried with it an idea that sin was a solvent of the soul ; it was concerned with the destroying of the soul. The social consciousness of sin, however, was long in finding its way into the minds of the people. The priestly cult had a good deal to do with the individual development of the idea of sin, and yet the author of the 51st Psalm deemed his sin not in its social aspect but only in so far as it seemed to him a transgression of human laws, an offence which Jehovah punishes very severely. We cannot follow the different phases of the development of the doctrine of sin, but down to a very late stage sin had not been doctrinally defined, though it was fully recognised. The matter which weighed most both with the people and certainly with the prophets, was the sin of infidelity towards God. Individual sin was never as fully recognised by Judaism as it is among Protestant Christians, and never certainly as it was in the Early Church. The reason was that Scripture and tradition had set down certain things as necessary to be done to be at peace with God, and this weakened the consciousness of sin. The Pharisees and Sadducees and other sects lived by what they did, and not by what they omitted to do. Not until the time of Maimonides did the Jews learn to say ' I believe.' What they claimed as distinctive was ' I am a son of Abraham, and I do this and that and the other ; I am not as other men are.' The most significant service that Judaism rendered to this great doctrine was by its national conception of sin, which accounted for the solidarity of the nation, and the national responsibility in the matter. ' And I turned my face towards the Lord God to seek (Him) by prayer, supplication, by fasting, sackcloth and ashes. And I prayed to Jehovah our God and made confession, saying, " Alas, Lord, the Mighty and

Great God, Keeper of the Covenant and kindness towards those who love thee and keep thy commandments, we have sinned, we have committed iniquity, we have acted wickedly, we have rebelled, we have departed from thy commandments and thy judgments. We did not hearken to thy servants the prophets who spoke in thy name against our kings, princes, and our sires, and against all the people of the land. Unto thee, O Lord, is (to be attributed) kindness, and to us shamefacedness, as at this day (so also) to the people of Judah, the inhabitants of Jerusalem, and to all Israel near and far, in all the lands whither thou hast scattered them because of their treachery, because they acted treacherously towards thee "' (Dan. ix. 3–7). It is difficult to make people realise that owing to racial or national solidarity the individual consciousness of sin was not developed among the Jews. ' We are the children of Abraham,' they argued, ' and in this way we stand and fall with the nation.' The national view taken of the conception of sin had a great deal to do with the development of Messianism. The priest could expiate individual sin when it was burdening the individual, by offering up a sacrifice for him, but the high priest offered for the whole nation, and this was the most solemn service of the year. In this respect alone did Judaism conceive of atonement. The Day of Atonement was a national day, not an individual one (see Lev. xvi.). The Day of Atonement has since our Lord's day become more individualistic in its nature, but the corporate national sense is very much to the fore even now.

Messianism.

While the priestly cult insisted on sacrifice as a means of expiation, the Synagogue and prophetic cult, though not objecting to sacrifice as such, had a different solution for the problem. The nation must be saved not only spiritually but materially too; indeed, the whole creation must be saved; the earth itself must share in the salvation, or redemption. The best example of this doctrine is found in Isa. xi. 1–10; xxv. 1–xxvi. 12 (these portions probably belong to 350 B.C.). In the Apocrypha and Pseudepigrapha the teaching about the Messiah is bewildering and contradictory. He is represented as a descendant of Levi, and in the same book (The Testaments of the Twelve Patriarchs) a descendant of Judah. The books of Baruch and the Zadokite fragments are no less misleading. They make the Messiah active and passive at the same time, pre-existent and yet ordinary man, contradictions which make great confusion. In the Apocryphal and Pseudepigraphic literature the following passages seem to me the most representative of the Messianic beliefs in the time of our Lord, and I quote them at length:

(1) And there I saw One who had a head of days,
 And his head was white like wool,
 And with him was another being whose counten-
  ance had appearance of man,
 And his face was full of graciousness, like one of
  the holy angels.
(2) And I asked the Angel who went with me and
  showed me all the hidden things concerning that
  Son of Man, who he was and whence he was
  (and), why he went with the Head of Days?
(3) And he answered and said unto me:
 This is the Son of Man who hath righteousness,
 With whom dwelleth righteousness,
 And who revealeth all the treasures of that which
  is hidden,
 Because the Lord of Spirits hath chosen Him,
 And whose lot hath the pre-eminence before the
  Lord of Spirits in uprightness for ever.
(4) And this Son of Man whom thou hast seen
 Shall raise up the kings and the mighty from
  their seats,
 (And the strong from their thrones)
 And shall loosen the reins of the strong, and break
  the teeth of the sinners.
 (Enoch xlvi. 1–4.)

(1) For wisdom is poured out like water,
 And glory faileth not before him for evermore.
(2) For he is mighty in all the secrets of righteousness,
 And unrighteousness shall disappear as a shadow,

And have no continuance ;
Because the Elect One standeth before the Lord
  of Spirits,
And his glory is for ever and ever,
And his might unto all generations.

(3) And in him dwells the spirit of wisdom,
And the spirit which gives insight,
And the spirit of understanding and of might,
And the spirit of those who have fallen asleep in
  righteousness.

(4) And he shall judge the secret things,
And none shall be able to utter a lying word before
  him ;
For he is the Elect One before the Lord of Spirits
according to his good pleasure. (Enoch xlix. 1–4.)

(1) There mine eyes saw a deep valley with open
  mouths, and all who dwell on the earth and
  sea and islands shall bring to him gifts and
  presents and tokens of homage, but that deep
  valley shall not become full.

(2) And their hands commit lawless deeds,
And the sinners devour all those whom they
  lawlessly oppress :
Yet the sinners shall be destroyed before the face
  of the Lord of Spirits,
And they shall be banished from off the face of
  the earth,
And they shall perish for ever and ever.

(3) For I saw all the angels of punishment abiding (there)
  and preparing all the instruments of Satan.

(4) And I asked the angel of peace who went with
  me : ' For whom are they preparing these
  instruments ? '

(5) And he said unto me : ' They prepare these for
  the kings and the mighty of this earth, that
  they may be thereby destroyed.'

(6) And after this the righteous and the Elect One
  shall cause the house of his congregation to
  appear : henceforth they shall be no more
  hindered in the name of the Lord of Spirits.

(7) And these mountains shall not stand as the earth
　　before his righteousness,
　　But the hills shall be as a fountain of water,
　　And the righteous shall have rest from the oppres-
　　sion of sinners. (Enoch liii.)

(23) Behold, O Lord, and raise up to them their
king, the son of David, according to the time which
Thou seest, O God ; and let him reign over Israel
thy servant ; (24) and strengthen him with power
that he may humble the sinful rulers ; (25) and may
purify Jerusalem from the Gentiles who trample her
down to destruction ; (26) so as to destroy the wicked
from my inheritance ; and to break their pride like a
potter's vessel, to break like a rod of iron all their
firmness ; (27) to destroy the sinful Gentiles with the
word of His mouth ; at His rebuke the Gentiles shall
flee from before His face ; and to confute sinners by
the word of their heart ; (28) that He may gather
together a holy people that shall exalt in righteousness : and may judge the tribes of the people whom
the Lord his God sanctified ; (29) and He shall not
any more suffer sin to lodge amongst them ; and no
more shall dwell amongst them the man that knoweth
evil. (30) For He knoweth them that they are the
children of God, and He shall divide them according
to their tribes upon the earth ; (31) and the sojourner
and the foreigner shall not dwell with them ; for He
will judge the Gentiles and the people in the wisdom
of His righteousness ; (32) and He shall possess a
people from among the Gentiles ; and they shall
serve Him under His yoke ; and they praise the Lord
openly over all the earth ; (33) and He shall purify
Jerusalem in holiness as it was of old time ; (34) that
the Gentiles may come from the ends of the earth to
behold His glory ; bringing her sons with them as
an honourable gift ; those who were scattered from
her ; (35) and to see the glory of the Lord wherewith
He hath glorified her ; and He the righteous king,
taught of God, is over them, because they are all
righteous, and their king is the Lord Messiah ; (37)

for He will not trust on horsemen nor on chariot ;
nor on the bow ; nor shall He multiply to Himself
gold and silver for war : nor shall He rely on a multitude on the day of war ; (38) for the Lord. (Psalms
of Solomon xvii. 23–38.)

Judaism and Zoroastrianism.

Before going on to the other points in the religious
development of our period, I must turn aside to indicate
the principles of another religion with which the dispersed
Jews could not but be familiar. How much it influenced
their conclusions we cannot estimate at this distant date.

Between the years 660–583 B.C. a prophet and reformer
came forward in Media and Bactria. He was a man of
very high ideals and apparently had a great following
both in Persia and the adjacent countries. His teaching
up to a point was Monotheistic, for he taught that Ahura-
Mazda or Mazda Ahura (which means the Wise Lord or
Lord of Wisdom) was the sustainer of the universe. He
was Lord of the Sun, Moon, Stars, Wind, Darkness and
Light. So far we can all go with this great prophet, but
the problem of evil was too much for him, and in seeking
a solution for it he blundered into dualism. He preached
the existence of two gods, Ahura Mazda (the god of
Wisdom), and Angro or Ahriman (the god of darkness,
evil thought, word and action). The world is the field
of conflict between these two gods, and man the object
of their desire. Man has a free will and can choose for
himself, but choose he must.

The Jews took this dualism over, but did not allow it
to replace their Deity. To them dualism became two
principles in life under the care of God. They are known
as Yetser h'-tov (the good persuader) and Yetser h'-ra
(the evil persuader). They even went so far as to locate
the good persuader in the right breast, and the evil persuader in the left one. Hence the Jew even to-day when
beating the breast in penitence will beat the left one to
keep his evil persuader in subjection.

This idea crops up in our modern psychology also, as
the split or dual personality typified in Robert Louis
Stevenson's story of *Dr. Jekyll and Mr. Hyde.*

In the conflict between Ahura-Mazda and Ahriman there are agents of each taking part in the battle. For Ahura-Mazda, good spirits (angels) ; and for Ahriman, Durj (the lie) and his dawas (demons). These doctrines are important, since it seems that they influenced the angelology and demonology of the Jews and the Christians.

This great prophet was the first to direct non-Jewish attention, among other things, to immortality of a personal nature, to a final judgment and to a resurrection.

Briefly his teaching was :

The dead go into the grave. The soul of a person hovers near the grave for three days, after which there comes a beautiful maiden who is the creation of his virtue and good life. The soul then passes through three courts —good thoughts, good deeds and good words—and then finds itself in the presence of Ahura-Mazda.

For him who had chosen Ahriman and Durj, after death his soul lingers for three days at the grave in great perplexity, when a demon comes and lassoes it. His sins are embodied for him in an evil-looking witch, and after passing through the three courts of evil thoughts, deeds and words, the soul is landed in one of the compartments of hell. The good and evil remain in their respective states until the appearance of Shaoshyant the Saviour. At his coming the dead will be raised, beginning with our first parents. This resurrection will take place as follows : the bones of the dead will be demanded from the earth, the blood from the water, the hair from the plants, and life from the fire. When the body is complete, the good will be separated from the evil for three days, the good going to heaven, and the evil to hell, to be tortured in the body for further three days. At the end of this time the great ox (Hælyos) and Haoma are given to all, and all become immortal.

The affinity of these beliefs to those commonly held by the Jews, with certain modifications, are such that it is impossible not to conclude that the Jews adapted the teaching of the prophet of Iran to the solutions of their own problems.

Angelology and Demonology.

The rise of the belief in angels and demons may be put in a sentence as being due to the fact that there was an external impersonal universe in which there were influences that affect one's life.

The belief in angels and demons, which is as old as history itself, may be traced in archæology to prehistoric times. The belief was universal in the ancient world, though it differed somewhat in outlook.

In the Old Testament teaching the belief in angels and demons may alike be traced to the belief in the transcendence of God, and not infrequently the belief becomes so unbalanced that immanence and transcendence, matter and spirit, are so merged in each other that it is very difficult to distinguish one from the other. These beings of the extra-material universe are messengers of God for good or evil, they never act without the will of God, though God allows them independence of action. The independence is exercised mostly by the evil beings, but the evil beings cannot act evilly unless given leave to do so. The best example of this conception is found in the Book of Job, especially chaps. i. and ii.

We cannot follow the development of the idea in the pre-exilic literature, for that would involve us in a consideration of the general Semitic conception of these beliefs ; nor need we spend much time in considering the post-exilic Scriptural teaching concerning these matters, for they generally follow the main Semitic view. One book only in the Old Testament Canon requires attention, the Book of Daniel. In chap. viii. the writer speaks first of ' a holy one,' verse 13, and in verse 16 the name of the ' holy one ' is given as ' Gabriel ' and his function is that of revealing the contents of his vision. In chap. ix. verse 21, Gabriel is spoken of as ' the man Gabriel.' The purpose of his appearance is again to impart the meaning of the writer's vision. Another vision is granted the writer which quite unnerves him, and in the end the individual concerned in this vision tells him that no one can be compared to him save ' Michael your prince.' Thus two separate individuals are mentioned so far. In chap. xii. verse 1, Michael is again distinctly the title of ' the great prince who is appointed over the children of thy people.' Other angels are seen by the writer in the course of his vision. The teaching of this book is unmistakable as to the belief in the existence of angels, and as to some of the functions they have to fulfil.

It will not be possible to go into great detail regarding the angelology of our period, but some general indications will be given. The most notable book for our purpose is Enoch, and from this book I shall give selected passages from Canon Charles's translation :

' And these, Michael, Uriel, Raphael and Gabriel, looked down from heaven and saw much blood being shed upon the earth . . . the souls of men make their suit, saying: " Bring our cause before the Most High " (Enoch ix. 1–4). Here we have two more individual angels named, and they are implored to act as mediators between God and man. Chapter xx. of the Book of Enoch is worthy of entire quotation, for, as will be seen, it deals with the sphere of seven of the named angels :

' " And these are the names of the holy angels who watch. Uriel, one of the holy angels, who is over the world and over Tartarus. Raphael, one of the holy angels, who is over the spirits of man. Raguel, one of the holy angels, who takes vengeance on the world of the luminaries. Michael, one of the holy angels, to wit, he that is set over the past part of mankind and over chaos. Saraqâêl, one of the holy angels, who is set over the spirits who sin in the spirit. Gabriel, one of the holy angels,,who is over Paradise and the serpents and the Cherubim. Remiel, one of the holy angels, whom God set over those who rise." '

Other quotations from the Apocrypha and Pseudepigrapha might be given ; for example, the Book of Tobit, the Testaments of the Twelve Patriarchs, etc. etc. This conception is not a past and forgotten one, but, as already remarked, very real to the orthodox Jew of the present. Every evening, apart from his other prayers, the following is said : ' In the name of Jehovah (this name of course is not pronounced in full), the God of Israel, on my right hand is Michael, on my left is Gabriel, in front of me Uriel, behind me Raphael, and upon my head is the Shekinah of God."

Demonology.

Just as the universe was inhabited by the good spirits, so it was by evil spirits, and God made use of these evil spirits, as He did of the good ones. The evil spirits, or demons, had their spheres of action, and they also had a chief, this chief being Satan. The demons have their names and functions, and could take up their abode in the beings of individuals. There was one great difference between good and evil spirits : while man had no control over the actions of good spirits, he had over evil ones. He could exorcise them, and could have their spell removed from him by a person possessed of great merit in goodness.

The question that presents itself concerning our Lord's belief and attitude to this problem is a very difficult one. Let us see what has been said about it.

(1) It has been argued that our Lord, being a child of His times, believed in good and evil spirits, or angels.

(2) That He knew better than to believe these things, but that He had to use the language of His day.

(3) That our Lord Himself did not believe in these things, but that the authors of our Gospels interpreted certain of His cures in the language of the times.

(4) That these demoniac possessions were forms of nervous ailments, and that the power of suggestion, and the impact of the personality of our Lord on the possessed, cured them.

I do not know if it is forgotten, or studiously ignored, that the Jewish theology involves belief in angels, and that some of the angels, or spirits, as they are sometimes designated, were good and others were evil. Take, for example, the theophany in Exodus iii. : it is the Malach (angel or messenger of Yahweh) who is involved in the first place. The theophany in Isaiah vi. is of the same nature. Indeed the whole range of Old Testament writers surely had enough reasoning powers to realise that their presentation of this matter leaves much to be desired if they do not mean what they say.

6

I have already pointed out that in the Old Testament we are not dealing with God as an individuality, but a Godhead which, put in terms of philosophy, amounts to a Divine Economy. Is it not possible that God used spiritual beings to act for Him in these matters, and that this is why we meet so often with what seems on the face of it to be anthropomorphism? Is it not possible to hold that the revelation made to man prior to the advent, and during the life of Him who came to reveal God as Spirit, was made through these agencies, good and evil spirits, and that since God dwelt with man in Jesus Christ, these agencies have been withdrawn, as they are no longer needed as a means of communication between God and man? Is it not further possible to explain the coming and continuance of the Holy Spirit with us?

I am aware of the grave problem involved in this matter of casting out evil spirits, and of belief in angels. If these were only figments of the imagination, or remains of older superstitions, I cannot imagine our Lord being silent about them or, by using the language of His day, allowing the people to continue an erroneous belief which ought not to have been allowed to continue. I am greatly drawn to the conclusion that it was essential that, before the advent of Christ, God should have had some means of real intercourse with man, and that, in fact, he did have these true spiritual beings which we call angels and demons, and that now since we can know Him through Jesus Christ, and since the Holy Spirit is in our midst, the other agencies used before the time of Christ are no longer needed to take the part they did in human affairs and they have been withdrawn.

The Jews have continued in this belief in angels and demons just because the greater revelation has not become part of their heritage. Other peoples, like the Muhammadans, still believe in these just because they do not possess the greater revelation. But when it dawns upon them, they will come to the fuller knowledge of God as manifested in Jesus Christ, and these beliefs which in the past were real but are no longer so to-day will disappear along with many other beliefs which cannot be held side by side with the final revelation of God in and through Jesus Christ.

The Future of Man and the Future Life.

Many Old Testament scholars tell us that the idea of a future life was not current among Old Testament writers or seers. But is that a fact? It is somewhat difficult to understand the action of Saul, who went to the witch of Endor asking her to bring Samuel up to him. If Samuel was dead and done with, how could she do that? While the passage in Isa. ix. 19 is not very clear and must be emended, it is yet clear that he protests against the people making inquiries from the dead on behalf of the living; he protests against the spiritualists of his day. We hear much from the same source about Sheol, and the passive existence of those that go down into it: we have yet to get an explanation of what this passive existence means. If there was any kind of continuity, no matter what form it took, existence after death was believed in. To say that a people do not believe in immortality because they do not believe in it in terms such as we do, is to go beyond the limits of reasonable assumption.

Again I ask, what was the meaning of Saul's campaign against such persons as the witch of Endor? Was it not that the people believed too much in the continued existence of the dead? What was the meaning of Isaiah's protest? Had it any meaning? The earlier writers of the Old Testament do not have very much to say about the matter doctrinally. Have we? Have we, in this day when the Resurrection of Jesus is an established fact, a doctrine which reaches down to the man in the street and yet satisfies a man like Sir Arthur Keith? Is it possible that a people who had come into such close touch with the Egyptians as did the Habiri (Hebrews) should have had no belief about this matter? On the contrary, the steps which Saul took show that it was so thoroughly believed in that parasites of the human species took advantage of it and used it as a means of livelihood. I maintain that it was so well established as a belief that it was a hindrance to the people rather than a help.

When we turn from the early Hebrew and Israelitish periods to the Jewish period, we are left in no doubt as to the existence of the belief. Every book in the Apocrypha and Pseudepigrapha is full of it. It becomes a settled belief in the resurrection of the body, a belief which may have been taken over from Zoroastrianism. Indeed the whole conception of the future life was so influenced by Zoroastrian thinking that it became a positive danger to Judaism. Many Old Testament scholars argue against the influence of Zoroastrian belief. In private discussion Dr. A. Peake maintained that it is just as likely that the idea of immortality had arisen in Judaism because the problem presented itself to the mind at that period. Dr. Peake argued with reason that such a passage as Job xix. 25–26 is a natural conclusion to the problem that the writer was faced with. I willingly admit this. The author of that divine drama was no doubt capable of reaching such a solution independent of any other mind. But my contention is that the other Old Testament writers, or at least many of them, and the people generally believed in immortality. It is to me altogether inconceivable that they should have thought that their heroes and prophets had been annihilated by death.

The question, however, is not that of belief in immortality or no, but that so tersely expressed in Dan. xii. 2 : ' And many who sleep in the dust of the earth shall waken up, some to age-long life, and others to age-long shame and abhorrence.'

The belief of pre-Christian times which was taken over into Christianity was not merely a belief in immortality, but, as the creeds show, one of the revivification of the body. For some the passage in Daniel may suffice to justify such a belief, and when the passages of the Apocrypha and Pseudepigrapha are added, the evidence seems complete. When the writings of the Early Church Fathers such as Justin or Athenagoras are studied, no doubt is left that they had taken the belief over in all its realism.

Without going into detail and multiplying quotations I will state the belief in a few words. The dead of the Hebrew race will be raised, when they will receive their former bodies. They will be judged, as the passage in Daniel cited above indicates. All will become immortal. Some will enjoy with their immortality God's full favour, others his full wrath. Elijah will come a few days prior to the revivification, and Messiah will act as the judge of the raised. More will be said in this connection when the sects of the time of our Lord are considered, but something must be added here about the view that Jesus took of the whole problem.

In seeking to ascertain our Lord's teaching on this matter, we come up against the eternal question of the validity of the testimony of the Fourth Gospel. For my part I shall proceed on the lines that the evidence of the Fourth Gospel is as valid as that of the Synoptists.

The first question is that of our Lord's belief regarding the doctrine in the Old Testament. This question was put to Him regarding a matter arising from certain usages of the Law. The answer is clear and to the point. Our Lord first tells the Sadducees that their disbelief in the Resurrection is due to a misunderstanding of the Law. So far as the resurrected body is concerned it is altogether different from that which we possess prior to death. It is like that of the angels. Having answered the question asked concerning a definite situation, our Lord goes on to treat of the question on the broader issues involved. In His revelation to Moses, God declared for immortality, when He called Himself the God of Abraham, Isaac and Jacob. Had these been dead, God would not have made any reference to them. So that, even as far as the Law is concerned, immortality is asserted (see Mark xii. 18–27 and the corresponding passages in the Synoptists). That our Lord believed that Abraham was alive during His ministry is indicated in the parable of the rich man and Lazarus. There is no question of resurrection there. The rich man, real or imaginary, is getting his reward ; so is Lazarus, real or imaginary as the case may have been.

The other passages dealing with the matter in a very definite form are : John xi. 25, where Jesus claims that He is the resurrection, and that faith in Him means eternal life ; John iii. 16 where we find the same claim attached to faith. To press this matter any further would lead to an argument about the belief of St. Paul. St. Paul's belief is stated distinctly enough in 1 Corinthians xv., and shows that he believed in immortality, and not in the bodily resurrection, when he wrote that passage.

It is evident that the prophets believed it, that the writer of Job believed it, that the writers between the Testaments believed it, and that our Lord demonstrated that this belief is based upon God's own Word, and further, that He demonstrated it by His victory over death.

The evidence cited indicates that belief in some form of continuity after death was established in the teaching of the Old Testament, and that it was a form more in keeping with the idea of immortality than resurrectionism. Also that in the teaching of the last three centuries before our era the belief took the form of resurrectionism, though whether this new development was due to the Zoroastrian doctrine is a point that cannot be decided. It is evident that the Jewish people in our Lord's time believed in resurrectionism rather than in immortality, and that the disciples shared in that belief. As to the question whether our Lord also shared in it, this must be answered by theology on the basis of all the facts. That St. Paul departed from the Jewish idea of the resurrection of the identical body which was laid in the grave is amply proved by i Corinthians xv.

CHAPTER IV

FEASTS, FASTS AND THE SABBATH

IT is difficult to distinguish between the religious and
the secular in Judaism. The reason is not far to
seek : the Jews do not recognise anything as secular. And
in this lay the real genius of the Hebrew and the Jew
alike, they took over primitive customs, traditions and
beliefs and adapted them to their own needs, being very
careful to give them a monotheistic stamp. We shall not
trouble to follow up the origins of feasts and fasts in remote
antiquity, for, interesting as this may be, it does not
affect their bearing on Christianity, with which we are here
mostly concerned.

The Passover.

This feast is of the greatest importance to Christians
for many reasons and will be considered in greater detail
than the others. Apart from the fact that the Passover
is the most ancient feast of antiquity which has come
down to us, and apart from the fact that it perpetuates
an historical incident of great importance in the history
and religion of the world, to Christian men and women it
has an appeal that no other feast in the Old Testament
can have, and this is due to the fact that our Synoptists
associate it with the Last Supper of our Lord which he had
with His disciples.

The Passover in the Old Testament.

That this feast was not fixed in every detail, but grew
in its development, it will not take long for us to find out.
The first passage in which the Passover is mentioned is
Ex. xii. 1–29. Briefly stated, the injunctions therein for
the observance of the feast are : (Verses 1–4) The month

in which the feast should take place is designated 'the beginning of months,' that is to say the New Year's month. This seems at variance with other passages which ordain that the New Year begin on the first day of the month Tishre, six months from that on which the feast of the Passover occurs, but the explanation is easy. There were two seasons which were looked upon as marking the beginning of the year—the one agricultural, the other ecclesiastical. We have the same thing happening in our own country to-day : the Government year does not begin on the first of January, but on the first of April. It was, therefore, quite natural that a nomadic people should have its interest centre round a different season from that of an organised society of town dwellers. Taxes always played their part in the ordering of the life of the community, and it was easier to get the taxes when people had reaped their harvest and had the wherewithal to pay them.

On the tenth day of the month Nisan an animal from the flocks was to be set aside for the Paschal victim. The animal was to supply the requirements of a family or household, but if neither of these units was large enough to need a whole animal for itself then they were to join with their neighbours in sharing the Paschal victim. This matter was to be regulated by the eating requirements of the individuals, seeing that the victim had to be eaten on the evening on which it was slaughtered.

(Verse 5) This verse specifies the kind of animal, and is important. It states that the victim should be either a lamb or a kid of the male sex, that it should be free from blemish, and that it should be a year old ; that is to say, it should be an animal born within the current agricultural year.

(Verse 6) The date for the slaughtering of the victim is given as the 14th of the month. This raises a difficulty which has remained unsolved. The day in ancient times, both among Semites and the Greeks, began at sunset, and not as the present European day, which begins at midnight ; and since the time is said to be ' bain H'arbaim,' *i.e.* between the evenings, it is difficult to say if by this is meant between the setting of the sun on the 13th when the 14th begins, or between the setting of the sun on the

eve of the 14th when the 15th begins. If we may take
the meaning attached to this passage from another dealing
with the same subject, namely, Lev. xxiii. 5–6, the understanding of the passage would seem to be put beyond
doubt, but even with this passage before us the matter is
not settled. The passage reads : ' In the first month, on
the 14th day of the month between the evenings is Pesach
unto Jehovah, and on the 15th of the same month is the
feast of unleavened bread ; seven days shall ye eat unleavened bread.' Now there seems a clear demarcation
between the dates, and yet the matter is very doubtful.
I have asked some very learned rabbis to explain the
matter to me, and the only answer I got was, ' The 15th
day begins when the 14th ends.' By that they meant
that the victim was killed at sunset of the 14th which
begins the 15th. It is stated in our passage that the
people should slaughter the victim. This deserves special
notice, since priests alone were allowed to slaughter any
animal that was deemed a sacrifice. The inference is very
pointed, and it is that this victim was not looked upon as a
sacrifice. This method of killing the victim by the people
themselves continued down to the destruction of the
second Temple.

(Verse 8) Ordains that the blood of the victim should
be sprinkled upon the doorposts and the lintels of the houses
in which the victim is to be eaten.

(Verses 9–12) The remaining injunctions are that the
meat must be consumed on the night of the slaughtering ;
must be roasted, and must be eaten with unleavened
bread and bitter herbs. It must not be boiled or seethed,
nor should the head, feet or entrails be eaten ; all that was
left over by morning must be burned. The manner of
eating is prescribed as follows : ' The loins girded, sandals
on the feet, sticks in the hands, and eaten in a hurried
manner,' for, it says, it is Pesach unto Jehovah. Many
meanings are offered for the word Pesach, but if we take
the word in connection with its context here, there can
be little doubt that it implies something done hurriedly,
which is expressed by the English word ' Passover.' The
chapter goes on to make further remarks about the killing
of the Pascha, and the eating of unleavened bread, but

adds very little to what has already been gathered from the passage we have examined. The only remark which calls for attention is that in verse 42 'Lel shemurin' (a night of watching) has been taken to mean a night that one must not sleep in.

A passage in Ex. xxxiv. 18, and the Leviticus passage quoted above add nothing to our knowledge, and so need not detain us.

Numbers ix. 1-15.

The main interest in this passage is the provision that is made for such as are Levitically unclean, or on a long voyage, and are therefore unable to celebrate the Passover on the stated date. It is enacted that in cases of such persons it shall be deemed lawful for them to celebrate the feast a month after the time appointed for its ordinary celebration, that is to say, on the 14th day of the month Eiar. Further, our passage states that the stranger and sojourner should also celebrate the feast. The eight days' duration of the feast does not seem incumbent upon those who had failed to keep it on its set date. The penalty for not keeping the feast is stated to be the cutting a man off from his people, that is to say, excommunication.

Deuteronomy xvi. 1-8.

In this passage we meet with a great many difficulties regarding the observance of this feast as compared with the others.

In verse 2 it is stated that not only could the paschal victim be sheep or goats, but cattle were also eligible for that purpose. It further states that the Pascha must be killed in the place that Jehovah will select for His name to dwell in, that is to say, at the central sanctuary, Jerusalem. In verse 5 it puts the matter of place beyond doubt, for it states very explicitly that the Pascha cannot be killed in any of their towns, but in the place specified above. The same verse clears up the question of the exact time of slaughtering, stating that the victim should be slaughtered in the evening as the sun sets. This time has been preserved by the Samaritans. I witnessed their celebration of the feast in 1926, but I was surprised to observe that they were using leavened bread. I do not know if this was simply to supply the non-Samaritans who visited them, but the food given us was certainly not unleavened. In verse 7 another difference occurs, the word ' bashal,' which, as a rule, is translated ' boil ' or ' seethe,' is used in a favourable sense, maybe inferring that roasting was not necessarily the only legitimate manner of preparation. But the word ' bashal ' has a larger meaning, and may simply be used here in the sense of cooking.

Other Old Testament Passages.

The feast is mentioned in Josh. v. 10, and from that period to the time of Josiah no mention is made of the Passover. The early prophets have nothing to say about it, the reason for this being given us in 2 Kings xxiii. 21-23 : ' And the king commanded all the nation, saying, Celebrate the Pesach unto Yahweh your God according to the written instructions in this book of the covenant,' and the passage adds : ' For the Pesach had not been celebrated since the days of the judges who judged Israel, nor in the days of the kings of Israel, nor of the kings of Judah.' The date of the celebration of the Passover in Josiah's reign is given as the eighteenth year : that means about 622 B.C. The writer of the Book of Chronicles, or the compiler, interprets this differently, for he waters down the statement to read that such a celebration as that in the days of Josiah had not occurred since the days of Samuel, nor did it occur during the time of the monarchies (2 Chron. xxxv. 18).

Ezekiel xlv. 21-24.

I will quote this passage in extension because of its importance from the priestly view-point.

' On the first month, on the fourteenth day of the month, ye shall observe the Passover, a feast of seven days' duration, during which unleavened bread must be eaten. On that day the president of the people (presumably the high priest) shall offer for himself and the people of the land an ox as a sin-offering. During each day of the feast there shall be offered up unto Yahweh seven oxen as a whole burnt-offering, and seven rams without blemish, these shall be offered every day during the feast, and a kid as a sin-offering.' The curious thing about this passage is that the paschal victim is not mentioned specifically : the prophet-priest is more concerned about the ordinary sacrifices, and the sacrifice for the purifying of the altar from any form of defilement, yet he does mention the eating of unleavened bread.

There are passages in Nehemiah (*circa* 444–400 B.C.) and Ezra (*circa* 397–370 B.C.) which indicate that the feast was observed. The last passage of value in the Old Testament is found in 2 Chron. xxxv. 1–19. If the authorship of the Chronicles be assigned to Ezra, the method of observation of the feast in his day is very illuminating, for it is practically as it was celebrated at the time of our Lord. In this passage we are told that the nation was divided into three sections, consisting of priests, Levites and people. We are told in this passage that the blood of the paschal victims was sprinkled on the base of the altar by the priest in the Temple at Jerusalem.

We note the evolutionary nature of the Passover as we move from passage to passage : no explanations are given for the modifications or changes, but it is taken for granted that the needs of the people and the times are sanctioned by God. This principle, which is often overlooked by students of the Bible, ought to receive more attention than it does, for it is a very far-reaching one. If it is understood and given proper place in the study of the Bible, many difficulties will be removed, and what some people term ' contradictions ' will be seen to be no more than changes of the needs of the times which the legislators deemed as quite within their right to make in the full consciousness that these had the approval of God.

The Book of Jubilees and the Mishnah.

The Book of Jubilees, which I believe was written about the year 180, though Charles and others would bring it down to the years 135–105 B.C., has a whole chapter on the observance of the Passover. In this chapter (xlix.) some very marked changes in the observance appear. The following are the more noteworthy. In verse 11 it states that the Pascha was eaten on the night of the fifteenth. In verse 6 the following occurs : ' And all Israel were eating the flesh of the paschal lamb, and drinking wine, and were lauding, blessing and giving thanks to the Lord God of their fathers.' In verses 10 and 11, the time for the slaughtering of the paschal lamb is given as from the third part of the day, that is to say, from 3 p.m., to the first part of the night, that is to say, till 11 p.m. It further states that the victim must be eaten before 3 a.m., and that it must be eaten in the sanctuary. It will be noticed that two new elements enter into the observation of the paschal feast. First that the time of slaughtering, instead of being at sunset, may take place at any time between 3 and 11 p.m. Second, that wine was used when the victim was being eaten. But the most amazing statement is that the victim must be eaten in the sanctuary. Such a thing could not possibly have been contemplated in the years which Dr. Charles assigns to the book, for in the time of Simon Ashmonai this would have been a physical impossibility. It points to a time when the people who observed the feast were few, and therefore before the time of the Ashmonaim. In this connection there is a passage in Josephus which runs as follows: ' So these high priests, upon the coming of their feast which is called the Passover, when they slay their sacrifices from the ninth to the eleventh hour (3 to 5 p.m.), but that so that a company not less than ten belong to every sacrifice (for it is not lawful for them to feast singly), and many of us were twenty in a company, found the number of sacrifices was two hundred and fifty-six thousand five hundred ' (*Wars of the Jews*, VI. ix. 3). Josephus goes on to compute the number present at the feast in question as 2,700,200. This computation has been questioned, but I think without any sound reason.

The Tractate Pesachim.

In dealing with this tractate we have to exercise special care, since it was not brought to completion till the second century A.D., though its main teaching goes back to at least 300 B.C. The contents are of very considerable value for the understanding of the whole matter. In the first place we must note the observation regarding engagement in work on the day preceding the Passover. Though it indicates that the customs of Judea and Galilee differed in this connection, it is clear that no work was permissible or was done from the afternoon of the day prior to the slaughtering of the Passover. This point is especially valuable in view of the mention in the New Testament that a person who was concerned with the crucifixion of our Lord was coming from the field, also that the women brought various things for embalming the body of our Lord.

The time of the slaughtering of the Passover is given. On ordinary days the Passover was slaughtered after the Thamid, that is to say, at 3.30 p.m., but if the Passover happened to fall on a Friday it was slaughtered an hour earlier, namely, at 2.30 p.m. It also states that the Passover was slaughtered by the nation in the three sections as mentioned in 2 Chron. xxxv. Each representative of a family or Chaburah (association) slaughtered its own victim ; priests stood with golden and silver vessels in which the blood of the victims was caught and passed from one to the other till it reached the officiating priest at the altar, who sprinkled the blood on the base of the altar. The Hallel (Psalms 113–118) was recited during the slaughtering and sprinkling of the blood. It is stated that no victim may be used for the needs of one person only, but Rabbis Judah and Josse say that one victim might meet the needs of a hundred persons.

In section x. 48b it is laid down that at least four cups of wine must be partaken of during the celebration of the Passover. Even the poorest person must have enough wine for four cups. Differences of opinion arise between the schools of Hillel and Shammai as to the blessings over the cups, the former maintaining that the blessing over the first cup must concern itself with the special significance of the day, while the latter maintains that it must be a cup of thanksgiving. There follows an elaborate description of how the meal was celebrated, what was said and done. The Hallel, or at least part of it, was recited, and the majority of the pious Jews remained feasting till the morning.

Summary.

It is quite evident from the passages and authorities that we have considered that the Passover was a national feast of the greatest antiquity ; that it was essentially a family or a friendly shared feast ; that its observance was obligatory upon all males of the Jewish nation ; that from the time of the Deuteronomic code it had to be slaughtered in Jerusalem ; that from the time of the composition of the Chronicles the blood of the victim had to be sprinkled at the base of the altar of the Temple ; that from the time of the authorship of the Book of Jubilees wine had to be partaken of when the Paschal meal was eaten ; that during some subsequent period four cups of wine were enjoined upon the celebrants ; that, apart from the historical incidents connected with the feast which they all engaged in reciting as the victim was being eaten, they also sang the Hallel.   Other factors such as the intercalation of the month of Nisan had much to do with the exact time of the observance of the feast, as also had the ripeness of the corn, the fatness of the paschal victims, and the spring equinox.

The New Testament and the Passover.

Our Synoptists join in telling us that our Lord was anxious to celebrate the Passover with His disciples before He suffered, and they infer that He did so.   The Fourth Gospel has nothing to say about the celebration of the Passover as such, but it is very clear as to the date of the Last Supper of our Lord with His disciples.   The account of the Fourth Gospel has been interpreted as being at variance with that of the Synoptists, but is that conclusion justified ?   The writer of that Gospel had nothing to say about the nature of the meal ; he leaves that to the writers of the Synoptics, who were in the field with their accounts before him, and simply states the date on which Jesus was crucified as having been the Day of Preparation—that is, the day on which the Pascha was slain.   But this evidence makes it clear that our Lord did not celebrate the Passover on the same day as the Jewish nation at large, and there is no reason at all why the records should not be made complementary.

All Jewish usage would point very strongly indeed to the fact that it was almost an impossibility that our Lord should have been dealt with by the authorities on a feast day. True, the entire trial was so illegal that it had not the remotest semblance to a regular trial ; but I doubt if the Jewish authorities would have dared to violate the feast in the manner that such a trial would necessitate. While the Synoptists do insist on the meal being a Passover meal, they have very little to say as to the date on which it was eaten. But we must turn to the accounts themselves.

St. Paul's Account.

The account given by St. Paul in his First Epistle to the Corinthians, chapter xi., is the first in point of time, as it belongs to the first few years of the second half of the first century A.D. In this account no mention is made of the Passover nor yet of anything connected with the feast : St. Paul is not concerned with that side of the question. He tells the Corinthians that on the night on which the Lord Jesus was betrayed He took bread and wine, that after giving thanks He gave to the disciples, telling them that these were His body and blood broken and shed for them, and that they should partake of these elements as a means of remembering His Last Supper with them and His death till He come again. The whole point in this account is that the partaking of these elements is a memorial to be observed till the return of Jesus.

We may also note here how this memorial was observed. The people of Corinth met at night ; they brought their ordinary meal with them and they partook of it ; some had too much wine with their supper so that they were not sober at the end of it ; and it was after they had had their ordinary meal that they partook of the elements of bread and wine in a sacramental fashion.

Turning to the Synoptics, I take the Lucan account first, because the manner of the observation of the Last Supper follows closely the account of St. Paul, and would therefore indicate that Luke xxii. 19–20 was derived from the same source. In chapter xxii. Luke tells us : ' And the day of unleavened bread came, on which the Passover must be sacrificed,' etc. Now this is a very strange statement, to say the least, for the words of Luke can only have one meaning, namely, that the feast of unleavened bread preceded that of the Passover. But we must take his state-

ment as we find it, and go on to the other Synoptics.
Mark is Luke's source here, and Matthew, as is often the
case, follows Mark word for word. So we are compelled
to conclude, on the basis of these accounts, that it was
on the first day of unleavened bread, *i.e.* the fifteenth day
of Nisan, that Jesus and His disciples observed the Feast
of the Passover. We ought, moreover, to note that all
the Synoptists record the resolve of the authorities not to
wait till the feast-day lest there be a tumult amongst the
people, that is to say, they did not mind acting in defiance
of the prohibition of the Law and Mishnah, but did not
want to face a rising among the people.

The Passover in the Gospels.

We come to the last source in our New Testament
narrative, written last of all the Gospels. The Fourth
Gospel has nothing to say as to the connection of the Last
Supper with the Passover, but in chapter xviii., verse 28,
it states implicitly that the Jews did not go into the
prætorium, as this would have made them unfit for the
eating of the Passover. This incident, we must note, took
place after Jesus and His disciples had had their Last
Supper, and so the confusion increases, and to clear it
we must determine which of the accounts are correct. To
do this we must first gather up the statements in the
Gospels themselves, and then turn to Jewish usage.

The following considerations emerge from an examination :

(1) The release of a prisoner. The release took place
on the eve of the feast, but when Jesus was before Pilate
the prisoner had not yet been released.

(2) The burial of Jesus. Had Jesus and His disciples
kept the Passover in the usual manner, the day following
it would be a holy day during which no burial could take
place. Jesus could not have been buried by any Jew.

(3) Luke tells us that the women returned after the
burial and prepared spices. Now this could not have
been the case if the day was that following the Passover.

When these facts, on the showing of the Synoptics themselves, are so contrary to what Jewish usage teaches us
as likely, and when the account of the Fourth Gospel is

7

added, the evidence against the meal having been the Passover is strong. The very terminology—' the first day of unleavened bread when the Passover was sacrificed '—is so utterly un-Jewish that it cannot be deemed possible that a Jew wrote it.

An examination of the text of the synoptic gospels, especially Matthew and Mark, leaves much to be desired. They begin by telling us that two days before the feast the authorities had made up their minds that Jesus must die before the feast, and instead of continuing their narrative, they bring in the story of the anointing at Bethany, which Luke omits. And the Fourth Gospel assigns this incident to the evening previous to His entry into Jerusalem when He was acclaimed by the people.

I always hesitate to reject a passage in the Bible as unauthentic, and require strong proof even to question a passage. I must, however, in face of a strong natural reluctance reject this passage, that is to say, Mark xiv. 12 and Matt. xxvi. 17. The story of the anointing in Bethany does not belong here ; it was inserted here by some hand not Jewish, and in order to pick up the course of the narrative the questionable verses were inserted. If these are eliminated and the verses are joined up to those at the beginning of the chapters we have the truer version of the actual course of events.

The question remains, Was the Last Supper a Passover meal ? It was in one sense only, in so far as it may have had a pascal lamb as part of it. There is nothing in the gospels to indicate that it was, save the remark that our Lord gave Judas the sop which He had dipped in something.

It is quite well known from the Talmud that Chaburoth (that is to say, associations of scholars) met at various times for a fellowship meal and discussion. The purpose of these meals or meetings was to welcome the Sabbath, to engage in religious conversation, or to say farewell to the Sabbath or a feast day. Such passages are quoted by Dr. Oesterley (*The Jewish Background of the Christian Liturgy*, pp. 167 ff.), and make the matter very clear. I hold that the Last Supper was a meeting of this nature, and that they may have anticipated the Passover and partaken of a paschal lamb.

It is a little difficult for Western people to realise the possibility of a change in the date of the feast, for its anticipation or postponement. But when the workings of the Jewish calendar are examined carefully this difficulty disappears. Taking the Passover as an example, we notice that its observance depended on many factors. The spring Equinox was an important factor ; others are tabulated for us in the tractate *Sanhedrin*, of which the following may be cited : (1) If the roads were unfit for travelling ; (2) if the bridges were broken down ; (3) if the conditions of the weather did not permit of fires being lit in the open for the roasting of the paschal victim ; (4) if those who had set out for the celebration of the feast in Jerusalem had been prevented from reaching the city (*Sanh.* i. 11a, English 7). In the same passages we are told that Rabban Gamaliel once had to go to visit the governor of Syria, and because he did not come back in time the Passover was postponed. Rabban Gamaliel himself gives the following reasons for changing the date of the Passover—the conditions of the victims, the ripeness of the corn, and the condition of the birds that had to be offered up—if these are not favourable the feast may be postponed. Further comment about the matter is unnecessary. If any of these things could change the date of the Passover, the Master would have no hesitation in anticipating the actual date of the feast in the face of the certainty of His death.

The Celebration in the Upper Room.

Jesus and his disciples gathered in a 'Katalyma' (an inn). They would wash their hands for the purpose of partaking of food, and this would be followed by the blessing over the cup of wine. It is clear from St. Luke that the first cup was partaken of in the usual manner, that is to say, He gave thanks over the cup, drank of it Himself and passed it to them to drink from. The blessing over the first cup was followed by the breaking of the bread, the ordinary method being to break off a piece of bread from the loaf, dip it in salt, and then pass it on to those present to partake of. In this case, however, our Lord accompanied the passing of the bread with the words, ' This is my body, which is broken for you, this do in remembrance of me.' From the account given by St. Paul and the first two gospels it would seem that the blessing over the cup followed immediately after, but this is hardly possible if the usual Jewish method was followed ; and since Luke tells us that the cup was the cup after the supper, we may take it for granted that a considerable time had elapsed between the two acts. What happened during the interval ? This we are not told in so many words, but we can nevertheless fill in the time. In Luke xxii. 24 ff. and John xiii. 1–18 we get part of the subject matter. The disciples again took up the question of who will be the chief in the kingdom. John and James were the leaders in that question. They had got their mother to ask our Lord for places on His right and left hand for her sons ; and now returned to this matter. Our Lord's answer that these places were not His to apportion did not seem to penetrate their minds, and to make the matter clear beyond doubt He girded Himself with a towel and washed their feet to teach them that humility and service alone will entitle men to high places in the kingdom of God. Other details can be gathered, for instance our Lord's perturbation at the presence of Judas. It was the sacred and time-honoured custom that if you had partaken of salt and bread with a person he became your friend, and even though he had killed a relative whom you had to avenge he was pardoned. Dipping in the same dish was, if anything, an even more sacred bond of friendship. Judas was breaking these pledges, and our Lord, troubled over this breach of the sacred symbols of the people, told Judas that He knew the thoughts of his wicked heart. What exactly He told him we do not know, and the disciples themselves did not know ; but it is noteworthy that the author of the Fourth Gospel says that the disciples thought that He was saying something to him about the preparations to be made for the feast. They could hardly have been eating the Passover and think that. Our Lord further told the disciples that they would forsake Him that evening, and Peter was told that He would deny

162A

any knowledge of Him if he did not forsake Him.   Other details might also be supplied, but these would have to rest on an opinion, and so are better left out.   The supper was drawing to an end, and was finished as usual with a blessing over a cup of wine (so, according to Luke xxii. 20 : ' Likewise also the cup after supper, saying, This cup is the new testament in my blood, which is shed for you '). They concluded the meal with the singing of a hymn.

Conclusion.

While many factors point to a paschal meal on the regular Passover lines, especially the sop which was given to Judas by our Lord and is considered as the bitter herbs, against this is the fact that the ' sop ' is mentioned in the Fourth Gospel only, and the writer of that gospel does not imply in a word or hint that it was a Passover meal.   Another factor which has led many to read the Passover into the meal are the words, ' And when they had sung an hymn.'   From this it is argued that the hymn was the Hallel (Ps. 113–118), but it is not explicitly stated what the nature of the hymn was.

Our main sources for the feasts, apart from the Passover which we have already examined, are Leviticus xxiii., Numbers xxviii.–ix., the Book of Jubilees, the Mishnaic tractates, the New Testament and the works of Philo and Josephus.

Other Feasts.
The New Moon.

Some scholars may demur at my calling the New Moon a feast, but I have no doubt in my own mind that it is one of the oldest and most sacred feasts in the calendar, and that the other feasts were regulated by it.   Its observance is lost in antiquity.   I will quote one passage from the Hemerology of an old inscription according to Professor Sayce's text :   ' The month of the second Elul.   The first day (is dedicated) to Anu and Bel.   A day of good luck. When during the month the moon is seen, the shepherd of mighty nations (shall offer) to the moon as a free-will offering (the Sumerian word here means ' the dues of the goddess,' the Assyrian word is ' Nidabu '=the Hebrew

word ' Nedabah,' free gift) a gazelle without blemish.
He shall make his free-will offering to the sun, the mistress
of the world, and the moon the supreme god.'

That the New Moon was a festival equal to that of the
Sabbath, appears very clearly from the following passages
—1 Sam. xx. 18 ff. ; 2 Kings iv. 23. Other passages might
be cited, but are not necessary. The observance of the
New Moon festival has continued to this day ; special
services are held in the synagogue ; special prayers are
appointed for the day, among which is the Hallel. In
Palestine on Saturday evening following the New Moon,
the evening prayer is said in the open fields or in the court-
yard adjoining the synagogue, and a special prayer called
' the New Moon prayer ' is recited. I have gone at some
length into this feast because of its great importance to
the Jewish calendar as a whole.

The Feast of Weeks (Pentecost).

This feast lives in the memory of Christians, for it was
during its celebration in Jerusalem that the Church was
started. The chief characteristic of this feast was the
bringing of the first-fruits to the Temple as an offering.

Tradition connects this feast with the reception of the
Commandments by Moses at Mount Sinai ; the Book of
Jubilees carries it back to the time of Abraham (Jubilees
xvi. 14). The feast occurs fifty days after the Passover.
That it had originally something to do with the sacred
number, seven times seven, is suggested by a study of
Assyrian sources. It is a joyous feast ; the houses are
decorated with green leaves of all kinds. Apart from
other special portions of Scripture, the Book of Ruth is
read, and the agricultural vocation of the nation is brought
to mind. The origin and birthday of the beloved Singer of
Israel is thought of, and the nation is reminded by the
example of Ruth that, if it can by its life commend the
faith it professes, there would be many Naomis joining
themselves to its practices and doctrines. It would seem
that the early Christians did commend the teaching of their
Master by their lives ; their witness was emphasised by
the gift of the coming of the Holy Spirit ; and more than
three thousand were added that day to the new community

of Jesus. If Judaism to-day could but learn the lesson of Ruth and Pentecost, great things for the good of the world might result.

New Year.

We are again reminded of the agricultural nature of the people by this feast, because the first day of the seventh month marked the close of the harvest and brought to an end the year's activities in the fields, orchards and vineyards.

The reader of the Old Testament is somewhat puzzled by the seeming contradiction about this matter, for he reads in some passages that Nisan, the month in which the Passover occurs, is the first month, and in others that this month Tishri is the month which commences New Year. He would be still more disconcerted to read in the tractate *Rosh H'shanah* (Of the beginning of the year) to find that there are four dates given as commencements of the year. ' There are four New Years, namely, the first day of Nisan, this is the king's New Year, and also the New Year for those who went up to the Temple. The first day of Elul is the New Year for tithing of cattle, Rabbis Eliezer and Simon say that this should take place on the first day of Tishri. And on the first day of Tishri is the New Year, from it are the Sabbatical and Jubilee years counted, it also is counted as the New Year in connection with harvest and vegetation. The first day in Shebat is the New Year for trees ; according to the schools of Shammai and Hillel it is on the fifth day of the month ' (tractate *Rosh H'shanah* i. 1–2).

It is quite clear from this statement that we have in Judaism what is practised in the modern world. The Government year in Great Britain starts on the 1st of April and not of January. Judaism also had its civil and ecclesiastical new years, as well as other new years, for special reasons. We may take it for granted that in its earliest form the New Year was a very important agricultural event, perhaps not always a joyous one. The state of the crops would determine the nature of the feast. Rabbinical and traditional Judaism have, however, given the feast a new significance. It is stated on their authority that it is the time of New Year in heaven, God appointing man's portion for the year on that day or the two days during which it is celebrated.

The Jew who does not darken the doors of the synagogue save on the Day of Atonement comes to the synagogue on this date to plead for the continuance of life and prosperity to him and his. In Palestine the people go to places from which the sea or some lake can be seen, and into these watery expanses cast their sins. It is a very solemn season for the Jew, and he certainly comes as a very humble penitent before his Maker. It is believed that on this day God reads up the records of every Jew, whose doings are kept in the book to which his soul goes every night to record faithfully, and that God either enters the name of the person in the book of life which is continued for the coming year, or that He fails to do so, and He ordains what the nature of death should be, drowning, burning, strangulation, etc., but that the ultimate sentence is not passed till the Day of Atonement. Therefore the days which separate New Year from Atonement are called 'the ten days of repentance,' and great is the number of prayers offered up during these days, and great, certainly, is the searching of hearts. It is not to be wondered at that we hear nothing of this feast in connection with our Lord's life or that of the Early Church. We need not concern ourselves with other matters connected with this feast, such as blowing the ram's horn, though to be sure this is a very important part of the service and is very awe-inspiring.

Feast of Tabernacles.

This feast, which is of eight days' duration, is an agricultural feast and must be of very ancient date. Its peculiar feature is the living of the people in booths. The summers in Palestine and in the adjacent countries are free from rain, and in the main very warm, if not excessively hot, so that most of the people engaged in agricultural pursuits live in the open. About the time of the feast the rain begins to fall, and it may be due to this fact that the booths, or in earlier times tents, were required. This meant that these agriculturists entered into their winter quarters. As this feast occurs on the night of the full moon it has been argued that it may also derive its significance from the autumnal equinox, a probability that seems quite reasonable. Whatever its original significance, we cannot say that either of the foregoing ideas had much to do with the celebration of the feast by the Jews of our period.

The use of the willow and myrtle both in the construction of the booth and in the ceremonies at morning prayers in the synagogue is significant, and though cabalistic explanations are not wanting as to the reason for this use, so far as I can trace, the meaning of it is purely agricultural, and the feast a harvest thanksgiving.

The winter months were very anxious times for the authorities, for the people took the opportunity during this time of inactivity to settle scores of enmity and to reopen blood feuds. The cycle of feasts was no doubt intended to get the people into a better frame of mind and to centre their thoughts upon the religious side of life. While the New Year and Atonement feasts were meant to bring them face to face with the omissions of the summer months, when toil and other preoccupations caused them to neglect their duties towards God, and to call them to repentance, the Feast of Booths was to bring them into closer human fellowship that might obviate many of the quarrels that would be revived for settlement during the winter months. Even to this day, blood feuds and other differences between various tribes are taken up in the winter months.

Rabbinical lore has attached new significance to the feast, and the living in the booths has been interpreted as that of being enveloped in the Shekinah, that is to say, in God Himself. He overshadowed each booth, and as the celebrants ate, drank and slept in these booths, so they did invisibly in the very being of the Deity. This conception of living is a very exalted one, and the booth ceases to be the bare thing that it appears outwardly. The best silk curtains procurable are brought, and the inside is a very beautiful mixture of highly coloured and fine textured silks, and other decoration. The genius of youth is allowed full scope, and friends come to admire the decorations of each other's booths. When St. Paul used the figure of speech of being baptized into Christ, dying in Christ and living in Christ, he must have had in his mind the thought in connection with his past life in the booths.

Feast of Dedication (Chanukah).

This feast, which lasts eight days, is not Biblical in origin ; it is kept to commemorate the victory of the Hashmonaim over the forces of the Seleucids. Its particular feature is the lighting of olive-oil lamps. The first night of the feast one light is lit, the second two, and so on, till eight lights are lit. This is said to be due to the fact that a small cruse of oil which was found in the Temple after its recapture by the forces of Judas Maccabæus was miraculously made to last seven days for lighting the Temple. The lights were formerly lit outside the house, with a view to publishing the supposed miracle to all passers-by, but in modern times the lights are kept indoors. In pre-Christian times the feast was kept in the same manner as that of Tabernacles : booths were erected outside the houses and the people had their meals in them. It was natural to give the extra-Biblical feasts some Biblical aspect, and in the case of this feast it was celebrated on the same lines as that which preceded it. Hence its duration of eight days. As a national feast which recalled the heroic days of the Covenant, our Lord shared it with the people and took advantage of it by teaching His contemporaries a lesson about Himself as ' the Light of the World.'

Fasts.

Among the Semites the idea of penitence was associated with that of self-affliction, which took the form of fasting. When anything was ardently desired from the Deity, fasting and praying were thought a sure means of getting what was wanted. This idea has been taken over into the Christian Church. It is therefore not surprising that many fasts of a national and individual nature should have had vogue in Judaism. It would be tedious to enumerate all the Biblical fasts, nor would that enumeration enlighten us much either as to the real value of these fasts or their effects upon those who engaged in them. We know that our Lord had some very sharp things to say about those who in His day fasted in order to appear pious and especially meritorious. And many took care to let every one know that they fasted, for they did not wash their faces, nor groom themselves : they fasted that they might be seen of man. The fast alluded to by our Lord would seem to have been the bi-weekly fast. Every pious Jew fasted on Mondays and Thursdays, because it was traditionally believed that on these days respectively Moses went up and returned from the Mount on which he received the law. Apar tfrom the bi-weekly fasts there were seventeen others, the most important of which were the Day of Atonement, the seventeenth day of Tammuz, and the ninth day of Ab.

The Day of Atonement.

This fast is of Biblical origin (Leviticus xvi.) and so does not need much explanation, yet many things and ideas were added to those connected with it. One of the more important beliefs about the day is that associated with the idea that on that day the Book of Remembrance, in which all the deeds of the year are written down, is examined. The examination is thought to begin on New Year's Day and to continue to the Day of Atonement. Either the provisional sentence passed on New Year's Day is confirmed or a reprieve is granted the individual for another year's life. The day is one of deep heart-searching, and the twenty-four hours it lasts are given up to prayer, confession and fasting. Many Jews do not leave their places of worship during the twenty-four hours, where they sit without their shoes. Every form of self-abnegation is practised, and some of the prayers prescribed during the ages for that day are very beautifully worded and their sentiment is very pure, breathing a spirituality that is worthy of Christian emulation. Many Jews who never darken the doors of the synagogue during the rest of the year turn their steps to them on that day. All are anxious to be on good terms with the Almighty on the day when their fortunes for the year are decided upon.

The tractate *Kipurim* ('Atonements') goes into the method of observance of the day very minutely, but we cannot enter into this here.

The Ninth of Ab.

This day is observed because on it the Temple is said to have been destroyed twice—first by Nebuchadrezzar in 586 B.C., and second by Titus in A.D. 70. This day is also observed as a fast during the twenty-four hours. On the eve of the fast, Jews resort to their places of worship, seat themselves on the floor, and among other things recite the Book of Lamentations. The cries that are heard on that evening are truly heart-rending. Need it be pointed out that it is a real lament that issues forth from the heart of a people feeling itself in exile from its home, deprived of its means of worship, the type of worship which its law enjoins and its heart longs for? In many cases sackcloth is worn and ashes are spread on the head. To the pious Jew this is the most solemn fast. Though the Day of Atonement is a personal day and of great moment in his life, yet this day of calamity for his people is one of greater sanctity to him, and he mourns deeply and earnestly.

Other Fasts.

Of the other fasts little need be said. The manner of observation of a fast is, however, interesting because of the allusion to it in the New Testament. The usual ablutions for the day are not permissible. Only the hands are washed—not the face, nor, of course, is the daily bath taken; the hair is left uncombed and neither water nor food of any kind is taken. It can readily be seen how some of those who sought religious merit made a great parade of these factors; and how our Lord denounced them as He did every other thing which was done that man might see and be awed by the piety of those who practised them. He had nothing to say against engaging in fasting, but He taught that God alone should be the witness of such fasting, and that He would respond to the waiting heart and the afflicted soul.

The Sabbath.

The battleground between our Lord and the Jerusalem authorities, especially the Pharisees and Scribes, centred round the Sabbath ; and even to this day many Jews are held back from Christianity because of the change which has taken place in the observance of the first day of the week by Christians as against the seventh day of the week enjoined in the Old Testament. To go fully into the history and development of the Sabbath would require a volume much larger than this book. We will try, however, to get a bird's-eye view of the matter.

The first point worthy of consideration is that the word ' Sabbath ' goes back to a Sumerian root ' SA-BAT-U,' which is equated by the Assyrian ' UM-NUH-LIBBI '=' day of rest of the heart.' Another equivalent to the Assyrian ' Sabbatu ' is the word ' GAMARU,' which means ' to complete, finish,' etc. The real difficulty about the word ' Sabbath ' is that Semitic scholars are not agreed as to its root or meaning, some holding that it is derived from a root which means ' to cease, finish,' and so on, the others that it is derived from a root which has to do with the number seven. In any case the Assyrian word leaves us in no doubt as to its meaning. The following quotation will suffice to demonstrate that the Babylonians observed days like the Hebrew Sabbaths. " The 21st day (is a day for) making the stated offering (to the gods) Sin and Shamesh. A lucky day and an evil day. The Shepherd (king) of wide-spreading peoples must not eat meat cooked over coal, nor bread cooked in ashes, must not change his garments, nor dress in white garments. He shall not offer libations. The king must not ride his chariot. The priestess shall not seek an oracle in the Holy of holies. The physician shall not lay his hands on the sick man. The day is unsuitable for making a curse. At dawn the king presents his offering to Shamesh, the mistress of the world, and Sin, the supreme god. His prayer will be acceptable to the god." This is from a document forming part of the *Western Asiatic Inscriptions*, vol. iv., Plates 32, 33. While it is difficult to date the document, yet it would seem to belong to pre-Mosaic days, probably to about

2000 B.C. It is to be noted that the 19th day is included among the Sabbaths. This would seem to be due to the fact that the month which is detailed was an intercalary month, that is to say, a month which was duplicated in order to bring the year into harmony with lunar requirements. Thus the 19th day would be the 49th day counting from the first day of the ordinary month, and since the 49th day would be a multiple of seven, that is, seven times seven, it had to be included among the days. It ought further to be noticed that in the case of our document the Sabbaths are not fixed to occur every seventh day of the week but rather every seventh day no matter what day of the week it happened to be ; and that the seven days were counted by the moon's rotations. While the similarity between the two will be clear, the differences will also be very evident.

The pre-exilic form of the Sabbath does not come into our sphere of study, yet it should be noticed from such passages as 2 Kings iv. 23, Amos viii. 4–6, Hosea ii. 13, Isa. i. 14, that the New Moon (that is to say, the first day of the lunar month) was observed as a Sabbath, and is mentioned by these prophets in the same passages. The post-exilic development comes more within our consideration, and we shall have to go more fully into it.

The Sabbath in Post-Exilic Literature.

We have in post-exilic literature the prophet Ezekiel, also the books of Isaiah of the Exile and Nehemiah, and the unclassified books, such as the Psalms, etc. Special care must be exercised in dealing with the prophecies of Ezekiel. He belongs to a period of history of the Jewish people which calls for a special message and a special messenger, and he was the first prophet of the Exile. He was led into captivity with his people as a young man, and they were now existing under circumstances very different from those of former days, for they were far from their home. We meet with a Judean here, a Galilean there ; the rich and the poor are on the same level. There had been a great transformation in the lives of the people, for there had been a readjustment to the new situation. The new situation created a tendency to forget Yahweh, and a new instinct of assimilation developed in the lives of the exiles. Under these peculiar circumstances God sends a peculiar man. Ezekiel is the leader of the Dia-spora ; he is the mouthpiece of the small community gathered around the river Chebar. He is more than that : he is the one to whom the captives look for guidance in their new surroundings. Far too much has been made of Ezekiel's legislative prowess. He has been made the father of the new priesthood. Indeed, there seems to be attributed to him from some critical quarters the setting up of an entirely new system. It is true that he had much to do with the organisation of the system, for Ezekiel is called upon to be more than a prophet : he is the leader of the people in their manifold religious activities. He is a prophet and systematiser of the customs and usages of the people as they existed in their homes, so that we have to consider Ezekiel as the last Judean and the first Jew. While a part of the nation becomes assimilated with the surrounding people, the other part turns in a new spirit and zeal to the faith of their fathers, for they believe in the promises of Yahweh. They hope to return to their home-land once again and they want to be kept in touch with the religious life of their people. Thus Ezekiel is the leader of the captivity reformation and the head of a new movement which acknowledged Yahweh as the only true God. Under these conditions we shall see the special direction to which the whole of his attention was given, and the new meanings that were assigned to old things.

It has been suggested by many that the Sabbath as an institution developed a new meaning in the times of Ezekiel, and that this prophet gave it the meaning which we find it to have in the post-exilic period. The passages in which he deals with the Sabbath are not many. They are scattered, but I shall pick out the most essential for quotation.

In chapter xx. he is speaking to a number of the leaders of the captivity who had come to seek an oracle of Yahweh by the mouth of the prophet. He reviews to them the history of the disobedience of their fathers and their constant falling away ; yet he points out to them Yahweh's continued blessing. In the 12th verse, speaking for

Yahweh, he says, ' And my Sabbaths also did I give unto them, that they might be for a sign between me and them, that I am Yahweh their sanctifier.' He goes on to talk about their disobedience in the wilderness. Amongst other things, in verse 13 he says, ' And my Sabbaths they desecrate.' And this charge the prophet repeats no less than four times in the chapter. He charges them over and over again with desecration of the Sabbath. In chapter xxii. the prophet again admonishes the people. He is speaking to the ' bloody city.' He is telling her of the fate which is awaiting her, and in verse 8 he enumerates, amongst other sins, the sin of Sabbath desecration. In the 26th verse the prophet again takes up the cause of the Sabbath. He is denouncing the prophets and the land, and amongst the impeachments he says, ' They have turned their eyes from the Sabbath.' So he also speaks of the Sabbath in chapter xxiii. 38. We meet again with the subject in chapters xliv., xlv. and xlvi., but not in a single place does the prophet designate any existing manner of observance, nor does he legislate for future observance. He does, however, legislate concerning the offerings for the Sabbath. The keynote of his attitude to the Sabbath is, ' You have desecrated the Sabbath : turn now to it and sanctify it,' because he looks upon it as an expression of holiness—an expression of the covenant which makes the Jews Yahweh's people.

I think that, without preconceived ideas, it is not possible to deduce anything more from the statement of the prophet than a treatment of the Sabbath from a purely altruistic point of view and an appeal for stricter observance. The prophets constantly enjoined the way in which it ought to be kept, but Ezekiel goes a step farther and tells them that Yahweh expected them to hallow the day.

We have another passage in the prophets which is just as insistent on Sabbath observance as is Ezekiel. It is the prophet of the Exile, whose writings are found under the writings of Isaiah. ' Thus said Yahweh, observe (the) precedents and do righteousness ; for our salvation is near to come, and my righteousness to be revealed. Happy is the man who doeth this, and the son of man who holdeth

fast to it.   He that observeth the Sabbath and doth not
desecrate it, and prevents his hand from doing anything
that is evil.   Let not the son of the stranger who hath
joined himself to Yahweh say, Yahweh hath separated
me from his people ; and let not the eunuch say, I am a
dry tree.   Thus saith Yahweh to the eunuchs that they
observe my Sabbaths, and choose those things which
delight me, and hold fast in my covenant.   And I will
give them a hand in the building of my house and walls.
And a name (better than that) of sons and daughters, an
everlasting name will I give unto them, which shall not
be cut off.   And the sons of the strangers who are joined
to Yahweh to serve him and love the name of Yahweh
that they might be his servants, all those who observe the
Sabbath from desecrating it, and hold to my covenant '
(Isa. lvi. 1 ff.).

It seems that there were some of the surrounding nations
that joined themselves to Yahweh and felt that they
ought to enjoy the common joys of Israel, but the people
treated them as strangers.   The prophet tells them they
are as precious in the sight of Yahweh as those who pride
themselves on being His sons and daughters.   Yahweh
will give them a name better than that, and will make
them share in the building of the temple and walls of
Jerusalem.   The Sabbath is here looked upon as part of
the covenant which these people took upon themselves
when they became Yahweh believers.

In chapter lviii. the prophet again refers to the Sabbath.
He is here describing the future bliss of the Jewish people.
He sets forth in very vivid and pictorial language the lot
of the nation that would turn to Yahweh, and says, ' If
thou wilt turn thy feet from the Sabbath, from doing thy
pleasure on my holy day and call the Sabbath a delight,
holy to Yahweh, honourable ; and thou wilt honour him by
not doing thine own work, refrain from finding thine own
pleasure or seeking thine own words, then shalt thou
delight thyself in Yahweh, and I will make thee to ride
upon the high places of the earth, and I will cause thee
to eat the heritage of Jacob thy father ; the mouth of
Yahweh hath spoken ' (Isa. lviii. 13–14).

Many commentators are inclined to treat this passage
8

as a late addition. As representative of this group Professor Whitehouse, the writer of the Century Bible volume upon Isaiah, persistently refuses to agree that anything that has to do with the Sabbath is of an early date. He rejects both passages in Isaiah as interpolations, though his reason for so doing is not clear. But we are not dealing here with the critical problem of the prophets, though allowance is made for these problems, and we must leave them to be solved by those who are specialists in the matter. But looking at the passage from our view-point, which takes cognizance of all these facts, these rejections seem unreasonable and prejudiced. And as far as our investigation permits us to go, we must accept these passages. We have passages of a much earlier date dealing with the Sabbath more thoroughly than do the passages from Isaiah of the Exile.

Before examining the last passages from the Old Testament we may look at a passage which probably belongs to the middle of the sixth century B.C. (Lam. ii. 6). The theme, purpose and aim of the book are too well known to need any comment. It is the great lamentation over the destruction of Jerusalem. While lamenting over other things, the author says : ' And he (Yahweh) hath violently taken away his tabernacle as it were of a garden. He hath destroyed his assembly. Yahweh hath caused his assemblies and Sabbaths to be forgotten in Zion, and hath despised in the wrath of his anger (both king and priest).' There may not be much in this passage to help us to solve our problem, but it is at least significant to learn that the author thought enough of the Sabbath to include it in his lamentations. The authorship of the book is in doubt. The traditions, LXX and the Targums maintain that Jeremiah wrote it, and this is very probable. But whoever wrote it, the date of the book cannot be much later than from about 580–550 B.C. It is more than probable that it belongs to the earlier part of the century. The fact is that the Sabbath is mentioned, and its being forgotten by Yahweh, as the author puts it, is sufficiently painful to be lamented.

We now come to the last book in the Old Testament dealing with the Sabbath. The Books of Chronicles also mention it, but in passages similar to those already quoted from Kings, so that for our purpose the Book of Nehemiah is the last in the Old Testament.

Here again I quote only the most essential passages.   In chapter ix. Nehemiah is reviewing to the people the goodness of God and His special providence for the nation. He begins with the progenitor of the race and goes right along, following the historical outline of Hebrew history. In the 14th verse he says : ' And thy holy Sabbaths thou didst make known to them.   The commandments, the statutes and the law didst thou command to them through thy servant Moses.'   In chapter x. he calls upon the people of Israel to renew their covenant with Yahweh, and amongst other things he asks them to bind themselves to the Sabbath (x. 31, A.V.) : ' That we may not receive from the hands of the people of the land (probably the Gentile farmers) any grain or wares which they may bring to sell.'   In chapter xiii. Nehemiah evidently relates the results of a tour which he made to ascertain the observance of the covenant which they took upon themselves in chapter x., and this is what he has to report : (xiii. 15–22) ' In these days I saw in Judah people treading the winepresses on the Sabbath day, bringing in sheaves and lading asses therewith, as also with wine, grapes, figs, and all sorts of burdens they bring into Jerusalem on the Sabbath day.   The Tyrians who lived in her (Jerusalem) brought in fish and all manner of ware and sold them on the Sabbath day.   And I quarrelled with the freemen of Judah and said to them, What is the meaning of the evil that you do to desecrate the Sabbath day ?   Is it not because your fathers did these that our God brought upon us and the city calamity, and continues to (bring) upon Israel because they desecrate the Sabbath ?   And it came to pass when it began to be dark before the Sabbath, I ordered them to lock the gates, that they may not be opened until after the Sabbath, and I stationed some of my youths upon the gates that no burden came in on the Sabbath, and the mercenaries contended, and all those who sold things outside the walls, and again and again they lodged outside the walls.   And I testified and said unto them, Why do you lodge outside the walls ?   If you insist on doing so,

I will lay my hands on you. From that time on they did not return on the Sabbath.'

These statements are quite clear and hardly need any amplification, yet the writer of Ezra–Nehemiah in the *International Critical Commentary* insists that the Sabbath was not regulated till after Nehemiah, or at least that it was not so fully amplified as it was later. It is interesting to notice that in the Hexateuch in Num. xv. 32 ff., we are told of a man being put to death for the desecration of the Sabbath. I think that even the most radical critics allow that that story could not have been written very much later than the time of Nehemiah.

Nehemiah puts the institution back to the days of Moses. He tells the people that for reasons such as the desecration of the Sabbath Jerusalem was destroyed, and he took measures to suppress Sabbath traffic. Hence he tells us that these mercenaries, after having had to lodge outside the walls again and again, did not come back.

The Book of Jubilees, chapter ii. 23–33, gives us the first clue to the Rabbinic Sabbath, and we shall quote it in full :

' There were two and twenty heads of mankind from Adam to Jacob, and two and twenty kinds of work were made until the seventh day ; this is blessed and holy ; and the former also is blessed and holy ; and this one serves with that one for sanctification and blessing. And to this (Jacob and his seed) it was granted that they should always be the blessed and holy ones of the first testimony and law, even as He had sanctified and blessed the Sabbath day on the seventh day. He created heaven and earth and everything that He created in six days, and God made the seventh day holy, for all His works ; therefore He commanded on its behalf that, whoever doth any work thereon shall die, and that he who defileth it shall surely die. Wherefore do thou command the children of Israel to observe this day that they may keep it holy and not do thereon any work, and not to defile it, as it is holier than all other days. And whoever profaneth it shall surely die, and whoever doeth thereon any work shall surely die eternally, that the children of Israel may observe this day throughout their generations, and not be rooted out of the land ; for it is a holy day and a blessed day. And every one who observeth it and keepeth Sabbath thereon from all his work, will be holy and blessed throughout all days like unto us. Declare and say to the children of Israel the law of this day both that they should keep Sabbath thereon ; and that they should not forsake it in the error of their hearts ; (and) that it is not lawful to do any work thereon which is unseemly, to do thereon their own pleasure, and that they should not prepare thereon anything to be eaten or drunk ; and (that it is not lawful) to draw water or bring in or take out thereon through the gates any burden which they had not prepared for themselves on the sixth day in their dwellings. And they shall not bring in nor take out from house to house on that day ; for that day is more holy and blessed than any Jubilee day of the jubilees : on this we kept Sabbath in the heavens before it was made known to any flesh to keep Sabbath thereon on the earth. And the Creator of all things blessed it, but He did not sanctify all peoples and nations to keep Sabbath thereon, but Israel alone ; them alone He permitted to eat and drink and to keep Sabbath thereon on the earth. And the Creator of all things blessed this day which He had created for a blessing and a sanctification and a glory above all days. This law and testimony was given to the children of Israel as a law for ever unto their generation.'

To this summary only the Zadokite Fragment adds some further information, and should be examined.

The Sabbath with the Rabbis.

During the time of Christ the ' fence around the law ' was so strict that it crowded out religion. The rabbis derived their authority from the people, but as soon as the first or second generation passed they claimed that that authority was God-given, and proceeded with their interpretation on the assumption that the people would accept them.

During the Exile the Israelites forgot their mother tongue or the Hebrew of the prophets ; they spoke Aramaic, and even their literature was written in that language. We have this exemplified in the books of Ezra and Daniel. The people, no longer understanding their Scriptures, called for an interpretation of them, and this was undertaken by the metargumin or official reciters, who produced the Targums. What the metargumin did for the Palestinian and other Jews of the Diaspora, the LXX did for the Hellenists. But these Targums were not deemed sufficiently strong because of the possibility of people misreading the Torah, and the Mishnah came into being.

The paradox of time repeated itself in history. I Kings xii. 14 : ' And he spake unto them after the council of the young men, saying, My father made your yoke heavy, but I will add to your yoke : My father chastised you with whips, but I will chastise you with scorpions.' Instead of making the law plainer to the populace so that they could understand it, these metargumins made it harder, and hid the meaning in such an intricate system of argumentation that even they themselves needed commentaries to have their writings explained to them. Instead of feeding the people on milk, they gave them indigestible meat. The people, in their ignorance of the Pentateuch, were led to accept the words of the rabbis as though they were given at Sinai. The result was Pharisaism and all the failings associated with the sect, including the composition of the Mishnah. Of the Mishnah, two tractates deal with the Sabbath. They are ' Sabbath ' and ' Erubim.' Thirty-nine laws were set down as a guide for the observance of the Sabbath. The questions taken up under these thirty-nine enactments are too full to be dwelt upon. For instance, in the fifth chapter of this tractate, laws concerning burden-bearing are dealt with : it is prohibited to bandage up an animal, since the bandage would make a burden. In the first chapter the laws deal with lights, and a discussion between the rabbis sets forth those lights that are permissible on the Sabbath, even the wicks being specified. One might go on quoting such examples, but it is not necessary for our understanding of the main issues.

It is, however, interesting to observe the scale of punishment meted out to an unfortunate transgressor of these Sabbatic laws. (1) For the first offence an offering was demanded. The offender had to bring the offering to Jerusalem. It is not hard to imagine what that meant to a poor Jew living in Rome or Athens, or indeed in any other part of the world. But the rabbis ordained this, and it had to be complied with. (2) For the second offence no particular punishment was prescribed. The offender was warned that there was a law of retribution and a moral law, and that God would punish him. (3) But if the person offended a third time, he was liable to be stoned to death. Such were the punishments meted out by the rabbis for the non-observance of their laws.

I think that a description of the Sabbath as observed by all classes will enable us better than a more scholarly study or an excerpt of rabbinical injunctions to appreciate Jesus' attitude to it. While Jesus may have never taken the trouble to learn all these laws as a pious Jew, he had to observe the Sabbath as all the others did.

In order to avoid any trespassing on the Sabbath, it was declared that the Sabbath ought to begin on Friday afternoon. All work was to cease after 2 p.m. All food to be consumed on Friday evening and during the Sabbath had to be cooked on Friday before sunset. The male members of the family were to repeat the portion of the Pentateuch assigned for that week (the Pentateuch was divided into fifty-two portions, thus making a portion for every week in the year). The reading was to be done in the Old Testament Hebrew ; each verse was to be repeated twice, and then once in Targumic Hebrew. This precaution was taken to ensure thorough understanding of the Hebrew. The males of the family went to the synagogue half an hour before sunset, and the females attended to the kindling of the lights. This ceremony is still attended to with great solemnity by all the females in the house. A newly wed girl is given a new lamp, and all the guests at the marriage-feast gather around her to see her perform this duty, which indicates that she is henceforth to be thought of as a mother in Israel.

In the synagogue there is elaborate ritual. The afternoon prayers are repeated, and with the setting of the sun, special evening prayers are begun. A special prayer is sung for the reception of the Sabbath. Mrs. H. Lucas gives a very good translation of it, and I will quote two stanzas from it. The prayer is called 'Lecha dody,' which means, 'Come forth, my friend.'

> Come forth, my friend, the bride to meet;
> Come, O my friend, the Sabbath greet,
> 'Observe ye' and 'remember' still
> The Sabbath thus,—His holy will
> God in one utterance did proclaim.
> The Lord is one, and one His name,
> To renown and praise and fame.
> Come forth, my friend, the bride to meet,
> Come, O my friend, the Sabbath greet.

> Crown of the husband, come in peace,
> Come bidding toil and trouble cease.
> With joy and cheerfulness abide
> Among thy people true and tried,
> Thy faithful people—come, O bride!
> Come forth, my friend, the bride to meet,
> Come, O my friend, the Sabbath greet.

Other beautiful prayers are repeated. On the return of the men from the synagogue the father or the oldest of the male members of the family makes a blessing over a cup of wine, repeating Gen. ii. 1–3 and other prayers. The evening meal is the best the family can afford, and many a family go hungry through the week in order to provide good meals for the Sabbath.

On retiring, the usual prayers of committing the soul to God for the night are said. These prayers are based on an elaborate angelology. Michael is asked to take his place on the right hand of the slumberer, Raphael on the left, and the Shekinah to cover the head. In the morning as soon as the eyes are opened, and before the usual ablution, a prayer thanking God for the return of the soul to the body is made. The name of God, however, is not mentioned till after the ablutions, when the prayer is continued. The male members and sometimes the older women in the congregation attend synagogue. Only coffee or tea is permitted to be partaken of before prayers. No food of any kind must be taken till after the prayers. Young people under twelve may go home and eat something after the first portion of the Pentateuch has been read.

The portion assigned for the week is divided up into

seven parts. There is an official reader. As he reads, different men are called upon to attend to his reading. The first to be called is a priest, *i.e.* a person who is a descendant of Aaron. The second one must be of the tribe of Levi. And the others are ordinary respectable people of the town. After the reading of a portion of the Pentateuch, a passage is read from the prophets. The prayers are ended about 11 a.m. The meal that follows is very elaborate, and the singing in between the courses very beautiful.

The afternoon is spent in reading the ethics of the fathers or any other ethical treatise. An early dinner is partaken of about 4 p.m., after which the male members return to the synagogue. The afternoon and evening prayers follow each other. The latter must not be engaged in until three stars are seen in the heavens. On returning home, a family meal is partaken of, most members of the family gathering at the house of the eldest member or in turns at the houses of the different members of the family. The singing and general conversation lasts till 12 p.m. Let us bear this meal in mind, as I think that in it we have a clue to the transition of the Sabbath to the Sunday.

Many Western, especially Continental, writers make the mistake of supposing that the Sabbath of the Mishnah was a burden on the people, which they bore unwillingly ; and a superficial reading of the New Testament supports their view. But let it not be forgotten that thousands of Jews were willing to give up their lives rather than fight on the Sabbath. Of this a good example occurred about the year 168 B.C. when four thousand Jews perished in a cave because they would not fight. Only a personal experience of the Sabbath observance in a pious Jewish home can give any idea of the absolute delight and joy the Sabbath is. Every Jewish home, no matter how scanty its food during the week, is provided with a four-course meal ; even the poorest of the poor have a bath on the Friday ; and no matter how patched the clothes are, clean clothes are put on. The house, which as a rule, consists of one room, is clean and brightly lit for the Sabbath. The hardest worked have their rest, and the women have their day of rest too, since no fire-making or cooking is allowed on the

Sabbath, and no labour which entails manual work of a tiring nature is engaged in.

Jesus and the Sabbath.

I cannot think that Jesus objected to the foregoing aspects of the Sabbath. He, who had to labour in the carpenter's shop from morning till late at night, day in and day out without respite, could not have grudged the day of rest to the worn and weary toiler, for the Sabbath is the poor man's day. To the Jew who lived in close communion with God, the Sabbath was a day to be looked forward to the whole week ; it afforded an opportunity to escape from the everyday hurry and bustle and to meditate upon the things which belonged to God. Jesus insisted that the day should be observed not only for deriving good for oneself, but for doing good to others. The rabbis in their blindness had so fenced the Sabbath about with laws that it became impossible to do good on that day, to tend the sick and the suffering. God ordained the Sabbath for man, and not man for the Sabbath. Very bold and extraordinary was His claim to be Lord of the Sabbath. Only one who had the Divine consciousness of his own authority such as Jesus had could make such a claim ; for the Sabbath was the holiest thing in everyday life, and Jesus wanted it not only to be holy but free. Jesus wanted to break down the fence that was so full of dangerous spikes in the nature of uncalled-for laws. These laws made the Sabbath, like the Law itself, a very frightening thing, which the conscientious person could not feel he was able to keep as he ought, and which thus, in his anxiety to keep every detail imposed upon him, deprived him of the real joy which the day was meant to bring and give. The change which took place in the Christian Church of the day should not make the Sunday less than the Saturday is to the pious Jew, but with the added assurance of immortality which the risen Christ brought to the Early Church should make it a day of the utmost joy and gladness, of rest, spiritual refreshment and remembrance.

CHAPTER V

PUBLIC AND FAMILY LIFE AND WORSHIP

Family Life.

OUR study of the political aspect of the Jewish period enabled us to realise that Judaism was born outwith Palestine ; that for only a very short period did it enjoy purely Jewish government ; and that it maintained itself in spite of its foreign origin and political vicissitudes. It also emerged that this was made possible by the very fact that the Jew was an exile, for through its exile the nation learned that Jehovah was alone worthy of worship.

In examining the religious development of our period we noted that the exile helped to broaden the nation's outlook ; that in coming in contact with such religious beliefs as that of the Zoroastrian religion it was set many problems which it had to face : and that, though the problems presented themselves in a Zoroastrian aspect, Judaism followed its own line of meeting these problems, and thus escaped the dualism of Zoroastrianism and the Polytheism of the Greeks and the Syrians.

When considering its literature we observed that it created a type of thought which was not only peculiar to its problems and theology but also native to its ideals. Its Messianism, its eschatology, its historic-religious novels, its traditions and outlook, though at times very confused, were yet in line with the teaching of its older prophets and seers, as well as its priestly cult. We further noticed that the new factor, namely, the synagogue, produced a literature of its own which was a merging of the prophetic and priestly, as well as an example of its hopes and aspirations for the future.

In our study of the Parties and personalities of the period, we shall note how the parties and schools of thought moulded the lives of the people, and at times so confined them within a fence which they erected around them in order to keep them without the limits of the Law, that only those who gave their entire lives to the study of the observance of these Laws could hope to attain to eternal life.

All the foregoing factors had much to do with the making of Judaism, but the Jew was made in his home. It was the home influence and the family circle that made Judaism possible, and it is into the home that we have to look to understand fully Judaism and the Jew. Muhammadanism is known to the world through its prayers and its antagonism to other religions. The Jew can only be known in his home life ; and it is because he was not and is not even now studied at home that he is an unknown quantity to his very neighbours, be they Christian, Muhammadan or of any other religion. So we must study his home life, his social life which arises from his home life, and his worship, to understand him, and by doing so we shall understand the Early Church and its ideals and ideas.

The Home Life and Ideals.

It must be realised very fully that Judaism was brought up on tradition, saga and legend. Those books of the Old Testament which belonged to the period prior to the Exile could not have been known to very many and could only have been possessed by a few. It is indeed very doubtful if the works of Amos, Hosea and the other prophets had been put into writing prior to the Exile ; their present corrupt state must at least in part be due to the fact that they had not been reduced to writing. One need not at this time point out that in those days the writing down of a document such as the Book of Amos necessitated a great deal of labour ; and apart from the labour the use by any large number of readers of what was written down would make the document blurred in a very short time, and this would also be a contributory factor to the making of mistakes in the course of transcription. We must, therefore, think of Judaism in a very different way from our habitual one. They did not have the pre-exilic literature on their shelves ready for use.

The bulk of the people did not even as much as see any written document. The teaching in the home and schools was of an oral nature, and naturally the history and traditions of the nation occupied the first place. There can be little doubt that the Psalms of pre-exilic date were known and recited in every home, also the Ten Commandments. Regarding the Law, as has already been indicated, it was known only to a very select few, and these few taught it according to their own understanding of it, and naturally put their own construction on its contents.

The Position of Women in Judaism.

There is no subject on which such lack of knowledge has been shown among Christian writers on Judaism as that of the position of women in the Jewish world. It has been assumed by many that the woman was looked upon as a mere chattel to be bought and sold, and that since girls did not attend the schools of the rabbis they were altogether ignorant of the Law. In point of fact it was the man who was bought as husband. Very few women without dowry could get well married, and it became a community obligation to find some money for every girl, and especially for orphaned girls, that they might not be left unmarried and thus be put to shame, for it was considered a shame for a woman to remain unmarried. An examination of the relevant documents in the Mishnah would show that both the (Te-na-im) marriage contracts made at the engagements and the (Keth-ub-oth) stipulations made and read on the day of the wedding, which laid down the conditions in case of divorce, gave the man and woman equal rights as regards the property each brought into the home. It is true that divorce laws favoured the man, but it is equally true, as our Lord pointed out, that it was because of the hardness of their hearts that these laws were at all necessary. In Law the man could divorce his wife if she was a bad cook, and some belonging to the lower strata of Jewish society availed themselves of this. But among the truly pious, divorce was rare, if indeed it ever occurred. The ideal of marriage had a very high place in the best circles of Judaism. It was believed that on the day of a wedding the names of those to be married were proclaimed in heaven, and that God Himself selected the parties to be wedded. With such an exalted ideal of marriage it may readily appear that a dissolution of the marriage bonds was not undertaken lightly or looked upon with favour by the great teachers of Israel. When our Lord stated that 'that which God had joined together man must not cut asunder,' he expressed the ideal which Judaism had set before itself in this matter.

It must be realised that the bulk of the nation was left outside Palestine. While the lists given to us in the Books of Ezra, Nehemiah and Esdras enumerate 49,000, many more than that must have remained in Babylonia; that is, so far as the earlier period is concerned. Books like Tobit indicate to us that the Dispersion was much wider than Babylonia itself, and in later times we find Jews not only in great numbers in Egypt, but also throughout Asia Minor. Thus it must be evident that while Jerusalem was the centre of the priestly cult, it was by no means the centre of the spiritual life of the Jew. It was a clearing-house to which every Jew brought his contributions. There they were sifted and emerged in their truly Jewish character. Within the limits of the Dispersion the men folk had to seek their daily bread, and it was therefore left to the women to educate or at least supervise the education of the children. We cannot at this time estimate how widely literacy was diffused among the women folk, but what they lacked in literacy was made up in traditional and superstitious teaching. The Jewish child was brought up first and foremost as a Monotheist, then in the full hope that Messiah would appear to free them from the Exile and usher in a new era in which the Jews would play a most important part. Angelology and Demonology formed a great part of the home education; the child was taught to live in a world in which angels and demons acted their part for good or ill. The fact that in the New Testament period we hear so much of demonology must have been due to this home atmosphere in which the children were steeped. If anything went wrong it was attributed to demon possession. Not only could human beings be possessed of demons, but places and things might also become possessed of them. Not only could people come into contact and be influenced by angels, but also things and places. The Judaism of our Lord's time was influenced by Demonology and Angelology because the home life was never free from it. Thus whether by day or night, at work or play, the Jewish child was left in the presence of the Unseen, of good or evil, according to its own conscience.

Education.

The education of the boy was the supreme concern of the nation ; everywhere schools were founded and paid for by the community. The school education was limited to learning, either from manuscript or orally, the first five books of Moses. At the age of ten or so, commentaries of the scribes and rabbis were added to that of the Law. These also were most likely orally transmitted. Regarding the prayers, the full discussion of them will be found in the section dealing with Worship. Alongside the learning of the Law and commentaries each Jewish child was taught some manual occupation, no matter what the position of the family was in the community. The male members had to be masters of some means of bread-winning. Since the Law and commentaries alone formed the basis of education, it became a common thing for many to know the Law at least by heart, also many of the Psalms, and in later life many parts of the prophets and commentaries. It follows that its religious education was the only education which the nation possessed or cared for. In spite of that, the Jews held high places in the business life of any community in which they found themselves, and did not lag behind in any other activities that went to make up the communal life.

The girls, naturally, were restricted even more than the boys to the home education : all that they needed to know their mothers were competent to teach them. The principles of Monotheism were deeply impressed upon them, as were also the common traditions and sagas of the nation. They were asked to observe but few laws, but these few they had to observe without deviation or modification. I have already said something about the position of women in the home. I only need add that not merely did the women reign supreme therein, but they influenced every phase of the community life. They did their work quietly and preferred always to remain behind the scene. They felt that the elementary education of their boys, the full education of their girls, and the general help they were able to render to the community provided a large enough sphere to satisfy all their longings.

We will now turn to individual matters which will shed some light on the New Testament narrative. Before proceeding I wish to remark that the New Testament itself is one of our main authorities for that period. Let us take the child from its birth. Every child born into a Jewish home was considered a child of Abraham. In the case of the male, on the eighth day it was brought into the full covenant of Abraham. In the case of the female, on the first or second Sabbath after its birth its arrival was announced in the synagogue, and the reader of the Law intimated to the congregation the name by which that child was to be known. It was also considered by this act to have become a child of Abraham. The belief was that every child had its guardian angel, and that from the very moment of its birth the guardian angel watched over it. It was only when the child itself tended to do evil that demons could take possession of it. I want to draw special attention to this last phrase. It was only when an individual sought freedom from the guardian angel that he or she was deemed to become possessed of demons. It was a matter of choice on the part of the individual, and so, when we read in the New Testament of demoniac possession, we ought to realise that it was looked upon as an act in accordance with the guidance of his or her guardian angel, and therefore demoniac possession was inherent sinfulness. Apart from the guardian angels, various other angels were deemed to take an interest in the affairs of the nation. The lot of women was not so hard as some have sought to make out. In spite of the fact that they were not expected to learn the Law and the Prophets, and in spite of the fact that they were not taught trades, they yet occupied high positions, both in knowledge of the Law and in the business world. It was considered essential that a girl of between sixteen and eighteen should marry, and her marriage was not only a family affair, but a community concern. When the girl was an orphan she was endowed by the community, and often the orphan girls were so well endowed that they were eagerly sought in marriage. There were in each community men and women who were called 'Shadchanim,' which means 'go-betweens.' These men or women familiarised themselves with both the community standing and the wealth of the individuals, and they proposed marriages between the young people. Their method was to approach the father and mother of the boy or girl and to ask if they would be prepared to affiance their child into such or such a family. If permission was granted, they approached the other family and began to offer or discuss terms. The young people were not generally consulted until most things were settled. It was usual for the bride's parents to buy and furnish the home and for the bridegroom's parents to contribute a sum of money, naturally depending on the position of the parents. In some cases the parents of the bride promised to keep the young people for a number of years in their own home and to supply all their needs. This was especially the case if the bridegroom had an inclination towards study. So far as the custom itself was concerned, it was and still is very laudable, for owing to the tender age of marriage the kindly guidance of the mother made for happiness in a home in which it might have been otherwise.

Engagements.

After both sets of parents had agreed to the marriage, and the young people had been consulted, and had also agreed, a date was appointed on which the engagement was celebrated officially. Friends of both families were invited to the home of the bride-to-be, and a rabbi and scribe were called in. The matters agreed upon with regard to dowry and any other arrangements were set down in writing, as were also conditions in case of divorce. The engagement was looked upon almost the same as marriage, and the breaking-off of an engagement had to go through a legal process similar to that of divorce. Readers

9

of the New Testament will understand Joseph's position from the foregoing; for though he was not married to Mary, she was yet counted as though she had already been in fact married to him, and consequently the calling of Jesus the son of Joseph was legally correct. The date of the wedding was set forth in the agreement made on betrothal and could not be departed from by either party without legal permission.

Marriages.

The wedding-day having been previously fixed, it was entered upon with great solemnity and heart-searching by both bride and bridegroom. The day was observed as a fast, each visiting the graveside of departed friends, and asking for intercession on their behalf from the departed. When both bride and bridegroom lived in the same city, town or village, each made their way to the synagogue court accompanied by their friends, and often by such music as was available in the place. Arriving at the court of the synagogue they were led under a canopy which was stretched out on four poles. The bride, heavily veiled, took her stand at the rabbi's right-hand side, the bridegroom at his left. The rabbi proceeded to read out the conditions formally arrived at by the parents, to which they nodded assent. Then the rabbi handed the bridegroom a ring which he placed on the fourth finger of the right hand saying, ' Behold thou art set apart for me according to the Law of Moses and Israel.' The bride and bridegroom returned to the home of the bride's people, accompanied by all who were formally invited through a messenger who had called upon them. But the house was open to all within the town or village. The poor, especially, were welcomed, feasted and, if the parents could afford it, made the recipients of sums of money. If either of the parties to be married belonged to a different town or village, the friends of the party residing in the place went out to meet the incoming party. Amongst those who went to meet them were young girls who chanted songs of praise of bride or bridegroom. Girls were, as a rule, married on Wednesdays, and widows on Friday afternoons. While there were many reasons for the custom of midweek marriages for girls, one of them seems to have been the reception of the incoming party. It was necessary for the girls who went out to meet the bride or bridegroom to provide themselves with lamps, which were lit by olive oil, and also to carry a small cruse of oil to replenish their lights in case of delay. The story of the wise and foolish virgins instances further usage in this matter. The wedding-feast lasted for seven days for those who could afford it, and naturally all strove to keep the festivities going for the full time. During that period friends sent sheep, goats, and, among the richer classes, cattle and other provisions. Most of those who attended sent wine to the feast. We find our Lord in Cana at one of these feasts, and the passage in that connection has been misunderstood, especially that part in which our Lord's mother made some remark to him. What she seems to have done was to draw His attention to the fact that it was His turn to send for wine, and His answer was, ' Never mind, woman ; I am keeping watch over the matter.'

The childless marriage was looked upon as calamitous, since it was believed that every Jew or Jewess must express themselves in child-bearing and upbringing, failure meaning that the individual would have to return to this world again in order to fulfil parental duties. Divorce was allowed in the case of a childless marriage, and was even deemed a duty.

The belief in the pre-existence of the soul had a great influence on Jewish thought. It was believed that each soul before its coming into the possession of a body made an appeal to the Almighty to allow it to remain in its pure state, but the decree of the Almighty always stood, and the soul was ordered to take possession of a body in such or such a home. It was also believed that the child prior to its birth was in communication with the angels and spiritual beings. Its coming into life was a great event, and much superstition surrounded that event. It was feared that the chief demoness, Lilith, sought to capture the soul of every child as it came into the world. To prevent this, amulets and texts from Scripture were hung round the room. The children belonging to the nearest school, or to a school in which one of the family was attending, were called into the home in which there was a newborn child. They chanted or recited Deut. vi. 4–13 : ' Hear, O Israel : Our God is one God, etc.,' and also the 91st Psalm. The visits of the children continued through the first seven days after the birth, but when the child was brought into the Abrahamic Covenant it was considered safe from evil spirits—at least as safe as its guardian angel could make it.

The social life centred round the home, the family being the unit. And since such things as the bringing of children into the Abrahamic Covenant, the time of the young boy becoming the son of the Law (which, in the case of an ordinary boy, was at the age of thirteen, and of an orphan boy, at twelve) and marriage were great events in the life of the Jew—these furnish the occasions for fellowship and goodwill. The feasts also formed a large part of the social life, and as these were numerous it gave opportunity for people, and especially family circles, to meet and join together in family joys. The centre of the community life outside Palestine and in Palestine itself was to a great degree the synagogue, while the centre of the religious life was the Temple. And since every Jew was expected to go up to Jerusalem thrice yearly, Jerusalem was a centre for the reception, as well as the emanation, of ideas and ideals. As has already been pointed out, though Jerusalem itself was often very sterile in thought and learning, yet all brought their contributions thither, to receive the stamp of orthodoxy. The village life in Palestine itself, as well as the settlements outside Palestine, centred round the synagogue ; and since every phase of the Jewish life was related to one standard only, namely, its agreeableness to the Divine will, there was nothing merely secular or social, but everything had to conform to the religious standard of the time.

It will be seen from the foregoing that the education of the Jewish boy, and his continued education as a man, was concerned entirely with the study of the Law and the rabbis. Neither science nor philosophy as such interested the Jew very much, and certainly never entered into his educational system. Even to this day many a successful Jew knows no more of mathematics than ordinary addition, subtraction, multiplication and division ; and yet one finds him everywhere dominating the business world and taking more than a little share in municipal and state affairs. The Jewish maxims of the whole round of life were put concisely for us in the words of St. Paul : ' In Him we live, move and have our being.'

Worship in the Temple and Synagogue.

Worship in Judaism was not uniform, but consisted of (1) Temple Worship ; (2) Synagogue Worship ; and (3) Unattached Worship.

To ascertain how much our Christian forms of worship owe to Jewish influence, a survey of the religious life of Jewry for a day at the beginning of the first century A.D. would serve best.

It would be natural to begin the investigation with the Temple. The Temple was the centre of the priestly cult, and therefore was given up to many ceremonies and much ritual that we cannot hope to investigate here.

The sacrifices as such naturally could not have any influence on Christian worship, but one type of sacrifice, usually designated ' the whole burnt offering ' (in the Hebrew, ' Thamid '), has its interest because it was, as the word indicates, a permanent offering ; and, secondly, because it was an offering for the nation, and the nation shared in it.

The Thamid was offered thrice a day : at 9 a.m., 3 p.m. and 6 p.m. (see Ex. xxix. 39 ; Num. xxviii. 3 ; Ezra iii. 3 ; Neh. x. 34). It is contended by some scholars that the Thamid was a morning and afternoon sacrifice only. Against the contention there are the following considerations : (1) The passages quoted read in full : ' And this shall ye offer upon the altar, lambs of a year old twice daily as a Thamid. The one lamb for the morning and the other lamb between the evenings ' (Ex. xxix. 38, 39) ; (2) ' And thou shalt say unto them, This is the burnt sacrifice that ye shall bring nigh unto Jehovah, lambs a year old, whole in body and limb, twice daily as a whole burnt offering, the Thamid. The one lamb shall ye make in the morning and the other between the evenings ' (Num. xxviii. 3, 4) ; (3) ' They offered upon it burnt offerings unto Jehovah, burnt offerings of morning and evening ' (Ezra iii. 3).

The great difficulty is to decide what exactly ' Bain-h'ar-baym ' means. Usually these words are translated ' twilight,' but many contend that it means any time in the afternoon.

In Neh. x. 34, however, it says : ' Unto the shewbread the Mincha of the Thamid and the holath of the Thamid.' It would appear from this passage that the Mincha was considered a separate Thamid, and that the other Thamids are mentioned alongside it.

In the Mishnah the question of the sacrifice of the Thamid is not given explicitly, but in the tractate *Pesachim*, division v. par. 1, it says : ' The Thamid was slaughtered at 8 (2 p.m.) and 8.30 (2.30 p.m.) and sacrificed between 9 (3 p.m.) and 9.30 (3.30 p.m.). On the eve of the Passover it was slaughtered at 7.30 (1.30 p.m.), and sacrificed at 8.30 (2.30 p.m.).' This passage is dealing with the sacrifice of the Thamid as such, and does not imply that it was a lamb offering. Amongst the Samaritans the Passover lamb, which is also enjoined to be killed at Bain-h'ar-baym, is slaughtered immediately after sunset (about 6 p.m.).

It is further to be remembered that the afternoon prayer in Jewry is known as Mincha. There is, furthermore, significance in the remark made about Dan. vi. 10, 11. ' And his windows were open in his chambers towards Jerusalem, and three times in the day he knelt upon his knees and prayed and gave thanks before his God.' We are thus justified in concluding that there were three Thamids a day—morning, afternoon and evening, and that the afternoon Thamid was a Mincha (meal offering).

We can now turn to the investigation of the Thamid as such. This is described minutely in the tractate *Thamid* of the Mishnah, pp. 188a–191a.

With some very minor exceptions, all three Thamids followed the same course. It cannot be said that our main source of information, namely, the Talmud, is clear on the question of Temple services ; indeed it is very often the case that the tractates are contradictory (I shall give you my own conclusions on the matter as I gather them from these sources). It is necessary to point out that, at the time we are considering, the people were divided into three classes—Priests, Levites and Israelites—and that each of these classes was again divided into twenty-four sections. When the Thamid was sacrificed, representatives from every part of the Diaspora present in Jerusalem, and the 'Mishmar' watch, whose turn it was to be present at the sacrifice of the Thamid, but who could not go with the order to Jerusalem, gathered in their synagogues at home. There they recited, amongst other things, separate pieces of Scripture on separate days of the week—Sunday, Gen. i. 1–5; Monday, vers. 6–8; Tuesday, vers. 9–13; Wednesday, vers. 14–19; Thursday, vers. 20–23; Friday, vers. 24–31; Saturday, Gen. ii. 1–4. These are marked in the M.T. by a Pe, and in the A.V. by a small indication at the side of the verse.

While the clothing of the priests does not, strictly speaking, concern us here, yet as some of it has found its way into the Church in a modified form, it may not be out of place to take note of it. It consisted of shorts tied at the thighs, over which was worn a close-fitting white garment reaching to the feet. This garment had sleeves like the modern university gown, but they were fastened together at the back. A multi-coloured girdle sitting rather high on the chest, with one end hanging down to the ankle, and a skull-cap, completed the attire. Since the serving priest had to wash his hands and feet frequently, and as the usual custom among the Semites is not to wear shoes in a place of worship, we are justified in concluding that during the service the priest did not wear any foot-gear. The garments, with the exception of the girdle, were of white linen, indicative of levitical and moral purity.

The work of the day for the officiating priests began before sunrise. The presiding priest came to the room of the inner courts, where the priests slept. They had already been up some time, and had performed their ceremonial bathing. The president would ask for volunteers from amongst them to clean the ashes off the altar of burnt offerings, but as there were numerous volunteers for this office, lots had to be drawn. While the chosen priests were attending to this task, and also putting fresh wood on the altar for the approaching sacrifice, the other priests repaired to a hall (Lish-Chath h'Gizah) outside the Temple area, where lots were again drawn, this time for (1) the slaughtering of the Thamid ; (2) the sprinkling of the blood on the altar ; (3) the removal of the ashes from the altar of incense ; (4) the trimming of the candles, etc., thirteen lots being drawn in all. Then one of the priests would be sent out to see if the sun had risen, and had lit up the country as far south as Hebron. If it had, the lamb to be offered as the Thamid was first given a drink from a golden bowl and then led to the north side of the altar, where it was sacrificed. Nine priests took part in the slaughtering and proper preparation of the victim. This done, they all retired again to the Lish-Chath h'Gizah, where the president called upon them to recite the prescribed prayers. While neither the Babylonian nor Jerusalem Talmuds tells us what the first prayer was, yet we gather it was the Yotser. This was followed by a second prayer, the H'Avah, and then followed the Shema (Deut. vi. 4–9, xi. 13–21 ; Num. xv. 37–41). There has been some dispute as to whether the whole of these passages were recited. As they were already included in the door-lintel parchment (Mezuzah) (Deut. vi. 4–9, xi. 13–21) and in the phylacteries (Tephilim), I think it is very probable that they were recited in full. The Ten Commandments were also recited at this time. Following this, the priests returned to the Temple precincts, and along with the people they repeated two prayers—Emeth Ve-yatsib (true and established) and the H'vodah (service). After this they gave the people the Aaronic blessing, to which the people responded, ' Blessed be Jehovah, the Lord God of Israel, from everlasting to everlasting.' Then the Magrephah (gong) was sounded (said to have been heard as far as Jericho), which was the sign for the priests, Levites and stationary men (representatives of the divisions of the people) to gather for the burning of the incense. This is when the priests hoped for a revelation from God for the people (Luke i. 10). At this time also the Thamid was laid on the fire ; and the high priest's offering, consisting of twelve half-cakes (the other halves being burnt at the evening Thamid), and the drink offering were also burnt on the altar. Meanwhile the president gave the signal at which a priest struck a cymbal, and the choir of the Levites, accompanied by instrumental music, began the psalm of the day.

This psalm was sung in three portions, and on the completion of each portion the priests blew three blasts on their trumpets, at which the people bowed down and worshipped. The psalms sung were : Sunday, xxiv. ; Monday, xlviii. ; Tuesday, lxxxii. ; Wednesday, xciv. ; Thursday, lxxxi. ; Friday, xciii. ; Saturday, xcii.

The Synagogue and its Polity.

Professor Causse of Strasbourg, in the course of a lecture which he delivered on the Diaspora (the collective name for the Jews dispersed after the Babylonian captivity) to an international gathering of Old Testament scholars at Oxford in 1927, remarked that ' Jerusalem was a centre into which all the ideas and ideals of Jewry flowed, and while it was the seat of authority, and its stamp was required for orthodoxy, yet the Diaspora was the original home of the great thoughts of Judaism.'

The synagogue was one of the gifts of the Diaspora, which had a very beneficient effect on the life of the people. The origin of the synagogue may be traced to the exilic period. It was not primarily a place of prayer, but rather a gathering-place for discussion of religious subjects and exposition of the Law. Such gatherings as are described in Ezek. viii. 1 may well have been its beginnings. It is not surprising, therefore, to find a claim put forth that the men of the Great Synagogue were the compilers of the books of Ezekiel, the twelve prophets, Daniel and Esther (tractate *Baba Bathra*, p. 10 in English, p. 15 in Hebrew).

To this early use of the synagogue as a place of exposition and compilation of Scripture was added the later use of it as a place of prayer. During the troubled times when the high priesthood was sold to the most influential family and to the highest bidder, any self-respecting Jew who wished to commune with God could not look upon the Temple as a fitting place for this purpose, and thus the synagogue became the home of spiritual Israel.

Its Government.

The officials of the synagogue were :

(1) The Rosh H'Keneseth (in Greek, Archisynagogos).
(2) Zekennim (in Greek, Archontes)—Elders.
(3) Segan—Prefect or Ruler.
(4) Gabaai Tsedakah—Those who had charge of the charitable affairs of the congregation.
(5) Chazan—Leader of Praise.
(6) Sheliche Tsebeer—The representatives of the community.
(7) Shamas—Steward.

The Talmud is very confusing about these officials, but the following will give an idea of their duties. The chief of the synagogue was responsible for the good conduct of the worshippers during services, and the Chazan and Shamas were answerable to him for the proper carrying out of their duties.

The Segan was a civil official, and represented the Persian, Seleucid or Roman authorities.

The elders were the ecclesiastical authority. They ruled not only in the synagogue, but in civil matters also. They had power to exclude any one from the synagogue. This exclusion took two forms—(1) exclusion for a given period ; (2) excommunication—exclusion for ever. This second form was naturally used very sparingly, but any one who has ever seen it cannot readily forget the picture. The synagogue, even to the lamps and the candles, is draped in black, and a curse is pronounced on the individual or individuals, who are henceforth outside the commonwealth of Israel. These elders could also sentence to a flogging, thirty-nine stripes being the limit of this form of punishment.

The guardians of charity had to care for the poor and provide hospitality, on ordinary days a meal and a night's hospitality, but on the Sabbath this had to be extended to three meals and two nights' lodgings.

The Chazan was the official leader in prayer and reader of the Law, but the Archisynagogos could invite any one he deemed fit to undertake these duties. The Chazan had always to be on hand, and he was a paid official.

The Shamas (steward) was responsible for the interior economy and was a paid official.

The Building.

The building was a plain one, simply furnished. It was evidently allowed to have signs of the Zodiac painted on the walls. The Great Synagogue in Jerusalem certainly has three signs painted on its walls, but I have never seen anything of this nature in any of the Galilean synagogues. Eagles of stone or metal also seem to have been allowed in some synagogues, but I think this was more an exception than a general rule.

The seats were so arranged that they faced the Temple (usually east). In the centre of the building there was a raised platform from which the Law and the Prophets were read and the preaching was done. In a corner of the building was a jar of water with a dipper and basin where the priest washed his hands before pronouncing the Aaronic benediction. This was also available for any member of the congregation who deemed it ceremonially necessary.

In the wall facing the east there was the Ark, containing the parchment scrolls of the Law, and near it stood a desk, at which the leader in prayer stood with his back to the congregation.

Attached to the synagogue was a separate compartment for the women worshippers. This was usually higher than the synagogue level, and under it was either the school or a sort of library (Genizah).

Worship.

Apart from the prayers given in connection with the Temple worship, six prayers called the H'middah were said standing. I fail to see how Schürer, Edersheim and Oesterley can argue for eighteen prayers (Shemonah Esre) being said, when we are told distinctly (*Berachoth* vii. p. 25 (Arabic 29a, Hebrew)) that Samuel the cotton-dealer collected these eighteen prayers just before the time of Gamaliel II. (*circa* 70–100 A.D.). The fact that some of the prayers may be traced in Ben Sira (Oesterley's *Jewish Background of Christian Liturgy*, pp. 55 ff.) proves nothing. The H'middah in the time of Christ consisted only of six prayers, namely, the first, second, third, seventeenth, eighteenth, and nineteenth prayers of the present-day Jewish Prayer Book. Strangely enough, Dr. Oesterley, whilst arguing for the eighteen prayers as pre-Christian, argues against the tractate *Thamid* in regard to No. 17. He apparently forgets that the Temple was destroyed twice.

It would seem that these prayers were first said silently by the congregation, and then loudly by the leader in prayer, for it was between the first three and the last three that others prayers could be inserted, and some rabbis took advantage of this permission to add their own prayers (Luke xi. 1).

Before the sixth prayer the Aaronic benediction was pronounced by the priest. The last prayer followed, and then the reading of the Law and the Prophets. For the Law the leader of the prayer left his desk and went to the Ark, in which the scrolls of the Law were kept. The first five books of the Old Testament were written on sheets of parchment about eighteen inches long, but of variable breadth. These sheets were sewn together and stretched upon two rollers working in saucer-like sockets. This parchment was usually covered by a silk cover. In many cases each scroll had a special case (tekah). The scroll was carried to the raised platform, and for this privilege sums of money used to be paid. The lesson from the Pentateuch was read by any one present whom the Archisynagogos deemed fit for the office. If none of the congregation was called upon, the permanent prayer leader (Chazan) did the reading.

The Pentateuch was divided into one hundred and fifty divisions, and one division was read every week, so that the whole was read through triennially. Originally, short lessons were read on festivals and extraordinary Sabbaths (Sabbath Sabbathou), but at this time biweekly readings on Mondays and Thursdays and on the Sabbath were the order. On the Sabbath day the portion was divided into seven portions. If there were priests or Levites present they read the first and second sections (see *Gittim*, ver. 9,

p. 96*a*, bottom). ' These words are said for the sake of peace, the priest reads first ; he is followed by a Levite, and he by an Israelite (one of the people).'

The following account from the tractate *Megillah* (sec. iv. pars. 1–4, pp. 66*a* and 66*b*) gives us a reasonable idea of how the reading was done : ' He who reads the scroll stands, he who translates may sit. There are found places where it is customary to say a blessing, then let him say it. Where this is not in vogue the blessing is not said. On Monday and Thursday morning and Saturday afternoon services (Mincha), three divisions are read, no more and no less, and no closing passage from the Prophets is read. He who reads the first section, and he who reads the last section must say a blessing at the beginning and end. On New Moon days and ordinary feast days four sections are read, no more and no less, the closing prophetic portion is not read. He who opens the reading and he who closes it, does so with a blessing. This is the rule for all ordinary times except feast days (extraordinary ones). On feast days five divisions are read, on the Day of Atonement six divisions, on Saturday seven divisions, no less, but there is added a portion from the Prophets.'

This is the blessing said in the synagogue at the present day, which I think is the same as that in the time of our Lord : ' Bless ye Jehovah, worthy of blessing.' The people answer, ' Blessed be Jehovah, who is worthy of praise for ever and eternity. Blessed art Thou, Jehovah, our God, God of the universe, who hast chosen us from all the peoples and given us His Torah ; praised be Jehovah, who gave us the Torah.' Then the closing blessing, ' Blessed art Thou, Jehovah, our God, King of the universe, who gave us the Torah of truth, and planted within us eternal life ; blessed art Thou, Jehovah, giver of the Torah.'

The reading of the Law, we learn from Luke iv. 17, Acts xiii. 15, and the above quotation, was followed by a short passage from the Prophets in the old Jewish sense. This term covered all the Prophets, and Joshua, Judges, the books of Samuel and Kings.

Before leaving this subject it must be explained that the phrase, ' he who translates,' in the quotation above, refers to the very necessary interpreter in the synagogue.

The Hebrew language was a classical language to most Jews in our Lord's day. The majority could read it, but did not readily understand it. They spoke the Aramaic, a cognate Semitic language, and thus it became necessary to have translators in the synagogue. While nothing definite is told us as to how this translation was made, I think that probably a specially appointed official sat on the bimah and read the translation.

After the portion from the Prophets (H'ftorah) was read, there followed a ' Derashah,' which can best be translated as ' an intelligent commentary.'

Other Forms of Worship.

We are well acquainted with such from passages in the New Testament, *e.g.* Luke xi. 1, and the innumerable occasions on which our Lord turned aside with His disciples to pray. The Acts, further, furnish us with many examples of private prayer in houses and by the riverside (see Acts i. 12–14, ii. 1, xii. 12, and many other passages). It ought to be noted also that the breaking of bread in the Apostolic Church took place at these private meetings.

I am not prepared to pass judgment as to which type of worship—the Temple, synagogue, or private—has influenced Christian worship most, nor yet to pass an opinion as to which of these forms is in accordance with the teaching of Christ and the Early Church. I need only point out that when taken point by point from the early prayers (which are represented by Matins), the burning of incense, the priestly blessing, the repetition of set prayers, the use of the Psalms, the reading of Scripture, the preaching, down to the worship in the home, not one single item but has found its way into Christian worship.

CHAPTER VI

PARTIES AND PERSONALITIES THAT INFLUENCED THE PERIOD

Parties.

The Priestly Party.

THE most important party in Judaism was undoubtedly the priestly party. While they were not a party in the strict sense of the word, since they identified themselves with each of the other parties that we shall deal with, and should be spoken of as a cult, yet as the people were divided into three sections, namely, priests, Levites and the rest of the people, it is difficult to find a term that would describe their place in the national life apart from the word 'party.' Into the complicated system of priestly descent and qualifications for service we cannot enter here. Suffice it to say that from an early date, say about 1000 B.C., they were a class which considered itself as the mediators between God and man, and monopolised the service of the sanctuary for their male descendants. Thus, when the Temple was built by Solomon, a family descendant from one Zadok, who claimed descent from the tribe of Levi and the family of Aaron the brother of Moses, obtained a monopoly of the service in the Temple. That this party should seek to monopolise the worship of God in the Temple they ministered in is no matter of wonder, and that this exclusive right to officiate in the Temple should lead to abuses is only to be expected.

The priesthood was not of Hebrew or Israelitish invention, for it was well established among the older civilisations of Babylonia and Egypt. That it maintained itself upon the superstition of the peoples it was supposed to serve, there can be little doubt. It is also very clear that it developed a tradition which was disseminated very carefully and ingeniously. Scholars have differed as to the relationship that existed between prophets and priest.

I have listened to the late Professor Francis Brown (one of the editors of the Oxford Hebrew Lexicon) and to Professor John Edgar M'Fadyen advocating with great power that there was no hostility between the two classes, but I am not convinced that this was so. I hold that there was grave conflict between the leaders of the synagogue party and that of the Temple party. The synagogue party taught that God can only be reconciled to man by means of personal achievement, while the priestly party preached reconciliation through sacrifice. From the days of Samuel the idealists of the nation preached obedience rather than sacrifice.

The priestly party as such was a spiritually sterile party, and it was also intellectually weak. Its appeal was in pomp, show and elaborate ceremonies; while the prophets, idealists and synagogue leaders had no such means. They appealed to the heart, and the heart of Israel was hard and unyielding.

As was pointed out in the first chapter, strife amongst the priests themselves began at an early stage in the history of Judaism. The Zadokites contested the claims of the priests who had remained in Palestine during the years of the Exile, and Zerubbabel sided with them. That the number of priests who returned was not very large is quite plain from all the authorities on this period, but that these, small as they were, soon became the most influential party in the community is also very evident. It is difficult to say at what period the registration of the priestly families began, but they certainly existed at the time of Nehemiah, and there is no reason to doubt that from that time on the register of descent of the priestly progeny has maintained itself as a distinctive part of the people. When the Law is read, the priest takes precedence in being called to the reading, and the priest also still pronounces the benediction upon the people.

The priesthood, as has already been pointed out, was divided into twenty-four sections, as were also the Levites, and the remainder of the nation. These sections took their turn in supplying the necessary members for the services in the Temple. Whatever may have been the case prior to the time of the Hashmonaim, from the date of the rededication of the Temple by them till after our Lord's time the high priesthood was not in the Zadokite family. It was given instead to the family that possessed the most political influence, and apart from the Hashmonaim themselves there was not a single high priest that stood out for any goodness, rather the contrary, judging by the Talmud, which makes some very bitter remarks about these leaders. Our Lord prayed the Father not to lay the charge of His death against His people, but I am not so sure that this prayer included the priestlings, for it was they who compassed His death. Little more need be said about this party. That there were good people among them goes without saying, but that they, their traditions, general conduct and character were unworthy of their people, cannot be denied.

The Sanhedrin.

Regarding this body of men, their origin, and even their very name, there is much doubt. Without taking the reader into the intricacies of this problem, we shall state in a few sentences what, on close examination of the most reliable authorities, the obvious conclusions are.

The word ' Sunedrion ' is of Greek origin and means a court of justice, so that at least so far as the name is concerned this court cannot be of an earlier date than the period of Grecian influence in Palestine. It is safe to assume that the constitution of this body is not earlier than the Roman period (63 B.C.), and, so far as our literature of the period is concerned, this assumption is supported by the fact that the name ' Sanhedrin ' is not found in the literature we have until the last half-century B.C. Then it occurs first in the Psalms of Solomon, and secondly in connection with Herod, who was cited to appear before that body while governor of Galilee.

Speculation as to its origin is rife among scholars of our period, and many passages of Scripture are, as usual, brought to the aid of the several theories that are advocated. But we will do well to disregard these theories, which mostly deal with the might-have-been, and confine ourselves to facts. Gabinius divided Palestine into five sections for the purpose of efficient government. ' He

(Gabinius) also parted the whole nation into five conventions (synods), assigning one portion to Jerusalem, another to Gadara, a third to Amathus, a fourth to Jericho, and the fifth division to Sepphoris, a city in Galilee ' (see Josephus, *Wars of the Jews*, bk. i. chap. viii. par. 5). This division took place between 57–55 B.C. It might be asked, What has this division to do with the Sanhedrin? In answer it must be pointed out that this division was for judicial purposes, and as we find that these districts had their Sanhedrin, it is almost conclusive that these synods were the origin of the jurisdictory power of the Sanhedrin which afterwards centred in the body in Jerusalem. Cæsar brought this arrangement to an end in 47 B.C. when he appointed Hyrcanus II. as prince of the whole nation. All the authority was then transferred to Jerusalem, and the Jerusalem synod, with the high priest at its head, became the chief body of legislators for the nation. When Herod, who was governor of Galilee, put to death some rebels in his province, the Sanhedrin at Jerusalem cited him to appear before them to answer for the usurpation of authority which they deemed to belong exclusively to themselves. This incident is the first recorded act of this body as a national body, and in the absence of further evidence we must assume that this was their first act of self-assertion.

Its Constitution and Functions.

There were five types of the Sanhedrist courts. The first consisted of three judges, who had jurisdiction over the following affairs : Cases of trusteeships, cases of common robbery, cases of injury, housebreaking and libel (some rabbis held that cases of libel, when these contained a charge of defamation of character, should go before the Sanhedrin court of twenty-three judges). Further, when any person was deemed worthy of flogging, for non-observance of the New Moon or New Year, these three judges dealt with the matter. Rabbi Simon, son of Gamaliel, held that cases of flogging should go through three courts, namely, that of the court of three, five and seven judges. Those persons sentenced to flogging could appeal from the lower to the higher courts. And so evolved the round of duties of the judicial bodies progressing from three members to five, seven, twenty-three and seventy-one. The Sanhedrist court of twenty-three had the power of passing the death sentence, though an appeal to the supreme body could be made from this lower court. The supreme body of seventy-one sat in Jerusalem in the court near the Temple. The tractate *Sanhedrin* states the special duties of the supreme court as being ' to judge tribal affairs, the case of a false prophet, and the case of a high priest.' They had also the exclusive right of declaring war, and had further special jurisdiction which does not concern us here. While other specially specified jurisdiction of the Sanhedrin is laid down, the three specific types given above are the only ones of importance. This should be noted clearly, for, if our Lord was brought before that body, it could only have been under the second caption, namely, a false prophet. While the four lower courts were strictly limited to the discharge of certain functions in their capacities as judges, the supreme court was not limited, and it was recognised by the Romans as a court which had the right of passing the death sentence, which the Romans had to carry out.

The place of meeting of the supreme Sanhedrin was the ' Lischat H'gizzah.' There is great divergence of opinion as to the nature of the building as well as the exact spot it occupied, but this is an unimportant matter. The question of real interest is the nature of the meetings held, and the method followed at trials. The place in which the Sanhedrin met was arranged like a crescent so that they could all see each other. Two recorders were present, one occupying the one end of the crescent, and the other the other end. According to Rabbi Judah it was necessary to have three recorders, one taking down the evidence of the prosecution, one of the defence, and one taking down both. The crescent-like arrangement had three rows in which future Sanhedrists sat. These students for Sanhedristic rank could not talk against any one standing on trial for his life, but they were allowed to point out anything which favoured the prisoner. The passage dealing with the question of trial (*Sanh*. iv. 12 ff.) makes a significant observation about trials for life. It says that Adam was created as a single man that it might ever be remembered that the world depends upon the individual, so that the taking of a life must be most carefully considered, for a wrong sentence may mean the destruction of a whole race.

Witnesses appearing against a person tried for his life had to answer seven questions: To what year did their charge refer ?   What month of the year ?   What day of the month ?   What day of the week ?   What hour of the day ?   What place ?   and What was the nature of the offence ?   If the witnesses disagreed on any of the foregoing questions their testimony was worthless.   It is added in the same connection that careful, consistent and accurate examination of witnesses is specially meritorious. The witnesses were examined and cross-examined separately, and their testimony had to agree in every detail. If one of the judges had said anything which seemed to imply that he believed the accused guilty, but changed his mind, he could withdraw and speak in favour of the accused ; but if he had spoken in favour he could not reverse his opinion.   It was natural with such a large court that some members were absent from it at various times.   It was, therefore, laid down that twenty-three formed a quorum and could, if they agreed and had a clear majority, pass the death sentence ; but if of the twenty-three twelve were for conviction and eleven against, other members of the court had to be called in until there was a clear majority of two against the accused, though even a majority of one was sufficient in favour of acquittal.   If the trial was over, and the accused was being led out to pay the penalty, and a witness turned up who had something to say in favour of the accused, he was brought back and the trial reheard. The accused could not be executed on the day of the trial, but a clear day given in which the sentence was proclaimed, and witnesses in favour of the accused still given an opportunity to appear in his favour.   No sentence could be carried out on a Friday afternoon, on the Sabbath or on a feast day.

The tractate *Sanhedrin*, which deals with the questions of the formation of courts, their functions, their methods and their jurisdiction, is a very absorbing one, but cannot be gone into here. The foregoing facts have been gone into because they bear on the so-called 'Trial of Jesus.' Other points, such as the time of the meeting of the courts, which had to take place during the daytime, might have been added, but the essentials in these matters so far pointed out indicate that the case of Jesus was remarkable for the absence of every rule required by the usages of Judaism.

The question as to whether the high priest was the president of the court of the Sanhedrin has been argued at great length. Personally, I feel that the answer is in the negative.

Schools and their Heads.

As far back as the time of Ezekiel we find the elders gathering in some place for the purpose of counsel (Ezek. viii. 1), and these gatherings continued from that time. As has already been pointed out in connection with the worship of the synagogue, the original purpose of these meeting-places was not so much for worship as for study and discussion of religious matters. In the course of time these places became the centre of learning for the nation, and it was only natural that some of these learned people should be recognised as leaders. This recognition went a great deal further among the Jews than it did among the other nations, and it was from these centres that Jewish thought and learning emanated. Though Jerusalem was the recognised centre of these schools, yet such schools existed in the Diaspora, and much that was noblest in Jewish thought came from those schools outside of Judea itself, though brought to Jerusalem to receive the stamp of orthodoxy. The earliest of these schools is known as 'Men of the Great Assembly,' and it was upon the dictum of this school that later Judaism sought to regulate its conduct. This dictum is given us in *Aboth* i. 1, 'Be careful in judgment; raise many disciples, and make a fence round the Torah.' The succession of these great teachers is almost unbroken, and men like Simon ' the just,' 219–199 B.C., Antigonus of Socho, 200 B.C., and many others whose names are given us in the *Aboth* were leaders in these schools. Their names are given in pairs, and their sayings are worth a close study. The later great leaders in these schools are Schemia and Abtalion, Hillel and Shammai. We cannot enter fully into the requirements for leadership and authority, but it should be borne in mind that these schools represented the seats of authority for the people, and that only those who belonged to these schools were deemed as sitting in the seats of Moses and the Prophets. That our Lord did not belong to any of these schools is fairly certain. Indeed, His task was to convince the people that one need not belong to these schools to have some contribution to make to the religious thought—a task that only personal achievement could accomplish.

The Scribes.

While individuals and schools led, the power of leadership in so far as it concerned itself with interpretation of the Law was vested in a class known as the Soferim, 'Scribes.' From the time of Ezra 'The Scribe,' scribism became the function of a large class of learned people. While it was not looked upon as a sect, as some scribes belonged to the Pharisean and others to the Sadducean parties, and still others to the other parties, it was yet a class by itself, just as are the lawyers of our own day. It was the legislative, as well as the predominating, class in Judaism. The scribes were not only the guardians of the Law and the Prophets, but the repository of a tradition which was more binding even than the Scriptures. They claimed to be the medium of a revelation which was greater than that made to Moses and the Prophets. It is true to say that Judaism, as we know it, and as our Lord knew it, was what the scribes had made it. Since the scribes were so large a class, and as they had such a great influence upon Judaism, it is not only difficult, but quite wrong, to generalise about them. True, they demanded a place in the national life next to that of God Himself. They put themselves above parent and family, and demanded the places of honour at all public functions. Though they had a great many other shortcomings, they also did much for the nation which most Christians either do not know of at all or do not realise fully. The New Testament picture of them is but a partial picture, and in the nature of things it could not be anything else, because our Lord dealt with the defects of their teachings and with the arrogance of spirit of which they were guilty as a class. But a detailed study of some individual characters among them shows us men of sterling character, of humble minds, of great and loving hearts and, above all, of deep learning. The scribes were concerned with the one question, ' How is man to make himself acceptable unto God ?   How is he to regulate and conduct his life in every matter that affects his life so that he may please God ? '   Thus the scribe made it his duty to set forth with greatest care the laws for the conduct of life.   Without an actual experience of this scribal type of life which, in the case of an orthodox Jew, starts the moment his eyes are opened in the morning and only finishes when he closes them in sleep at night, during which time his life must be guarded and regulated according to the will of God, the scribal view-point cannot be understood.

The difference between the teachings of the scribes and that of our Lord may be summed up in a few words.   Jesus wanted man to yield his will to the will of God, which was to be achieved not by following so many rules which made life a burden, but by reserving one's right to do what the dictates of conscience demanded under certain circumstances.   This is best illustrated in the parable of the man who was robbed on the road between Jerusalem and Jericho.   The scribe would have told the priest and Levite that they must under no consideration go to the aid of the stricken man lest they become levitically unclean.   Jesus shows that a hated Samaritan, who had not the restrictions of scribal teaching upon him, fulfilled the law of mercy and the law of God by doing what was incumbent upon him to do by all the laws of humanity and God.   The scribes made the will of God a burden which was unbearable.   Jesus made the will of God a joyous self-expression.   Neither Sabbath nor any other fixed law was allowed to interfere with this freedom of the will, but in the willing and free exercise of it, according to the needs of life, God was served in deed and in truth. After all is said about the scribes that can and ought to be said, justice demands that we should bear in mind that they were the product of evolution of a system (Judaism) which had over and over again shown itself incapable of the exercise of freedom. ' Make a fence to the Law ' was not a mere expression of opinion, but a dire need. The scribes were too elated with their privileges to be conscious of their responsibility and opportunity, and so every step had to be safeguarded, and they themselves had the making of these guards.

Jewish Sects.

Since the political life was merged in the religious life, and both land and people were looked upon as the property of God, it was natural that parties should be divided on religious rather than political grounds. Nothing could exist apart from religion. If this principle could be borne in mind in connection with the study of every phase of Jewish life, the task of clearly understanding this and the subsequent history and outlook of the Jew would be greatly simplified.

The Samaritans.

This people lived in central Palestine, which formed part of what was the northern kingdom, known histori- cally as ' Israel.' It was Semitic by race, yet belonging to a different branch of the race from that to which the Jews themselves belonged. When Samaria fell in 722 B.C., the Assyrians followed the policy of transporting the conquered inhabitants into various centres of their empire and resettling the land with their own people. Naturally the colonists brought their own religious beliefs with them into their adopted home. The Semite, whether Jewish, Assyrian, Babylonian or any other section of the race, held to the belief that each tract of country had its own special presiding deity, and no matter how many other gods were worshipped, the territorial god was a very important factor in the pantheon. The Assyrian settlers seem to have taken some time to make up their minds as to the form the territorial god should take, but a sudden invasion of their territory by lions led them to think that the god of their territory was angry with them, and, not knowing how to propitiate him, they sent a delegation to Jerusalem asking the Judeans to send them priests who would instruct them in the forms of worship suitable for the land. The Judean authorities granted this request and sent some priests to instruct them in Yahweh worship. That the worship of this deity did not lead to monotheism there can be little doubt. Still in time, the general beliefs of the neighbouring kingdom must have influenced them to such an extent that they did become monotheistic. They would seem, however, to have maintained their own traditions and customs, and did not become merged into the main stream of Judaism.

The points on which they differed most from the rest of the Jewish people were : (1) They did not accept the writings of the Prophets as part of their own literature; (2) when Jerusalem became the central place of worship and its Temple the central sanctuary for all Jewry, the Samaritans maintained their own worship on Mount Gerizim, and there they had their central shrines.

They were nonconformists and provincial, and that these two factors should have caused diversity which amounted to hatred cannot be wondered at. That the fanaticism of Nehemiah, who would not let them share in the rebuilding of the second Temple, had something to do with the ultimate estrangement between them and the Jews there can be no doubt, and that their own action in hindering Nehemiah's building of the walls round Jerusalem further caused the breach to widen may also be reasonably assumed. They carried the feud into the Dispersion, and in Egypt these feuds between Jew and Samaritan had gone so far as to make it necessary for the king to intervene. The result of the dispute in Egypt was that the Samaritan champions were ordered to be put to death, and finally the last act which made the breach complete was the destruction of the Temple on Mount Gerizim by John Hyrcanus I. From that time onward the Samaritans and Jews had no dealings with each other. Herod, a half-Jew himself, knowing that he would find support more readily among the Samaritans than he was likely to do among the Judean Jews, favoured them. He

rebuilt their city of Samaria, naming it Sebaste, and showed
them other favours. The help that the Samaritans gave
Herod in his establishing himself on the throne of Palestine
was not forgotten and never forgiven by the Jews. The
enmity was so bitter that the Jews avoided the very soil
on which the Samaritans trod.

The Galileans.

That the Jews were not opposed to the Samaritans
because of their non-Jewish origin may be gathered from
the fact that the inhabitants of Galilee were also non-
Jewish. It will be remembered that Aristobulus in his
short reign undertook the conquest of the northern parts of
Palestine, that is to say, the regions beyond Samaria.
We must quote Josephus fully here, for it is upon his
information that our view-point of the Galileans is based.
' He (Aristobulus) was called a lover of the Grecians, and
had conferred many benefits on his own country, and made
war against Iturea, and added a great part of it to Judea,
and compelled the inhabitants if they would remain in that
country to be circumcised, and to live according to the
Jewish Laws ' (*Antiq.*, Book XIII. chap. xi. par. 3). This
information comes from Strabo, who in turn got it from one
' Timagenes.' While we cannot enter into the argument
between Sir George Adam Smith and Professor Schürer
as to who the Itureans were, their geographical location,
etc., yet it is quite evident from what we have ascertained
that, so far as the returned Jews were concerned, they were
gathered mostly within an area of not more than about
twenty square miles round Jerusalem. They had spread
in the time of the Maccabees to the south, and even to
Transjordania, but during the whole struggle for liberty
in the second century we hear very little of Jews from the
northern district. From 2 Maccabees v. we learn that
Simon, Judas's brother, was sent to Galilee to protect those
Jews who were found there. We are told that he brought
back the entire Jewish population of Galilee to Jerusalem.
From this we cannot help but conclude that the Jewish
population of Galilee must have been very small, and taking
this factor in conjunction with the quotation from *Antiquities*, we cannot avoid the conclusion that when Aristo-

bulus went north there were no Jews there, and, whether the Itureans were actually the Galileans or not, their conversion by force must have taken place at the same time as that of the Galileans. Even in our Lord's time we find many Gentiles in the northern districts, and while it would seem that the Itureans were Arabs, there were not a few Greeks in the district who had settled there during the supremacy of the Seleucids.

Galilean Jews

I consider the question of the racial and religious origin of the Galileans one of great importance in its bearing on Christianity. The fact that eleven of the disciples of Jesus were Galileans must have some significance. The attachment of these men to Jesus while the only Judean (Judas Iscariot) betrayed Him means something, also the fact that His ministry was more successful in Galilee than in Judea. Hebrew of the Hebrews though I am, I am inclined to the feeling that had the propagation of the Gospel of Jesus been left to the Judean Jews, it would not have fared so well. It was the broader mind and the wider outlook of these people who were descendants of Arabs and Greeks, and their daily intercourse with the Gentiles in their everyday life, that made the Gospel that came from them so broad and universal. True, Peter had to get a special vision to make him go to the Gentiles, and Saul the Pharisee went to them when Peter would not go, but Saul had lived his early life among the Gentiles, and had learned that they had souls that needed to be saved.

Any one who knew the Palestine of thirty years ago knows how a similar state of affairs was existent then. The Judean Jews were always at war with their Moslem neighbours. They would not take the trouble to learn the Arabic, nor to understand it, whilst the Galilean Jews not only knew the Arabic, but in many cases knew it far better than Hebrew, which to them was only a classical language in which they read the Old Testament and their prayers. They spoke and read the Arabic as their common medium, and also went out and lived among the Arabs and traded with them. The north seems to have bred men with a wider outlook and a more tolerant spirit, and Judea a narrow and intolerant type. It is precarious to argue on the meagre evidence we have, but as a personal opinion

I suggest that in the selection of the Galileans for the great new venture of the kingdom of God, our Lord's decision was influenced by the fact that these men were not far removed from their Gentile ancestry, and had what were lacking in the Judean Jew, a broad heart and receptive mind that only needed His influence to yield their fruits for the Gentile world.

The Pharisees.

A learned American theologian has asked us to discredit the gospel story about the disagreement between Jesus and the Pharisees (*Jesus and the Pharisees*, by Donald W. Riddle). This is because tbe scholar has studied Pharisaism in the library and cloister, rather than the Palestine of Jesus' day and to-day.

Pharisaism was nothing less than what its Hehrew meaning (Perushim='separatists') implies. Its origins are found in the Nivdalim (separatists) of the days of Nehemiah. Its separatism did not mean so much a separation from the worldly elements of life as the exclusion from its society, and even from the world to come, of every one who did not think as it did. It did not lack in spirituality or goodness—far from that—but it deserved and got the criticism of Jesus. Its fanaticism, its bitterness, its intolerance, in spite of its light, made it more blameworthy than would have been the case had it not been so fully capable of making its light shine in the dark places of the earth. Pharisaism was not a political creed, though it sought to import its creed into politics and suffered very grievously for it. It was not a sect, for it included Scribe, Priest and Herodian. It was a view-point which based itself on the doctrines of the Old Testament and the traditional teachings of the rabbis, which did not allow of expansion or liberty of thought. It held to the letter of the Law and lost its spirit. It was extremely nationalistic, that is to say, it believed that God had only one concern in existence and that was the glorification of Judaism, and that this glorification would work out in the advent of a Messiah who would bring the entire world to believe and think as it did, and I am not very sure but that they wanted God to take their view-point too. Those who find in Christ the Greek, the Roman, the Cosmopolitan, and every other thing, but fail to find in Him the supreme Jew, also fail to recognise that it was just that which brought Him into conflict with the only party in Judaism that could render spiritual service to the world. Their failure was the greatest blow to Judaism. If an example were needed to show us what Pharisaism plus Christ would have meant to the world, we need only look at St. Paul. The imagination cannot even conjure up a picture of the might-have-been.

While not a political party, the Pharisees yet tried to control the State for the purpose of religion. They sought to control every channel that lent itself to the control of the life of the people. When they were in power they did not persecute nor abuse that power, but they sought to make the hand of the law firm against those who disregarded the Law and traditions. They were politically what they were in their ordinary daily life, strict with themselves and others for the observance of God's laws as they understood them.

If the new estimate alluded to above is the result of a study of the Pharisee in the secluded chambers of Oxford, the general estimate of this sect is a little unjust. The Pharisee was not a hypocrite, nor yet a pedant such as the schoolman of the medieval ages was. He did not concern himself with the number of angels that could sit on the point of a needle. The Pharisees of Judaism were the backbone of the nation, for they sought to keep the nation clear of the besetting sins to which it was prone, and they did everything within their power to make it impossible for the erring to stray far. They made great and elaborate fences round the Law and so elaborated every commandment that life under the Law was very tedious and burdensome. It is said in the Law ' thou shalt not boil a kid in its mother's milk.' The Pharisees argued that this is too broad a principle, and they laid it down that milk and meat must not be cooked together, nor must milk and meat be cooked in the same vessel. In case of a mistake in pots being made, the rule was laid down that if the contents of the pot were cold, and they contained meat, and by mistake milk had been poured in, unless the quantity of the milk was less than an olive could hold, it was unlawful for consumption, and even the pot itself had to be put through a process of purification. Other laws of the same nature were made and were equally difficult of observance. Let it not be thought, however, that these people did not delight in observing these things themselves ; they did, and had no greater joy in life than the fulfilling the Law in all its possible shades of meaning. The more commandments, they said, the more merit in observing them. The more difficult a thing to observe, the greater the reward for observing it. The charge of our Lord that they made burdens which they were not themselves prepared to bear, but imposed these on others, was a just charge. They argued that they could be safely allowed some latitude in the observance of the commandments, for they were sure of themselves, but they could not be sure of others. They trusted themselves and in themselves, but they did not trust others. We shall say something about the special doctrines they laid stress on, but before doing so it must be said that Pharisaism was the despair of the Master, as Judaism must have been to God. It was spiritual, it was mystical, it was orthodox, it was noble, but it lacked catholicity, it was ultra-Jewish, it was too nationalistic, it was just what its name implies— separatist. One had to be not only a Jew but a Pharisee to be worthy of immortality. The Pharisees went so far as to think themselves defiled by the touch of those whom they considered sinners. How was the kingdom of God to be ushered in by such men and women ? This, and this only, was the reason that our Lord came so often into conflict with them.

As to definite beliefs, we know from the New Testament and Josephus that there was the certainty of the future life. It is true that this belief involved the idea of the resurrection of the body, but here we deal with a question that is still unsettled by Christian thinkers and theologians, and though I am not afraid to face it, I do not feel called upon here to enter into controversy on the question. I will only say that, though I was brought up in the belief of the resurrection of the body, I do not believe it to be an essential Christian doctrine, and that

my understanding of Jesus' teaching, that it is immortality
that He gives to those who believe on His Name, has been
the greatest truth in Christianity to me. Not that I
think that the body is evil—far from it. I do not think
that God has made anything that is evil, but I feel that
Jesus did not teach it. Yet I recognise that the doctrine of
a future life was the special contribution of the Pharisees.

The other important doctrine that the Pharisees held
fast to and developed is that which has philosophically
been called ' Predestination.' It has been styled by
others, Josephus among them, ' Fatalism.' Yet, in
Josephus, as in the teaching of those who we know held
the Pharisean principles, ' Free Will ' is insisted upon. It
is difficult to persuade Western thinkers that these ideas
or philosophic principles have a content different from
that which they had among the Greeks and have for
modern thinkers. It is not an easy matter to give exact
expression to the Jewish conception of the content of this
principle, but I shall try. The Jew thinks of life as lived
entirely in the care of God, and therefore whatever happens
to him is with the consent of the will of God. But, though
all that occurs in his life is within the providential care of
God, he is not thereby deprived of the exercise of his own
will. The question that philosophy would ask in this connection is, Where does God's providence end and man's
freedom begin ? This the Jews as a whole, and the Pharisees
in particular, never tried to answer; indeed, could not
answer. They took life as they found it ; they insisted
that it was man's duty to submit to the will of God, to
regulate his life by the will of God as revealed in the Law ;
and yet they fully realised that they could do things
contrary to the will of God. But they willed to submit
themselves to His will. It was not blind fatalism that
made them submit to God, but the belief that God was
mindful of their needs, and was interested in the very
minutiæ of their lives ; and it was their privilege to submit
their lives to Him in faith that their doing so would call
forth His care and aid in the affairs of their lives. Disregard of God's will did not mean the loss of God's interest
in them. He continued to care for them in spite of their
disregard of His will, but He no longer aided them in the

working out of the plans and purposes of life. They hated
the ungodly for living outside the Divine circle, and were
carried so far by this hatred that they would do nothing
to help repentance from ungodliness. This was the plain
outlook of scribe and Pharisee, but they also probed more
deeply into the matter, and St. Paul gives the clearest
philosophical aspect of it in Rom. ix. 20, 21. The potter
must have both the clear conception of the article he is
to make, and the use to which the article is to be put.
Foreknowledge and predestination are essential in all
creative functions. St. Paul argues that God could not
have asked man what he would prefer to be like, and what
destiny he would choose, before he was made. The
maker must of necessity form His own judgment in the
matters of form and destiny of the thing He is making.
St. Paul and the thoughtful scribe and Pharisee seem to
me to have possessed a much deeper grasp of the philosophy
of 'Free Will' than have had the schools of philosophy of
the past and the present. Philosophy takes man as it
finds him, and says he ought to have a free will, and then
goes on to explain what it means by free will. St. Paul
argues that since man is a creature of God, just as the pot
is the creation of the potter, the issue is not whether the
pot is what it is, but is what it is made to be, since the
potter must in the ultimate have the making of the pot.
Theology since Augustine, especially in the Calvinistic
schools, and philosophy have failed to appreciate the
deepest aspect of the issue. While St. Paul uses the pot
to illustrate his concept, he of course has humanity in
mind as the real factor. The Genesis story of the creation
of man goes very much more deeply into the root of the
matter than is seen on the surface. Man is made perfect,
but is given the power of exercising his will for good or
evil. In that God went much farther than a potter. The
pot can have no choice, but man could. St. Paul brings
the federal element into play, not because of his nationalistic tendencies, but because he was a universalist in the
broadest sense of the word. God did not will to make
each individual apart from every other individual; life
and progress could not be carried on on that basis. It is
St. Paul and the Pharisees who are the evolutionists in

this respect. Like begets like ; Adam's children must be like Adam, and if Adam acquires or selects a certain way of life his children would inherit it from him.

Of course there is much more in this problem than we can here enter into. There is the question of the pre-destination of the individual, as the cases cited by St. Paul (Ishmael and Isaac, Esau and Jacob). Since humanity must be grouped federally, there are bound to be cases in which there would be apparent injustice, but even in these cases the potter, so to speak, is working out his plan and purpose with a view to the whole. The matter resolves itself into the infinite knowledge of God, who has to keep in view humanity, and who has to so shape and form it that it will in the end achieve a noble and high purpose. Jesus gives it the possibility to do so now.

Regarding the origin of the Pharisees, little can be said with confidence. The most that can be said is that they existed as a party or sect in the latter part of the second century B.C. and that their most active days were the first century A.D.

The Sadducees.

The Sadducees were the aristocrats of the nation, and they combined conservatism and liberalism to the same extent that most aristocratic classes do. They were liberals in their attitude to, and interpretation of, the Law, and they were conservative in its application.

One of their main points of difference from the rest of the nation was belief in the future life. Of this they took a purely materialistic view. Since the Sadducees main-tained that only the Pentateuch was authoritative both as to conduct and doctrine, and that the Prophets had prophesied for the past only, immortality did not concern them as an issue. They brought this matter to our Lord, and the answer He gave them is hardly grasped by com-mentators. Our Lord's answer implies that the Penta-teuch teaches immortality, inasmuch as God is called the God of Abraham, Isaac and Jacob. Since the Sadducees believed in the Law, they had no answer to this strong argument. We would do well to take particular note of this, but we should further note that they did not subscribe to the doctrine of the 'resurrection' in the crass sense that Pharisaism held it. Those who died entered a state of life like that ascribed to angels—that is to say, a spiritual state free of the material.

It would be tedious to enumerate the various matters on which the Sadducees and Pharisees differed, or wherein they both erred in their interpretation of Scripture. If it is understood clearly that the Sadducees were not only an aristocracy but also a priestly sect, and were very deeply concerned with the Temple, it will be clear that, while they differed from the other sections in one thing and another, they were essentially a Temple party, and everything which concerned the glorification of the Temple was a matter of concern to them. Because the Prophets did not glorify the Temple but the God of the Temple, and because the majority of them believed and taught that salvation would come by the intervention of God in the affairs of the nation, the Prophets had to be discarded. And because Jesus said that if the Temple was broken down He would raise it in three days, He had to pay with His life for it. Stephen was also charged with speaking against the Temple, and he had to die.

The Sadducees have been charged with coming strongly under the influence of Hellenism. I doubt if this could be established in fact. They did show tendencies which were not otherwise found in Judaism, but these were Jewish to the core. As an aristocratic party and as an hierarchy they were strongly nationalistic, and since they belonged mainly to the priestly cultus they were confined to Palestine, and therefore did not come so much into contact with foreign influence as did, for instance, the Pharisees and the Galileans. While as a State party they did come into contact with foreign opinion, they were not always in power in the State. In the nature of the case they could not be progressive, for the Temple, with its worship and ceremonies, was the ultimate goal of life. In this there could be no changes, though it might be made more elaborate.

Because they did not believe in the current angelology and demonology, they have been charged with being 'Moderates' and worldly. This charge is more easily made than substantiated. Josephus, who is our main authority for these charges, was on his own showing a Pharisee in spite of his priestly descent ; and it is hardly fair to take an opponent's testimony as altogether an unbiased statement of fact.   We would hardly take it as gospel truth if a member of the Labour or Liberal parties or a Communist told us that the common people (or shall we call them the manual labourers ?) alone were spiritually inclined, or that the religious ministry of the country was worldly. Just as to-day there are very deeply spiritual people among the aristocracy, and as in the priestly orders there are bad men as well as good, so among the Sadducees there were materialists and spiritually minded. That they did not find followers among the working classes is not to be wondered at. The Pharisees had politically a Utopia to promise. The Messiah was their offer to the people, and, if not the Messiah, a resurrection after death which would bring with it material bliss. In these matters the Sadducees' platform was poor ; all they could afford was a satisfaction that comes from a consciousness of having done one's duty, and the rest must be left to God.

Regarding the origin and size of the party there has been great speculation. It is asserted by some that the word 'Tsdukim' is derived from Zadok, a priest of the time of Solomon, and that in consequence of this the party was almost, if not altogether, confined to the priestly cult. While some evidence is offered by those who advocate this view, their contention is very far from proven. It would indeed be strange if this party, which claims such ancient origin, had not been heard of before, especially in the early Maccabean times ; and, if the party was purely priestly, that so much should be heard of it in Jewish and New Testament writings. I take it that the name of the party is derived from the word 'Tsadik,' righteous, and that it was given to them as a nickname by their opponents ; also, that they were a fairly large body, and that they were not confined to the priestly cult. They were the national-istic aristocrats of Jewry, who were not so much concerned with the future life, or Messianic hope, as with the present and with the Temple and its services. They were inelastic, and in many cases, such as Law observances, they were much stricter than the Pharisees. They had nothing to offer to the common people save the Temple and its services, and their own authority. They believed in themselves, and did not see the need for any change in the affairs of men. Their view of their own importance led them to take a very strong view of the freedom of the will; they believed themselves to be capable of acting rightly without being helped or coerced by God into doing so. We usually think of the Pharisees as the self-righteous. Their self-righteousness was based upon the belief that they were doing the will of God; but the Sadducees were far more self-righteous, for they believed that they could do and will rightly by personal effort. The Temple was not so much the dwelling-place of God as a place in which they allowed God a share with them in their special domain. As priests they saw to it that they shared with God in the sacrifices that were offered, and in the glory of the offering. That our Lord did not come more often into conflict with them seems to me to be due to the fact that He realised that there was very little gain to be hoped for from such controversy. When He sought to cleanse the Temple, He knew that the consequences for Him would be very dire. Our Lord's message was mainly to the common people, for among them alone was there both the need for it and the hope that, when the matter was cleared up, they would be the ones to see the true value of it, and to take it unto the ends of the earth.

The Pharisees wanted a Messiah for their own glorification—a Messiah who would bring the nations of the earth to their view-point. The Sadducees were too well off; they felt that the order of things they made was good enough for them, and they neither wanted nor needed a Messiah.

Zadokites and Essenes.

It will no doubt come as a surprise to those who divide the New Testament Jewish world between Pharisees and Sadducees, to find that Jewry had so many divisions, sects and schools of thought. The Pharisees were no doubt the largest party in Jewry, and the Sadducees very influential politically and religiously, but they by no means

represented the entire nation.   They made up in verbosity
and self-assertion what they lacked in numbers, and
certainly thought that between them they owned not only
the Jewish people, but the God of Israel.   The Zadokites,
Essenes, Zealots, Herodians, Galileans and especially the
Jews of the Diaspora, who did not necessarily belong to
either of the larger parties, were an integral part of the
nation, and to understand the real state of things in the
Palestine of the last two centuries B.C. and the first century
A.D. we must take these into consideration.   Even then
we shall by no means have exhausted the theological
schools, or the party divisions which existed during the
period under consideration.   There is a tendency to refer
all literature of our period to the larger parties, but we
should be careful in accepting these conclusions ; they do
not always work.

The Zadokites.

This party was altogether lost sight of for many centuries,
and only the discovery of some MSS. in the Cairo Genizah,
by Dr. S. Schechter, has enabled us to get some idea of
its outlook and beliefs.   The Schechter MSS. are only
fragments of a larger MS., and one has to be very careful
in drawing conclusions from them.

It would seem that the name of the Zadokites is derived
from that of a priest of the time of David who is first
mentioned in connection with the appointment of David's
first cabinet.   Zadok and Ahimelech are the joint chief
priests, and Zadok played an important part in connection
with the care of the Ark of the Covenant.   Again, when
the succession was in question just before David's death,
Zadok took his part in the anointing of Solomon as
against Adonijah.   From this fact we gather that Zadok
held the highest place in the priesthood of Judah.   Again,
in 572 B.C., Ezekiel tells us (Ezek. xl. 46) that the Zadokites
were the guardians of the Temple altar, and the same
prophet emphasises the place of the Zadokites in chapters
xliii., xliv., xlviii.   In Ezra vii. 2 we find that the Zadokite
succession is still continued.   Thus, for the course of six
hundred years, the Zadokite priesthood is to the fore, and
we may take it for granted that it continued till such a

time as there was some radical change in the constitution of that body.   This we know took place when the Seleucids became masters of Palestine.

Turning from Biblical notices of this family to those of the Fragments themselves, we get a date which is of some importance, in verse 5 of chap. i. in the A. Fragment, where we read, "And in the period of wrath three hundred and ninety years after He had given them into the hands of Nebuchadnezzar, the king of Babylon, He visited them.' I think that we may take it for granted that the party as a party with its special doctrines was started at that time, *i.e.* 196 B.C.   The political situation allows us to conclude that a movement from Palestine at this time is quite within historical probability, for Antiochus III., as we have seen, had transported two thousand families from Babylonia into Asia Minor, and the settlement of Jews in Syria at that time is quite in keeping with events as we know them. These Zadokites settled in Damascus.   Dr. R. H. Charles puts the migration to Damascus in 176 B.C., which suits the situation very well historically, and may be accepted as the most probable date.   The most interesting, as well as the most astonishing, doctrine of this party was its belief that the Messiah was to be a descendant of the priestly tribe of Levi and of the house of David.   This is even more surprising in view of the fact that the party was Biblical, that is to say, that it gave the prophetic writings equal status with the Law.   Were it unique in its doctrine, one would be apt to look upon it as a heretical party, but the Book of the Testaments of the Twelve Patriarchs and the Book of Ecclesiasticus teach the same doctrine.   While many inferences are possible regarding this strange non-prophetic doctrine, the most logical conclusion is that the priestly cult was so strong that it claimed for itself the leadership of the nation even in the Messianic hopes of the nation and in spite of Biblical teaching.

The extent of the party is impossible to gauge at this time, but it must have been fairly wide, and must have embraced not only priest and Levite, but also Jews who did not belong to these orders, and even proselytes, and seems to have had adherents in many towns in Palestine.

The Zadokites differed from the Sadducees in many points, but especially in their firm belief in immortality. They also differed from the Pharisees, but chiefly in their disregard of traditionalism.

Among other peculiarities of the party, the following are noteworthy : (1) Their belief that one of their teachers was the ' Star ' spoken of in Numbers xxiv. 17 ; (2) that a Lawgiver such as is promised in Gen. xlix. 10 (Me-cho-kek) to the tribe of Judah had actually arisen among them ; and (3) that they were led by a Teacher of righteousness.

Their organisation was provided for in every way, and in each place where they were found there was a judicial body consisting of ten persons, possessing all authority under the Law. There was also an inquisitor, whose authority was very extensive, for to him belonged the right to admit people into the party, to exclude from the party, to regulate the business of the community and to sit as judge in suits involving capital offences.

The strict observance of the Sabbath laws and also the feasts was another strong feature of this party, and in this respect they were stricter than the Pharisees.

The Essenes.

The origin and tenets of this party are alike very obscure, and the discussions which have raged around them have brought to the problem not only historians and theologians, but also eminent writers on the history of philosophy.

Some of the problems that were formerly raised in connection with this party have now quite definitely disappeared from the practical issues of New Testament problems. It is no longer asserted by any competent New Testament scholar or historian that either Jesus or John the Baptist were Essenes. The elimination of these possibilities, however, does not detract from the interest for the student of this period.

In spite of Lightfoot's erudite and classical treatment of the matter in several articles, but especially in his commentary on Colossians and Philemon, pp. 353-417, I feel that there is much to be said for Zeller's theory that the Essenes had many things in common with the philosophic teachings of Pythagoras of Samos. Pythagoras, the son of Mnesarchus, a gem-cutter, migrated from Samos (*circa* 530 B.C.), and started his school of philosophy in Croton (Southern Italy). About Pythagoras himself little need here be said, save that he was one of the profoundest thinkers of the world. He was the founder of the sciences of arithmetic, geometry and harmonics, and he was also a religious reformer who deserves to occupy a very high place in the annals of religious evolution.

While we have to depend on Philolaus, a writer of the end of the fifth century B.C., for our information, we can yet get a clear understanding of the main principles of Pythagoras's philosophy. Foremost among his doctrines we may place Theoria, which taught contemplation of the Divine order of the universe, and self-enlightenment, which came by special revelation made to Pythagoras. To become possessor of the foregoing it was necessary to be initiated into the cult, and admission was gained only after purification, the observance of ascetic rules in connection with food and dress, and also by developing the mystical side of life. There was thus a dualism of the world and the soul. In the world there are two principles ever in conflict, namely, Light and Darkness; in the soul, the conflict between Good and Evil. Apocatastasis was a feature in the teaching of Pythagoras, but the soul ultimately, according to him, reached a sphere in which there was unity and rest. He taught the necessity for ' Homilia,' that is, converse with the Divine (prayer), and ' Mimesis,' that is, the imitation of the Divine.

We may now examine the specific doctrines of the Essenes. It may here be mentioned that there is no party either in Judaism or in any religious system to which have been attributed so many qualities and theories as the Hasidim of the pre-Maccabean period. The Pharisees, the Sadducees, the Zadokites and the Essenes are all supposed to descend from them, but it is more likely that none of them did, and therefore I will here leave the Hasidim out of the discussion.

It should be pointed out that our only authorities for the doctrines and organisations of the Essenes are Philo of Alexandria, Flavius Josephus and Pliny (the Younger). These writers do not agree in some details, but in the main they give us a comprehensible account of the party. The great bulk of the party lived on a communistic basis at En-Geddi, near the Dead Sea, to the number of about four thousand. They were also found in many of the country towns, though not in the larger cities, for these they considered too immoral to live in. They had four orders, the lowest of which was that of the novitiates, and any one who joined them had to spend a year in this state. He received three articles—a spade, an apron and a white dress—each of these symbolising a doctrine. The second order was the order of lustrations, the third was of meditation, and the fourth was of full communisation. When he reached his fourth year he was allowed to partake of the common meal, which was looked upon as a sacrifice, and approached very nearly to the Sacrament of the Holy Communion.

The Essenes of the fourth order had to be celibate, but they permitted themselves to adopt male children so as to keep the community alive.

The Essenes did not take part in the sacrificial rites of the Temple, though they visited it. They shared with the Zadokites a great reverence for the Sabbath. They refused to take oaths, considering their word as good as their bond. They held the name of their founder or teacher in great reverence, and did not disclose that name to outsiders. They had secret books which they guarded very zealously, and they gave special attention to the medicinal value of herbs and practised cures with them. They also exorcised ills by recitations of certain formulæ. They were dualist in so far as they recognised the existence of Good and Evil, of Light and Darkness, as opposing principles in the universe. This dualism led them to sun-worship, but just exactly what the worship of the sun meant we cannot say. The probability is that they merely worshipped towards the sun, as it represented light in its mystical sense. They had an elaborate angelology and demonology, and also a very clear doctrine of immortality. Since they looked upon matter as impure, they were forced to think of the body itself as impure, and taught that the soul's redemption would come with the gaining of its freedom from the body.

Other peculiarities of this party might be mentioned, but it will not help us very much in coming to any conclusion as to their origin and standing in Judaism. I would venture the opinion that they were a prophetic Jewish party, who believed that God was more fully satisfied with obedience than with sacrifice. It is quite probable that they were a pre-Jewish sect; that they were part of the Exile which did not accept the P. section of the Pentateuch; that they came into contact with Zoroastrianism during their sojourn in Persia or Media; that they also came into contact with Pythagoreanism; and that they combined the three systems into the one they practised. How much Christianity learned from them it is difficult to say, but there is at least the attempt of the early Christians at communism, which might be regarded as likely to have been borrowed from them; and, as has already been pointed out, the common meal, which was a kind of sacrifice, may have had a great influence upon the Communion service. Their adherence to the Temple while rejecting its sacrifices may also have been very helpful to the early Christians in their attitude to the Temple. To draw further conclusions is very dangerous, and unless archæology unearths some new facts for us about this party, our knowledge of it will remain meagre. And yet, with all the lack of first-hand knowledge, we can say of the Essenes that they were a highly moral mixture of propheticism and philosophy with not a little superstition.

Herodians and Zealots.

The advent of Antipater and his sons into the political world of Jewry had momentous results, but in no part of the country so much as in Galilee. Here two parties came into being, one an intensely nationalistic party which came to be known as ' Zealots,' and the other a party of compromise which came to be known as ' Herodians.'

It will be remembered that Herod was cited to appear before the Sanhedrin for the execution of Hezekias, who is described as ' a leader of robbers.' That there were freebooters in Galilee during the early governorship of Herod we may take for granted, for in point of fact their successors have only recently been cleared out of their caves by the

British. But that there was fierce opposition to the
assumption by these Idumeans, such as Herod and his
brother, of leadership in Jewry is also quite patent. The
fiercest opposition to Antipater and his sons came from the
Galileans, a number of whom formed themselves into a
party to oppose any non-Jewish government in the
country; indeed, they would recognise no one as entitled
to reign in their beloved country save the Messiah. This
party (the Zealots) would have nothing to do with either
the half-Jew Herod or his masters at Rome ; and they
carried their opposition into effect with a fanaticism that
embarrassed both friend and foe. Their intense nationalism did not permit them to call any one in the political
world of their time lord or master, for they stood out for a
purely Jewish kingdom with the Messiah as head of the
State.

While their religious principle was as strong as their
purely nationalistic hatred of Herod and Rome, Herod
during his own reign was able to keep the Zealots in check.
But the fire of their nationalism was never quenched.
After Herod's death, and while his sons were in Rome
pleading their cause under different wills which Herod had
left, the Zealots took advantage of the general unrest of
the country, and under the leadership of Judas (a son of
Hezekias whom Herod had put to death) they collected
their following and led them to the royal arsenal in Sepphoris
(probably modern Safad). Judas took this and distributed
the arms to his followers, after which they overran the
whole of Galilee. Josephus (*Antiq.*, XVII. x. 5) has some
very uncomplimentary comments on Judas and his Zealots,
but we need not heed these too much, as Josephus always
suffered from a Roman complex that made him blind to
anything in Judea which was unfavourable to Rome.
The general revolt in the country was put down, and the
Zealots were scattered for a while, but they were not
destroyed, and they maintained themselves in spite of the
might of Rome.

During the year 6 A.D., Quirinius, who had already had
charge of a census in Palestine in 7 or 6 B.C., was again
sent to carry out another census in Palestine while governor
of Syria. At first the whole nation was opposed to this

census, but Joazar, the high priest of the period, persuaded the populace to submit to the decree of the Emperor, and the majority submitted. But not so Judas and his Zealots. Along with a man named Zadok he raised the standard of revolt in Galilee, but again the might of Rome prevailed, and the Zealots had to desist from their aims.

How this party influenced the destiny of Judaism a quotation from Josephus will indicate, for, as will be seen from it, Josephus lays at its door the ultimate destruction of the Jewish state: 'But of the fourth sect of Jewish philosophy, Judas the Galilean was the author. These men agree in all things with the Pharisaic notions; but they have an inviolable attachment to liberty; and they say that God is to be their only Ruler and Lord. They also consider as without value dying any kinds of death, nor indeed do they heed the deaths of their relations and friends, nor can any such fear make them call any man lord. Since this immovable resolution of theirs is well known to a great many, I shall speak no further about the matter. Nor am I afraid that anything I have said of them should be disbelieved, but rather fear that what I have said underrates the resolution they show when they undergo pain. It was in Gessius Florus's time that the nation began to grow mad with this distemper. He was procurator and occasioned the Jews to go wild with it by the abuse of his authority, and to make them revolt from the Romans. These are the sects of Jewish philosophy.'

The Herodians.

This party is not mentioned by Josephus, nor do Jewish sources generally have anything to say about it. The New Testament mentions them in passing, but, reading between the lines, we feel that this party must have been a very strong one in the land. It was just what its name indicates, ' pro-Herod,' and must have been found in every part of the country. It was natural that some of the people should have thought it better to have half a Jew as king than a Roman. We noticed that Herod's governorship of Galilee was not altogether devoid of success, and attracted many of the people to him. In Judea and

Samaria he also found favour with the people.   Apart from their feelings for the house of Antipater, the fact that it had allied itself to the Maccabeans would carry weight with many of the people, but in the ultimate it was perhaps the recognition of the inevitable that must have led many to become Herodians.   Herod was on the throne through no choice of theirs—Rome was mistress of the land ;   and to oppose Herod was to ask for trouble, whilst to support him was to have at least a capable ruler who claimed an adherence to Judaism.   It is true that many of the people accepted the Herods passively, but it would be altogether unique in history if the house of Herod should not have had some friends in the country.   Even the might of Rome could not have kept the crown on his head had that not been the case.   We can thus easily conclude what the political principles of this party were.   It was to maintain the Herods on the throne, and to do this they had to make a show of friendship for Rome.

The attempt of many writers to identify the Herodians with the Sadducees is as ineffective as it is lacking in reasonable conception of the state of political matters in the Palestine of that period.   To claim that there were no Herodians among the Pharisees, as Farrar and some others do, is to say that the Sadducees alone supported the house of Herod, which is on the face of it a contradiction of historically known facts of the period.

The question which the Herodians put to Jesus on the last occasion He visited the Temple gives us the best clue to this party's political outlook : ' Tell us, therefore, what thinkest thou ?   Is it lawful to give tribute to Cæsar or not ? '   Is it better to have half a loaf or no bread ?   Of course there was more than that in the question.   There was an attempt to entangle Jesus in the political issues of the day, but the question is the fullest expression of their political faith.   It has been noted fully enough by many commentators that, so far as the compassing of the death of Jesus was concerned, the Herodians are not mentioned, and probably as a party they had nothing to do with it. They had been satisfied with the answer of Jesus that Cæsar had his rights in the political affairs of the country, and if Cæsar had his rights so had the Herods ; but they must also have been assured that Jesus had nothing to do with politics. He was neither Zealot, anti-Herodian nor Herodian. Little more need be said about this party, which, though it did not gather the taxes for Cæsar or Herod, believed that the acceptance of the inevitable was the only safe road to national continuity. Many of them may have been real admirers of Herod and his house, and for that we cannot blame them, for there were some admirable points about Herod, and even about his sons, at least so far as political matters went.

Personalities.

Philo of Alexandria.

Hellenic influence on Judaism is not confined to Essenism and is seen at its best or worst in the writings of Philo of Alexandria. This great thinker, who deserves much better of historians than any Jewish thinker of our period, is just coming into his own. The new edition of Philo's work, which is being issued by the ' Loeb Classical Library,' deserves the grateful thanks of English-speaking students. The Greek text with its parallel English is done in admirable and masterly fashion and will, I am sure, receive the support it deserves from Old and New Testament scholars.

Philo was born about 20 B.C. in Alexandria, the home of Hellenistic Judaism. He belonged to a wealthy Jewish family, his brother being the Alabarch of Egyptian Jewry. Philo himself was more interested in the spiritual than in the political issues of his period, but, like many another scholar, was drawn into politics because of his integrity of character and worth to represent his nation in urgent matters touching upon their freedom and existence. Thus we find him in A.D. 39–40 pleading the cause of his co-religionists before the Emperor Caligula against the governor, Flaccus of Alexandria, who was persecuting the Jews in Egypt to gain favour with the anti-Jewish element. But Philo learned, if he indeed needed to do so, that the tender mercies of the wicked are cruel. The mad Caligula treated him and his companions with insolence and contempt, and they were even in danger of losing their lives. Such an experience must have had a terrible effect on the scholarly mind and loving heart of our philosopher, and, I doubt not, killed him.

Philo was first and last a Jew. His Judaism sought larger spheres of knowledge and broadening in Greek thought. Greek poetry as well as prose appealed to him, as he was interested in their philosophy ; and though he did not belong to any particular school of Greek thought, he combined knowledge of the various schools in his system. He was no mere borrower of other people's thoughts, but had a contribution to make of his own, and, typical of the best tradition of Judaism, he made his contribution to religion instead of to philosophy pure and simple. Indeed it might be said that Philo was a pioneer in the realm of the philosophy of religion, or, to put it more accurately, philosophical monotheism. He brought his ripe and rich knowledge of Platonism, Pythagoreanism, Stoicism and even Epicureanism to an interpretation of the Bible, especially the Pentateuch, and laid the foundation for the Alexandrianism of which the Fourth Gospel is the best example.

Philo, Hellenist that he was, retained the strongly Jewish conception that religion must occupy the first place in both heart and mind, and he made his wide philosophic knowledge serve him in his religious struggles. His unbounded admiration for Moses enabled him to retain an admiration for philosophy and general learning, and yet keep an open mind in the things which concerned religion. Socrates, Plato, Pythagoras, Aristotle and Homer were relegated to the background when Moses was in the company.

Philo's main service to religion was the introduction of the allegorical method, based on Grecian thought and method. The rabbis also employed the allegorical method, but their allegories were lacking in elasticity and even in common sense. Philo recognised some truths that many even at this time cannot bring themselves to see. He allowed for the mythological tendencies even in his beloved Pentateuch, and he argued against the anthropomorphisms with great power. An example or two from his own writings will best serve to illustrate his method, and also give scope to the personal judgment of the reader.

' " And Adam and his wife hid themselves from the presence of the Lord God in the midst of the forest of the garden " (Gen. iii. 8). He (Moses) introduces a doctrine showing that the bad man is an exile. For if virtue is a city peculiar to the wise, the man who has no capacity to partake of virtue has been driven away from the city, in which the bad man is incapable of taking part. It is accordingly the bad man only who has been driven away and sent into exile. But the exile from virtue has, by incurring such exile, hidden himself from God. For if the wise, as being His friends, are in God, it is evident that all bad men slink away and hide from him, as is to be expected in men who cherish hatred and ill-will to right reason.' Another excerpt which will give an example of his anti-anthropomorphism is herewith given. ' " And God planted a pleasaunce in Eden toward the sun-rising, and placed there the man whom He had formed " (Gen. ii. 8). By using many words for it, Moses has already made it manifest that the sublime and heavenly wisdom is of many names ; for he calls it beginning, image and vision of God ; and now by the planting of the pleasaunce he brings out the fact that earthly wisdom is a copy of this as an archetype. Far be it from man's reasoning to be the victim of so great impiety as to suppose that God tills the soil and plants the pleasaunces. We should at once be at a loss to tell from what motive He could do so. Not to provide Himself with pleasant refreshment and comfort. Let not such fables even enter our mind, for not even the whole world would be a place fit for God to make His abode, since God is His own place, and He is filled by Himself, and sufficient for Himself, filling and containing all other things in their destitution and barrenness and emptiness, but Himself contained by nothing else, seeing that He is Himself One and the Whole.'

The number 7 played a great part in Philo's thoughts, as did the entire question of numerals in a mathematical sense. He was also greatly interested in harmonics. I will close my quotations with his appreciation of the number 7 :

' We must pass on to the other kind of 7th, that which is contained within the decade. It exhibits a marvellous nature, not at all inferior to that of the former kind. For instance, 7 consists of 1 and 2 and 4, which have two relations making specially for harmony—the twofold and the fourfold—the one producing the diapason harmony, while the fourfold relation produces double diapason. 7 admits of other divisions besides these, in pairs like animals under a yoke. It is divided first into 1 and 6, then into 2 and 5, and last into 3 and 4. Most musical is the proportion of these numbers also, for 6 to 1 is a sixfold proportion, but the sixfold proportion makes the greatest distance that there is (in music), the distance from the highest to the lowest note, as we shall prove, when we pass from numbers to the proportion in harmonics.'

For New Testament students the greatest contribution of Philo is found in his exposition of the Logos. The Logos to Philo is like the Memrah in rabbinic teaching, yet it is more fully defined. To him it is the active Divine intelligence; it is more what the Christian would understand as the Holy Spirit, and yet a passage like the following points to the Logos as set forth in the New Testament: ' How can you hesitate, friends, to hate war and love peace, you who are called by the name of the same father, not a mortal but an immortal, a divine man, who, being the Logos of the Eternal, is himself of necessity imperishable ? ' Philo further asserts that the Logos is the high priest who intercedes for the world with God. But it would be erroneous to claim for Philo a doctrine of the Logos such as the Fourth Gospel postulates. The Fourth Gospel starts with a Personality as its basis and applies to it the attributes which Philo vaguely applies to some individuality or theory. The Fourth Gospel defines the Person of Jesus of Nazareth as the Logos and goes on to clothe Him in the Judo-Hellenistic garment. Philo has the garment, but cannot make it fit any personality within his knowledge, and thus the Logos with Philo remains an indefinable something, while the writer of the Fourth Gospel and the Alexandrian Christians find Jesus of Nazareth the ideal person whom the doctrine of the Logos fits to perfection. Philo must be read : he must be read with a Judo-Hellenistic background, and with a deep sympathy. To quote him further may only lead to a misunderstanding of his position as well as of his deep piety and great longing after God. He has been included in this survey because to have omitted him would have been like leaving out an important stone in a building.

Certain books of Philo's are mentioned in Eusebius's *Ecclesiastical History*, bk. ii. chap. xviii. ' This author, who was copious in language, comprehensive in thought, sublime and elevated in his views of the sacred Scriptures, has made his exposition of the sacred books equally distinguished for variety of matter and manner. On the one hand he expounds the history of Genesis, in the books that he calls *Allegories of the Divine Laws*, following the order of the book ; and on the other he forms particular divisions of the chapters, according to the subject of the Scriptures, with the objections and solutions ; in which same books also he prefixes the tables of the questions and solutions both in Genesis and Exodus respectively. There are also, besides these, treatises on certain problems particularly discussed, such as two *On Agriculture*, and two *On Drunkenness*, and some others distinguished by a different and peculiar title, such as *On the Things that a Sober Mind earnestly Desires, and those which it Execrates* ; also, *On the Confusion of Tongues*, and the treatise *On Flight and Discovery*, and that on *Literary Convention*, and *On the Question, " Who is Heir to things Divine ? "* or *On the Division of Things into Equal and Unequal*, also the treatise on the three virtues, which Moses records with others. Beside these, there is one *On those whose Names are changed, and wherefore their Names have been changed*, in which he says that he wrote also on the First and Second Covenant. There is also a work of the same author, *On Emigration, and on the Life of the Wise Man perfect in Righteousness*, or, *On the Unwritten Laws*. Also, *On Giants*, or, *On the Immutability of God*. And also, *On the Proposition that Dreams, according to Moses, are sent by God*—five books. These are the books that have come down to us on Genesis, but on Exodus we are acquainted with the first five books of *Questions and Solutions* ; also that *On the Tabernacle*, that also *On the Ten Commandments* ; also, the first four treatises on the laws referring particularly to the summary heads of the Ten Commandments. Also, the treatise

On the Sacrifice of Animals, and the Forms of Sacrifices;
that also, *On the Rewards proposed in the Law to Good Men,
and the Punishments and Curses to the Wicked.*

' Besides all these, there are single books extant by the
same author, as the treatises *On Providence*, and the book
composed by him *On the Jews*, and *The Statesman*. To this
may be added *Alexander*, or *On Irrational Animals evincing
Reason*. Besides these, *On the Proposition that a Wicked
Man is a Slave* ; to which is subjoined the book, *That every
Good Man is free*. After which he added the book *On a
Contemplative Life, or the Devout*, from which we have
related the circumstances respecting the life of the
apostolical men. Also, the interpretations of the Hebrew
names in the Law and the Prophets are said to be the result
of his industry. The same author, in the reign of Caius,
coming to Rome, is said to have recited before the whole
senate, in the reign of Claudius, what he wrote on the
impiety of Caius, to which he humorously prefixed the
title, *On the Virtues*. And the discourses were so much
admired as to be deemed worthy of a place in the libraries.'

The Venerable President.

If Philo was the pioneer in Judo-Hellenic religious
philosophy, Hillel was the founder of the Halachic method
which continues in Jewry to this day. No account of our
period would be complete without an account of Jewry's most
lovable teacher, most saintly sage and most patient scholar.

Our information concerning Hillel comes altogether
from the Talmud, so that one has to wade through many
passages in this maze of literature, always with the feeling
that much of the information may be highly coloured and
unreliable, but that, even so, much may be accepted as
reliable for the reason that what is related is natural and
unconventional.

The date of the birth of the Great President of the
Sanhedrin is not known, nor indeed can the term of his
office be ascertained with any degree of exactness. All
that can be said is that it was during the reign of
Herod I. That Hillel was a descendant of David has
been disputed, but the numerous places in which that
claim is made (*Sanhedrin* i. 5, *Kethuboth*, *Kidushin* and

other places) compel us to accept the veracity of these statements. Hillel was brought up in Mesopotamia, but came to Palestine to acquaint himself with the teaching of its sages. He was poor in this world's riches, but rich in his desire to gain knowledge. He attended the rabbinical school (Yeshuba) after his day's work as a seller of kindling wood was done. Entrance to the school was obtained by making a small payment daily. On one occasion Hillel, not having earned enough money to pay for his entrance, climbed up to the roof of the school and listened through the window. But it was a cold night, and Hillel was almost frozen when he was discovered ; and though it was the Sabbath day, the sages ordered that a fire should be kindled to bring him back to life. Never was the Sabbath broken for better purpose by the rabbis than when they saved the venerable Hillel.

Curiously enough, Hillel reached fame through a decision which concerned the Sabbath. The Passover happened to fall on a Sabbath day, and the question arose, Can the Paschal offering be slaughtered on the Sabbath ? No one being able to answer that question in Jewry, Hillel intimated that he had it on the authority of his teachers (who were very highly respected for their learning) that it was lawful to slaughter the Pascha on the Sabbath. His pronouncement was acted upon, and Hillel became an authority in Jewry second to none. One cannot go into details about the activities of Hillel nor yet quote many of the illuminating sayings attributed to him. A few, however, will not be out of place. ' That which is hateful to thee, do not to thy neighbour.' ' Man should be clean so as not to offend his guest. The soul is man's most cherished guest ; within us to-day, it may be with God to-morrow, and it would be calamitous if it were to report to God that it lodged in an unclean body.' ' Be of the disciples of Aaron, who loved peace, loving mankind, and attracting them to the Law.' ' Judge not thy neighbour till thou standest in his place.' ' Say not I will repent when I have leisure, for you may never have leisure.'

Hillel was the Elijah of traditionalism, and he restored, simplified and to a certain extent codified the mass of tradition that had become very chaotic during the last two centuries before the Christian era. He is said to have classified the traditional law into six sections, and thus laid the foundation upon which the Mishnah was afterwards built. He laid down a regular system of hermeneutics, upon which the interpretation of the Law in the rabbinic sense is based. If Hillel's descent from David may be questioned, there can be no doubt about his offspring. There were Gamaliel first, second and third, and Judah the Prince (Ha Nasi). The Gamaliels will be familiar to all New Testament readers ; and who can forget the services one of these rendered to Christianity as the teacher of Saul of Tarsus ? Hillel was to rabbinic Judaism what Philo was to Hellenistic Judaism ; and though we have none of his writings, Jewish literature is full of his teaching, wisdom and sane thought.

The question whether Hillel influenced Jesus has been argued at length by many scholars, but I feel that Hillel lived too near the time of Jesus for his teaching to have influenced Him. If one cares to gather up every saying in the Talmud and other Jewish literature, one might find sayings very much like those of Jesus ; but our German scholars, who are followed by some British and American scholars, have gone far wrong in their search for Talmudic sayings with a similarity to the sayings of Jesus. Most of the sayings in the Mishnah or Talmud which are offered as parallels to sayings of Jesus are of much later date than His time. It would not have been derogatory even for Jesus to have made use of some of Hillel's sayings, but the fact is that there are very few sayings of Hillel that can be said with certainty to have emanated from him, and it is much safer to leave this supposition alone. If Talmudic and Mishnaic knowledge must be displayed, it might be done at the expense of lesser personalities than Jesus or Hillel, for each of them can stand on his own ground and achievement.

General.

Jewish Missionary Activities.

That Judaism was a missionary religion is denied only by those Jews to-day who take exception to the activities

of Christian bodies engaged in missionary work among
Jews.   The glory of Abraham is to be found in his missionary inclinations, and so is that of the Prophets.   But
we have ample proof during the Maccabean period at
least that Judaism was not only a missionary religion,
but also Islamic (in its method).   The inhabitants of Jeb
were thus forced into Judaism by Judas Maccabæus, as
also were the Itureans by Aristobulus, whilst Simon
Maccabæus converted in the same manner many of the
southern cities of Judea.   Apart, however, from the forcing
of converts, there was missionary propaganda of a highly
organised character, as is evident from the writings of
Plutarch, Tacitus, Seneca, Juvenal, Dion Cassius, Josephus
and the New Testament.   There is even stronger testimony
from the Old Testament itself.   The words for these converts are part of the Hebrew language as much as the name
of the people themselves, and it is too late in the day for
those who object to the missionary activities of Christians
and Muhammadans to claim that Judaism has never been
a missionary religion.   When one reads the literature of
the last two centuries B.C. and finds that most of the Jews
in Palestine could be gathered into Jerusalem during the
wars of the Covenant, or that it was possible (as would
seem the case from Jubilees xlix.) that the Passover victim
could be eaten within the sanctuary by the entire nation
domiciled in Palestine, one is bound to ask whence came all
the Jewish population found about 100 B.C.   What had
become of all the occupants of the towns and villages of
Palestine who, on the showing of the Books of the Maccabees, were Gentile in 167 B.C. ?

It would be a waste of time to quote passages illustrative
of this in an effort to convince those who will not see.
Judaism looked forward to the day when all the world
would accept its religious tenets, for that ideal was part
of the prophetic vision and was very much to the fore in the
Messianic doctrines of all times.

The Requirements of Judaism for Admittance into its Fold.

Three things were essential for entrance into the heritage
of Abraham.   The first was circumcision, which brought
the convert into the family of Abraham in a national and

covenantal sense. Even at so early a stage as that of Jacob's lifetime, this was made a requisite (see Gen. xxxiv. 14 ff.), at least so the author of that section tells us. The second demand was baptism, that is to say, immersion in water. This was the cleansing sign, not of levitical purity, but of the washing away of all Gentile uncleanness. The third requisite was the offering up of a sacrifice. This was an indication of the convert's recognition of personal sin, and of his acceptance of the levitical code. These three things brought the Gentile male into the full and absolute fellowship of the Covenant of Abraham, Moses and the priesthood, whilst in the case of women converts the last two only were required.

There were some who would not enter quite so fully into Judaism, and these Judaism did not reject altogether. It made certain provision for them which enabled these converts to share with Judaism in its blessings. Many Christian as well as Jewish scholars have written on this subject. Schürer and Edersheim make many inaccurate statements in this connection. The subject is dealt with fully in the small tractate *Gerim* in the Babylonian Talmud. The commentary on this tractate gives the fullest references in Jewish literature concerning this subject. After the most careful examination of relevant literature I have come to the conclusion that while post-Christian Judaism ceased to be aggressively missionary, pre-Christian Judaism was not wronged by Jesus when He told the Pharisees that they compassed sea and land to make one proselyte (Matt. xxiii. 15). Of course the language is figurative, but it was nevertheless a true estimate of the missionary tendencies of the Pharisees.

In my own experience I can speak of two converts to Judaism. The one, a Russian woman, who had long been a convert when I came to know her. She was a very saintly woman, and was held in the highest respect in the community in spite of the fact that her children, especially one of her daughters, were a disgrace to it. Had this girl been the daughter of a Jewess by birth, her mother would have been liable to suffer many indignities ; and, even more, had she been a non-Jewess. But this converted woman, in spite of her misguided child, was held in very high respect by the whole community. The second was also a Russian, who had worked for Jews, but came to Palestine to be made a Jew. I was present at his reception into the commonwealth of Israel. Circumcision and baptism were the two acts by which he was admitted, and, of course, he was expected to observe all the commandments.

Judaism prepared the way for Christianity in respect of its missionary work, and it was Saul the Pharisee who was the most active missionary that the world has ever known. But the debt of Christianity to Judaism in this great matter is to be found further in the fact that many of the Gentiles who could not altogether ally themselves to Judaism, though attracted by its monotheism and general morality, found Christianity less difficult to accept, and thus Judaism served to bring a great multitude into the infant Church of the Apostolic and early sub-Apostolic times.

I must revert for a moment to the question of Baptism. I am often asked if I know of a custom among the Jews in which the living are baptized for the dead ? I suppose that those who ask this question have in view the passage in I Cor. xv. 29. I do not know of any such custom, nor do I find it mentioned in Jewish literature in so far as know that literature. I came across an incident which may have some bearing on this matter, and will relate it as I saw it.

A man by the name of Nathan lived in Safad, Palestine. He was partly blind, but he could see enough to get about, and he made his living by begging from house to house. He used to visit the Jewish colonies to beg there. Whether while going to or coming back from one of these colonies was not established, but he was attacked by some wild beast, killed and partly eaten. As it is the custom to wash the body before burial, and as this was not possible owing to the state of disintegration of the body, the matter was brought before Rabbi R. Zilbermann. The rabbi decided that the dead man's son should be baptized (for that is the form of washing of the dead : they are immersed, or baptized) instead of the dead man himself. I noted the fact, but was too young to be interested in the reason that guided the rabbi to his decision. Looking back upon the incident, I am of opinion that the reason was somewhat on the lines which the practice mentioned in the passage in 1 Corinthians followed. As there would be a good many converts to Christianity from Judaism, and probably also from among the Gentiles, whose parents would die outside of the faith, it seems not improbable that their children were baptized in their stead, and thus they were deemed as brought into the New Covenant. Prayer on behalf of departed parents, and the giving of alms on behalf of dead people, suggest the idea of substitutionary benefit. As the Church became more the organised body of believers, whole families being in it whose parents had themselves been Christians, this custom would fall out of use, and hence the silence about it in the Patristic Church.

CHAPTER VII

RETROSPECT

FROM the view-point of the student whose interest
in the period is both historical and theological,
the material which has been gathered leaves a bewildering
impression. Taking for instance the various peoples with
whom Judaism came into contact, Neo-Babylonianism
is followed by Medo-Persianism, which is in turn succeeded
by Hellenism and Neo-Hellenism (*i.e.* Syro-Hellenism),
and it again is replaced by Roman influence which is tinged
with Idumeanism. But the changes within Jewry itself,
and the divisions, are the factors which almost take one's
breath away. Jewry, which generally considers itself
a unity, is found to be a most heterogeneous conglomeration, not only as to its parties, but also as to its composition.
The reader of the New Testament generally thinks of
Jewry as divided into two sections—Pharisees and
Sadducees—but when he learns of the Essenes, Zadokites,
Zealots, Herodians, Galileans, Hellenists and Proselytes
(this by no means completes the list), he just wonders where
indeed to look for that Judaism of his conception, the
Judaism of authority, sitting in the seats of Moses and the
Prophets.

The truth of the matter has been put into a nutshell for
us by Professor Morris Jastrow, jun.: ' A pure race, if it
exists at all outside the brain of some ethnologist, is a
barren race. Mixed races, and mixed races alone, bring
forth the fruit that we term civilisation with social, religious and intellectual progress ' (*Religious Belief in Babylonia and Assyria*, p. 5). Had Judaism remained on its
own soil and been confined to its own literature, it might,
like Babylonia, Assyria, Egypt, Greece and Rome,
Carthage, Etruria and Phœnicia, have died, leaving a noble

heritage, but it was forced to live by the providential care of its God, to assimilate the best of all the ancient civilisations, and to receive into itself the virility of Hellenism and Arabianism, and forge them into a unity that could not be broken.

It is noteworthy that the forces which held Judaism together are so evident. In spite of the endless number of parties or sects, and of the differences of interpretation even among the parties themselves, there were a few outstanding things that cemented Judaism into a solid whole which the might of Babylonia, the strength of Media and Persia, the intellect of Greece, the fury of Syro-Hellenism and the legions of order and law of Rome failed to break. The principles which bound Jewry into that unbreakable unity were :

(1) Its belief in Jehovah, and that as the only true God He had a universal mission for it that must be fulfilled.

(2) Its racial solidarity, which was expressed in the Abrahamic sign of circumcision.

(3) Its Sabbath, the emblem of freedom, antiquity and possession of a religious personality which had to be satisfied by rest and worship.

(4) Its central shrine at Jerusalem, which was its emblem of the immanence of God, and the ultimate acceptance of Him by all the peoples of the earth.

(5) Last, but not least, its body of tradition and history contained in the Old Testament.

Had any of the other nations possessed even two or three only of the foregoing they would have continued with us to this day. For contemporary Judaism has only two of the foregoing left, namely, its belief in the universality of its God, and its hope of restoration to nationhood as its traditions teach it. When Judaism loses these it will itself be lost.

Judaism was never a religion which demanded conformity : it was nonconformist in every possible direction. It believed in the maintenance of the race very strongly, but it possessed a party that practised celibacy. It believed in the sanctity of Palestine, but it lived very happily and very vigorously outside it. It despised the Gentile world, but borrowed from that world all that could enrich its intellectual life as well as its religious tenets.

It turned towards the Temple thrice daily in every place of its Dispersion, but it found its God in its synagogues as fully as in the Temple, and, what is more, it sought and found Him in the home, not by outward representations of statues and likenesses, but in an atmosphere of spiritual essence. Its meals were sacred offerings, eaten not so much to satisfy the needs of the body as to provide an opportunity for thanking the Giver of all good and perfect gifts (this was not confined to the Essenes, but was true in the case of all religious Jews). Judaism lived in Jerusalem, but stayed everywhere it was allowed to get lodging. It despised the Samaritans because they lived and lodged in Gerizim, and tolerated its Sadducees who in common with the Samaritans rejected the Prophets; but the Sadducees at least lived in Jerusalem and offered their homage at the central shrine of Jehovah.

Did Christianity Inherit any of these Things ?

With the main doctrines of Christianity we are not concerned here, but with some of them we cannot refrain from dealing, because Christianity is to our mind the natural successor of the Judaism we have been studying.

The most precious thing that Christianity has taken over from Judaism is the belief in the universality of God, in whom ultimately all mankind will come to believe and worship. The sharpest division between the Founder of Christianity with His immediate followers and Judaism was the universality or the immanence of God. The Jews wanted to keep that immanence confined to the Temple, whilst Jesus and the disciples taught that God is to be found everywhere in a real sense, and that the heart of man, the temple not made with hands, was the dwelling-place of God. For that doctrine Jewry compassed the death of Jesus, stoned Stephen and drove the Christians out of the Holy Land.

So long as Christianity kept this principle to the fore as one of its doctrines, it made true and enlightened followers ; but when it transferred its allegiance to Rome and sought a vicar of God and a seat of authority it lost its power, and that power is still lacking in the greatest section of the Church.

The Sabbath.

Judaism could not tolerate or forgive the breaking up of its Sabbath and all that it stood for. Christianity, accepting the views of its Founder on this matter, insisted that freedom was made for man, and not man a slave of freedom. Just as the body required food and rest at certain times, which times were not set by a hard-and-fast rule, so the soul must be free to make its own Sabbaths, its own times of communion and worship. The followers of Jesus elected to make the first day of the week, which was to them a day of memorable happenings, their sign of freedom, the freedom of life from its material Temple. The Risen Christ spoke to them of a freedom far greater than the redemption from the slavery of Egypt or the creation of the world. God became to them not only the Creator of life, but the Restorer of the life which nature had worn out by pain and decay. Of this the early Christians were as sure as they were of their own existence, and they made it sure for future generations by their making the Sabbath the emblem of immortality.

The Sacrificial Meal.

Like the Essenes, the Founder of Christianity made all meals opportunities of thanksgiving. The meal in the oldest Semitic sense was an act in which the Deity partook with the individual. Not only did the Essenes look upon their meals as sacrificial emblems, but many pious Jews gathered on weekdays as well as Friday afternoons, and on the Sabbaths, to partake of love-and-praise meals. The life-giving food of the body was joined to the life-giving food which the soul received by communion with God. Just as the body was eating the common elements of the earth's produce, so the soul was figuratively eating or feeding itself on the Divine. ' I am the living bread which came down from heaven ; and if any eat this bread he shall live for ever ; and the bread that I will give is my flesh, which I will give for the life of the world '

(John vi. 51). Jesus' last meal with His little band of intimate followers was on the day before the Passover ; they were having both the Pascha and the common sacrificial meal. He reiterated at that meal the doctrine which they had held in common, regarding the food of the soul, which accompanied all meals eaten with proper regard and understanding of the needs of the soul. In the breaking of the bread (a means by which some of His followers recognised Him after His resurrection) and the drinking of the cup of blessing Jesus again emphasised that they should henceforward look upon His sacrifice as the food of the soul, the sacrifice of Himself and the shedding of His blood as the way into the very presence of God, and He enjoined them to hold these sacrificial meals with the same sacredness as they had held them with Him in His earthly life. The Christian Church in many of its divisions has imported strange things into that loving sacrificial meal. The magic of the priest, the disruption of natural laws, the mysteries of the Divine life have all been forced into that simple and gracious meal with heart-breaking results. For those who can follow the fuller meaning of the sacrificial meal of the Essenes, the Chaburoth and Chasidim, the other importations have no meaning or value ; it remains the simple and inspiring association of the believers with the Deity, when they hunger and thirst after God.

Baptism.

We saw that the convert to Judaism had to perform three things. He had to enter into the Abrahamic Covenant, to be baptized, and to offer a sacrifice. Jesus continued the second as a sign of entrance into the fellow-ship of His circle. Circumcision He said nothing about, since those who followed Him or entered into His small circle were already in that Covenant. The Early Church was in two minds about this matter : some wanted the continuance of this sign, and others objected to it. The first Council of Jerusalem decided the issue. The Gentiles were entering into a new covenant, not that of Abraham, but of Jesus, and they no longer needed that sign of the flesh. It said nothing of baptism, because it took it for granted that it was to continue, for it stood for purification from the Gentile past. Regarding the third, the Council made a definite ruling, *i.e.* that the Gentiles must abstain from offerings such as they were in the habit of making to their idols. To ensure this the matter of sacrifice (even had it been essential in their thinking) would have had to be discontinued, because it would only have led to the same sad distortions as that of the sacrificial meal. Could the Council have foreseen our modern difficulties it would no doubt have made provision for them, but their concern was mainly with the situation in their own day. That they continued to practise the rite of baptism is amply proved in the Acts of the Apostles, and that baptism meant something more than the ordinary purification act of Jewish usage is made clear from such passages as Acts xix. 1–4. That baptism to St. Paul at least was something more than a sign of repentance is quite clear, not only from that passage, but from others. St. Paul seems to have taken baptism in its rabbinical and mystical form. The use of the praying shawl (Thalit) and the dwelling in booths during the festival of that name seem to have been an analogy which St. Paul used in his conception of baptism. In each of these cases the mystical value of the act lies in the being enveloped in the Godhead, an indwelling in the Godhead, to be buried to this world and to be alive unto God.

We cannot enter here upon the question of infant baptism. A very recent investigation of this matter is contained in *Zeitschrift für die neutestamentliche Wissenschaft*, 1929, pp. 128–142. In its rabbinic meaning, which St. Paul seems to have shared, it professes that the act of baptism was that of being brought into an indwelling in Christ, and that children of Christian parents should be given this holy privilege. The assurance that the Saviour loves them is not certainly wanting in the New Testament writings.

Worship and Organisation.

The Temple and synagogal forms of worship have been dealt with at length. That the Apostolic Church continued the synagogal type we may safely assume, for the

Church was born in the synagogue. It was to the synagogues that the early missionaries of the Church went to lay down the claims of Jesus as the Saviour Messiah, and it is almost certain that, when the final breach between Church and synagogue took place, the Jewish converts at least did not depart very much from their former organisations. Indeed, the question of caring for the poor, which came to the fore at an early stage of the Christian life, was solved on the lines which we know to have existed in the synagogue, for the appointment of a diaconate to deal with the problem was in keeping with the lines followed by Jewry.

Christianity was not an appendage of Judaism, but a religion which based itself on two facts : (1) That Jesus of Nazareth was the promised Messiah ; that He was the Saviour of all who accept His teaching and will to do His will. (2) That Jesus of Nazareth was crucified in Jerusalem ; that He died and was laid in the grave ; that He rose from the grave and was seen by many who had known Him during His earthly life and by others ; and that He has ascended to the Father. That, therefore, Jesus of Nazareth is the crown of all Jewish and human aspirations ; that He fulfilled the visions of the Prophets and the pure ideals of all that was finest in Judaism ; and that He was no provincial Jew who was to be reckoned among the great of Jewry, but the ' Word ' made flesh for the world's sake, that it may through Him have the fullest fellowship with God and the Holy Spirit.

Reflections and Summary.

In the distant background stand Babylonia and Egypt, their presence being felt rather than seen, their influence sure but eluding definition. They are in the shadow of a great light, ' Monotheism,' and so long as that light keeps its effulgence, Egypt, Babylonia and the other indistinguishable shadows on our canvas will remain mere shadows, and nothing more.

Nearer the foreground, but not clearly distinguishable except in parts here and there, stand the figures of Abraham, Moses, Joshua, Samuel, David, Elijah and Elisha. It is most unfortunate that even our greatest

Biblical artists have not succeeded in clearing away the mists which surround these important figures. We do not despair that the light that pervades the whole picture will be strong enough and that some keen-sighted and gifted Biblical connoisseur will in time clear away this fog and bring them into the full light of the picture.

Before these again we see Amos, Hosea, Isaiah and Micah, where the light shines upon them in full and unmistakable clarity. They are known to us by definite characteristics—Justice, Inextinguishable Love, Righteousness, Piety and Humility. Doom and Hope, these two words appear to be written in large letters alongside our figures, summarising their great contribution to the religion of Jesus.

Still nearer stand the Weeping Prophet-Priest, the Priest-Prophet, the inciter to action, and destroyer of the Davidic line. Jeremiah sheds bitter tears, but predicts that out of the remnants of Judah and Israel shall come forth Judaism, which will form the immediate background of the entire picture and suffuse the whole of it. The Priestly-Prophet we see in imagination laying the first stone in the Temple structure upon which he would inscribe 'The Glory of Yahweh,' but it remains for Haggai and Zechariah to see the structure reared and worshippers from all the Dispersion crowding to its doors. With the Temple completed we observe Zechariah driving Zerubbabel into the edge of our canvas, and with him the Davidic line passes into obscurity.

The most outstanding object of this part of the background of our picture is, however, nameless. This nameless figure holds an inscription in his hand with the word 'LIGHT,' and towards this the Gentiles, though as yet in the far distance, strain their eyes. This figure on our canvas is, however, in spite of his very indistinguishable personality, a very intriguing figure, for comfort and suffering alike are characterised in the same representation, and the only possible conclusion that the mind can gather from this representation is REDEMPTION THROUGH SUFFERING.

The next group, though much nearer the centre figure of the picture, and therefore more in the light than the shadow, is yet puzzling and indistinct. The builder of the walls of the Holy City and the mighty Scribe are too intent on their own affairs to allow us a clear look at their faces. The one is surrounded by a multitude of working and fighting men, and we cannot be sure which he inclines to : the other is deeply immersed in his scribal work, his face is turned towards the parchment on which he is writing, and we are prevented from looking into his eyes to learn if there is originality in his work, or if he is simply the transscriber of the records of the past.

The nearest group to the centre is a confused and confusing conglomeration of Jewry, priestlings always struggling to the fore, men in garbs belonging to remote ages masquerading in our picture and seeking to pass themselves off for the Enochs, Jacobs, Solomons, Daniels, etc. Mighty conquerors, puppet princelings, brave, sturdy Covenanters, and effete Judo-Hellenists. In this group we see East and West meeting to part, and parting to meet again, the mystical and apocalyptic crowding out the practical and sturdy propheticism. This group is the despair of the beholder, and gaze as long and as often as he will, he can gain but a very imperfect impression of it. How indeed can any accurate impression be formed ? The group is most elusive, for what is Syro-Hellenistic for a while is turned into Judo-Galilean, and what is purely Idumean at first is then fully turned into Judean and wears the crown of David. That the group is a fantasy is the only concrete impression that the mind can grasp, but the solution of this riddle is at hand.

The centre of the picture is the ' LIGHT WHICH LIGHTENS ALL.' This Light brings out into fine relief every group, so far as the Great Artist has meant it to emerge, and ' IN HIS LIGHT WE SEE LIGHT.' We note groups of puny warriors hurling their darts and arrows at the Light, but though these make very imperceptible marks, the marks nevertheless remain. Time and the Great Artist will restore the light on our canvas to its original perfection, and humanity for the present must hold and make what it can of this portrayal of itself, its destiny and its hope.

Judaism has nothing to be ashamed of in its contribution to the great religions of the world. It has handed down a noble heritage from Lawgiver, Prophet, Sage and Priest. How noble that heritage is may be deduced from the fact that after two thousand years of sterility it still lives. It is true that it lives on the past, but the past was so very rich that, unlike the India or the China or the Japan, or even the Muhammadanism of to-day, it only requires to be true to the past to be again a real factor in the noblest conceptions of mankind. It needs to shed nothing of the past but its gabardine and its exilic complex, and it will be a mighty factor in humanity's thought and life. Its Propheticism, its Hierarchy, its Apocalypticism and Rabbinisms are the background of the light upon which the Light of Jesus shines.

With Judaism as the main background, the light which Christianity sheds on man's struggle towards God is understandable, without it it is not and could not be. The pity, the inevitable pity, is that in the course of its development Christianity has not taken as much of Judaism into its make-up as it ought : it has gone far afield for many of its conceptions and usages. The magic of the priests of Greece and Mithras have appealed more to some sections of it than the plain common sense of the Galilean fishermen and the Tarsian Hebrew. The philosophy of Pythagoras and the Neo-Platonist have appealed more than the unpretentious wisdom of Sirach and Hillel. The plain interior of the synagogue could not hold its place in the face of the gorgeous temples of Greece and Rome, the simple polity of the synagogue could not compete with the Pontifex Maximus of Rome, and to crown the insult to that simple polity of Jesus Himself, Peter has been placed on the chair of Roman magnificence.

Judaism has added nothing of worth to its noble heritage since it refused the Kingship of Jesus. Christianity has added much which it must discard if it is to come back to its pure source. Judaism needs to take a step forward to make all the difference between a sterile and ineffective creed and a living and fruitful one. Christianity must take a step backward to become the creed of the universe—the creed of humanity that seeks to realise itself in God, and God in itself.

BIBLIOGRAPHY

PROFESSOR W. MANSON, who has kindly read the proof, feels that there ought to be a Bibliography, and I quite agree. I append herewith a list of books and portions of books from my own bookshelves. This list is bound to suffer from the sin of omission, but on the other hand it will be confined to material which I have read and re-read, and can confidently recommend to those who want to get a serious grip of the subject. When all is said, the following books are sufficient and indispensable. There are, of course, to be added to this list the books mentioned in the course of comment in this volume.

ISRAEL ABRAHAMS.

    Festival Studies. 1906.
    Judaism. 1907.
    Studies in Pharisaism and the Gospels. 1917.
    Some Permanent Values in Judaism. 1924.
    The Glory of God. 1925.
    'The Jewish Interpretation of the Old Testament,' in
        The People and the Book. 1925.

W. E. BARNES.

    'The Development of the Religion of Israel from the
        Return to the Death of Simon,' in *The People and
        the Book* (edited by Peake). 1925.

J. VERNON BARTLET.

    'The Religious Background of the New Testament
        Writings,' in Peake's Commentary on the Bible.

P. V. M. BENECKE.

    'The Political Background of the New Testament,' in
        Gore's Commentary.

E. R. BEVAN.

    House of Seleucus. 1902.
    Jerusalem under the High Priests.
    A History of Egypt under the Ptolemaic Dynasty. 1927.

E. R. BEVAN (*Continued*).
> 'Syria and the Jews,' in the *Cambridge Ancient History*,
> vol. viii. chap. xvi.
> 'Environment,' etc., in Gore's Commentary, *Apocrypha*,
> pp. 1–30.

BEVAN, SINGER, and Others.
> *The Legacy of Israel.* 1927.

G. H. BOX.
> 'Old Testament in Relation to New,' in *The People and
> the Book.* 1925.

L. R. BROWN.
> *Early Judaism.* 1907.

F. C. BURKITT.
> *Jewish and Christian Apocalypses.* 1914.

C. F. BURNEY.
> *Israel's Hope of Immortality.* 1907.

G. A. CARTER.
> *Zoroastrianism and Judaism.* 1913.

R. H. CHARLES.
> *Eschatology.* 1913.
> *Religious Development between Old and New Testaments.*
> 1914.
> *The Book of Jubilees.* S.P.C.K. 1927.
> *The Book of Enoch.* S.P.C.K. 1929.

CHARLES and Others.
> *The Apocrypha and Pseudepigrapha of the Old Testament.*
> 2 vols. 1913.

T. K. CHEYNE.
> *Jewish Religious Life after the Exile.* 1898.

S. A. COOK.
> 'The Fall and Rise of Judah,' *Camb. Anc. Hist.*, vol. iii.
> chap. xviii.
> 'The Inauguration of Judaism,' *Camb. Anc. Hist.*, vol. vi.
> chap. vii.; other articles in same by Professor Cook.

A. E. COWLEY.
> *Aramaic Papyri of the Fifth Century B.C.* 1923.

S. Daiches.
> *The Jews in Babylonia in the Time of Ezra and Nehemiah.*
> 1900.

H. Danby.
> *The Tractate Sanhedrin.* S.P.C.K.

James Drummond.
> *Philo Judæus.* 2 vols. 1888.

A. Duff.
> *A History of the Religion of Judaism,* 500–200 B.C.

A. Edersheim.
> *The Temple, its Ministry and Services.* 1874.
> *Life and Times of Jesus the Messiah.* 1900.

W. Fairweather.
> *The Background of the Gospels.* 1908.
> *Jesus and the Greeks.* 1924.

Foakes-Jackson and Kirsopp Lake.
> *The Beginnings of Christianity.* 3 vols.

M. Gaster.
> *The Samaritans* (Schweich Lectures). 1923. Pub. 1925.

T. R. Glover.
> *Christ in the Ancient World.* 1930.

G. B. Gray.
> ' The Foundation and Extension of the Persian Empire,'
> *Camb. Anc. Hist.,* vol. iv. chap. i.

G. B. Gray and M. Cary.
> ' Reign of Darius,' *Camb. Anc. Hist.,* vol. iv. chap. vii.

J. Rendel Harris.
> *The Odes and Psalms of Solomon.* 1909.

A. Hausrath.
> *A History of the New Testament Times.* 1878.

T. Herford.
> *Pharisaism.* 1924.

J. H. HUNKIN.
> *From the Fall of Nineveh to Titus* (Schweich Lectures).
> 1926.

M. R. JAMES.
> *Biblical Antiquities of Philo.*

FLAVIUS JOSEPHUS.
> Works, many editions, indispensable.

KLAUSNER.
> *Jesus of Nazareth : His Life, Times, and Teaching.* 1925.

P. P. LEVERTOFF.
> *Midrash Sifre on Numbers.*
> *Love and the Messianic Age.* 1923.

H. LOEWE.
> Article ' Judaism,' in 14th ed. of *Ency. Brit.*, and other
> articles in same. Also Appendices in Montefiore's
> *Rabbinic Literature and Gospel Teaching* (representing
> the Orthodox Jewish view).

C. G. MONTEFIORE.
> *The Synoptic Gospels.* 2 vols. 2nd edition. 1927.
> *Rabbinic Literature and the Gospel Teaching.* 1930.

G. F. MOORE.
> *Zoroastrianism in History of Religions.* 1914.
> *Judaism in the First Centuries of the Christian Era.* 2 vols.
> 1927.

W. O. E. OESTERLEY.
> *Evolution of the Messianic Idea.* 1908.
> *The Books of the Apocrypha.* 1916.
> *The Jewish Background of the Christian Liturgy.* 1925.
> *The Wisdom of Ben Sira* (*Ecclesiasticus*). S.P.C.K.
> *The Wisdom of Solomon.* S.P.C.K.
> *Tractate Sabbath.* S.P.C.K.
> *Sayings of the Fathers.* S.P.C.K.

W. O. E. OESTERLEY and G. H. BOX.
> *The Religion and Worship of the Synagogue.* 1911.

W. O. E. OESTERLEY and T. H. ROBINSON.

Hebrew Religion : Its Origin and Development, part iii. 1930.

O. S. RANKIN.

The Origins of the Festival of Hanukkah. 1931.

M. ROSTOVTZEFF.

' Ptolemaic Egypt,' *Camb. Anc. Hist.*, vol. vii. chap. iv.
' Syria and the East,' *Camb. Anc. Hist.*, vol. vii. chap. v.

SCHECHTER.

Studies in Judaism. 1st Series, 1896 ; 2nd Series, 1908.
Certain chapters in these books which are readily
distinguished from the material dealing with later
subjects.

E. SCHÜRER.

A History of the Jewish People in the Time of Jesus Christ.
2nd ed. 1885.

M. SEIDEL.

In the Time of Jesus. 1885.

D. G. SIMPSON.

' Judaism the Religion in which Christ was Educated,'
chap. vi. in *Christianity in the Light of Modern
Knowledge.*

Sir GEORGE ADAM SMITH.

Jerusalem. 2 vols. 1907.
Geography of the Holy Land, 2 vols., revised edition. 1931.

W. W. TARN.

' The Struggle of Egypt against Syria and Macedonia,'
Camb. Anc. Hist., vol. vii. chap. xii.

R. CAMPBELL THOMPSON.

' The New Babylonian Empire,' *Camb. Anc. Hist.*, vol. iii.
chap. x.

C. C. TORREY.

Ezra. 1910.

TOY.

> *Judaism and Christianity.* 1890.

LUKYN WILLIAMS.

> *Tractate Berakoth.* S.P.C.K.

To this list must be added the articles in the various Encyclopædias and Bible Dictionaries, especially Hastings' works.

INDEX

Abar-Nahara, 6, 7.
Abtalion, 37, 150.
Agamemnon, 17.
Alexander of Macedon, 12 f.
Alexandra Salome, 32 f., 40.
Alexandria, 15.
Ammonites, 8.
Amram, 60.
Anshan, 4.
Antigonus, 17 f., 36 f., 149.
Antiochus I. (Soter), 17 f., 21.
Antiochus II. (Theos), 18.
Antiochus III. (The Great), 16, 18, 166.
Antiochus IV. (Epiphanes), 20.
Antiochus VII. (Sidetes), 30.
Antipater, 33 f., 170.
Antony, Mark, 34 f.
Apollonius, 15.
Arabs, 8.
Aristias, 15.
Aristobulus, 15, 31, 33, 182.
Artaxerxes I., 8.
Artaxerxes II., 9.
Ashdod, Ashdodites, 8, 34.
Ashurbanipal, 11.
Athenion, 15.

Babylon, Babylonia, 4, 5, 9, 10, 13, 16, 17, 19, 126, 143, 166.
Bacchides, 28.
Bagoas, 12.
Balas, 28 f.
Bardia, 5.
Baruch, 74.
Berenice, 14.
Bertholet, Prof. A., 72.
Box, Canon, 47.
Brown, Prof. F., 144.

Cæsar, Julius, 35.
Callimachus, 15.

Cambridge Anc. Hist., 4.
Cambyses, 5, 10.
Causse, Prof., 137.
Cecil, Lady, 11.
Cendebæus, 30.
Chanuka, 26, 106.
Charles, Dr. R. H., 46, 49, 52, 92 f., 166.
Chazan, 138.
Chebar, 111.
Cleopatra, 32, 38 f.
Cœlosyria, 16.
Crassus, M. Licinius, 34.
Crete, 12.
Cypros, 35.
Cyrus, 4 f.

Darius, 6.
Darius Codomannus, 13.
Delos, 18.
Demetrius I. (Soter), 27 f.
Demetrius II., 28.
Demetrius III. (Nicator), 29.
Diaspora, Dispersion, 15, 111, 118, 126, 135, 137, 149.
Dios, 34.
Dira, 34.

Edersheim, 139, 183.
Egypt, 10.
Ein-Geddi, 169.
Elephantine, papyri, etc., 5, 11, 12, 66.
Encyclopædia Biblica, 4.
Esarhaddon, 11.
Essenes, 164, 189.
Euergetes, 16, 18.
Exile, 3 f.
Ezekiel, 10.
Ezra, 8 f.

Gabinius, 34, 145.

Gabriel, 80.
Gadara, 34.
Gaumata, 5.
Gaza, 34.
Gessius Florus, 172.
Gorgias, 25.
Greece, 12.

Habiri, Habiru, 2, 83.
Haggai, 6, 10.
Hananias II., 15.
Hananias III., 21 f.
Haran, 2.
Harris, Dr. J. Rendel, 51, 70.
Hashmon, Hashmonaim, 24 f., 106, 144 f.
Hasidim, 22 f.
Heliodorus, 20.
Hellespont, 17.
Herod, 35 f., 170.
Hezekias, 170.
Hibrim, 2.
Hillel, 150, 179 f., 195.
Hippos, 34.
Hyrcania, 6.
Hyrcanus, 30, 34, 159.
Hystaspes, 6.

Ipsus, battle of, 17.
Itureans, 182.

Jaddua, 13.
Jakim (or Alcimus), 28.
Jamnia, 34.
Jamnæus, 32.
Jason, 21 f.
Jastrow, Prof. M., 186.
Jeremiah, 9.
Joazar, 172.
Jochebed, 60.
Jonathan, 28.
Joppa, 34.
Joseph, 16.
Josephus, 13, 34, 154, 158 f., 163, 168, 171.

Keith, Sir A., 83.

Longinus, C. Cassius, 35.
Lucas, Mrs. H., 119.
Lysias, 25, 27.

Maccabees, 24 f., 49 f., 182.
McFadyen, Prof. J. E., 144
Machærus, 38.
Malachi, 7, 10.
Malalas, 17.
Manetho, 15.
Marcellinus, L., 34.
Marduk, 5.
Mariamne, 36, 40.
Marissa, 34.
Mattathiah, 7, 24.
Michael, 79 f., 120.
Mishnah, 181, 121.
Mithridates, 5.
Mond, Sir Robert, 11.
Moore, Prof. G. F., 71.
Muhammadans, 82, 124.

Nathan, 184.
Nebuchadrezzer, 3, 5, 108.
Nebu-shezibanni, 11.
Nebuzaradan, 3.
Nehemiah, 8.
Neo-Platonism, 195.
Nephayan, 12.
Nicanor, 25, 28.

Octavius, 36, 38, 39.
Oesterley, Dr., 47, 98, 139, 140.
Onias. See Hananias.

Parthia, 6, 9, 10.
Peake, Dr. A., 84.
Pella, 19, 34.
Perdiccas, 13, 14, 16.
Persia, 6.
Petrie, Sir Flinders, 14, 15.
Pharisees, 32 f., 40, 72, 118, 156 f.
Philip of Macedon, 13, 19.
Philipus, M., 34.
Philo of Alexandria, 2, 168, 174 f.
Philolaus, 161.
Phœnicia, 16.
Pliny, the Younger, 168.
Polybius, 16, 27.
Pompey, 33 f.
Psammetikus I., 11.
Ptolemaius, 30.
Ptolemies, 12, 46.
Ptolemy Lagi (Soter), 14, 17.

Ptolemy II. (Philadelphus), 14.
Ptolemy III. (Euergetes), 15 f.
Ptolemy IV. (Philopator), 16, 19, 20.
Ptolemy V. (Epiphanes), 19.
Ptolemy VI. (Philometor), 31.
Ptolemy X. (Lathyrus), 32.
Pythagoras, 167, 195.

Quirinus, P. Sulpicius, 41, 171.

Raguel, 80.
Raphael, 80, 120.
Raphia, Battle of, 16, 50.
Remiel, 80.
Restoration of exiles, 4 f.
Rhodius, 15.
Riddle, D. W., 156.
Rome, 19, 25 f., 33 f., 40, 145 f.
Rostovtzeff, Prof. M., 25.
Roxana, 13 f.

Sachau, Prof., 11.
Sadducees, 32, 72, 85, 161 f., 172 f.
Safad, 184.
Sa-gas, 2.
Samaria, Samaritans, 3, 8, 31, 34, 90, 134, 151 f., 172, 188.
Sanabassar, 5.
Sanbalat, 8.
Saraqâêl, 80.
Sargon II., 3.
Satrap, satrapy, 6 f., 12.
Saturninus, C. Sentius, 41.
Sayce, Prof., 11.
Scaurus, 34.
Schechter, Dr., 47, 52, 165.
Schemia, 150.
Schürer, Dr., 139, 154, 183.
Scipio, L. (Asiaticus), 19.
Scythopolis, 34.
Seleucia, 17.
Seleucids, 12, 17, 106, 155.
Seleucus I. (Nikator), 16.
Seleucus II. (Callinicus), 18.

Seleucus IV. (Keraunus), 18.
Seleucus IV. (Philopator), 20.
Septuagint, 15, 114, 118.
Shammai, 150.
Shekinah, 81, 105, 120.
Shemaia, 37.
Simon the Just, 149.
Simon Maccabæus, 28 f.
Sirach, 195.
Smith, Sir G. A., 154.
Socius, C., 38.
Stevenson, R. L., 77.
Strabo, 16.
Strathius' Tower, 34.
Syria, 15 f., 19 f., 171.

Tachpanes, 11.
Targums, 114, 118.
Theocritus, 15.
Timagenes, 154.
Tobit, 126.
Trypho, 29 f.
Tyrians, 115.

Ugbaru, 4.
Ur, in Mesopotamia, 2.
Uriel, 80.

Ventidius, 37.

Waidrang, 12.
Whitehouse, Prof., 4, 114.

Yeb, 5, 11 f., 182.

Zadok, Zadokites, 143 f., 164 f.
Zadokite Fragment, 117.
Zealots, 170.
Zechariah, 6, 10.
Zeitschrift f. d. n.t. Wissenschaft, 191.
Zeller, 167.
Zerubbabel, 7, 10, 144.
Zoroastrianism, 77, 84 f., 123, 170.

PRINTED BY
MORRISON AND GIBB LTD.
EDINBURGH AND LONDON